MEDITERRANEAN
MTBs
AT WAR

Lt L.C. Reynolds RNVR.

Sub Lt H.F. Cooper RNVR.

MEDITERRANEAN
MTBs
AT WAR

SHORT MTB FLOTILLA OPERATIONS 1939–1945

L.C. REYNOLDS AND H.F. COOPER

FOREWORD BY REAR ADMIRAL SIR M. MORGAN-GILES

SUTTON PUBLISHING

in association with
THE IMPERIAL WAR MUSEUM

First published in the United Kingdom in 1999 by
Sutton Publishing Limited · Phoenix Mill
Thrupp · Stroud · Gloucestershire · GL5 2BU
in association with the Imperial War Museum

British Library Cataloguing in Publication Data
A catalogue record for this book is available from the British Library

ISBN 0 7509 92274 5

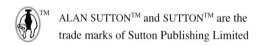

ALAN SUTTON™ and SUTTON™ are the
trade marks of Sutton Publishing Limited

Typeset in 10/13 pt Sabon.
Typesetting and origination by
Sutton Publishing Limited.
Printed in Great Britain by
Butler & Tanner, Frome, Somerset.

CONTENTS

LIST OF MAPS

FOREWORD

BY REAR ADMIRAL SIR M. MORGAN-GILES

This book casts new light on a long neglected aspect of naval history. The authors both had years of wartime operational experience in Coastal Forces in the Mediterranean. They describe the gradual build-up from frustrating early days until, by 1944, MTBs and MGBs on the west coast of Italy and in the Adriatic were playing a vital part in supporting the Allied armies in Italy and in driving enemy forces out of the Balkans.

Coastal Forces' operations facilitated the invasion of the 'soft underbelly of Europe', and in the Adriatic they did much to ensure that Tito wrested power from the Germans in Yugoslavia. The long-term importance of the latter event was not fully apparent until later – for without Tito in Belgrade it would have been the Soviet armies who occupied Yugoslavia in 1945. Then, during the Cold War, the Soviets would have possessed direct access to the Mediterranean.

The book describes how Coastal Forces worked to achieve these ends. The officers and men were of course the greatest factor – all very young, almost all Volunteer Reservists and wartime sailors. Their courage and endurance and fighting spirit were beyond praise. In these small crews each individual carried vastly more responsibility than their opposite numbers in larger ships: they 'engaged the enemy more closely', and much more frequently.

Even now, half a century later, it is easy to imagine the thrill and excitement for a young officer in his early twenties to be given command of a magnificent gleaming new 70-ft torpedo boat, with 4,000 roaring horsepower, very effective armament and a keen and well trained crew.

But in writing thus one must be careful to avoid appearing to glorify war. The authors have wisely avoided doing so; they have included no false heroics – merely a factual and extremely interesting detailed record of events, and of fast-moving close-range actions. This is not an exercise in nostalgia. But surely it is a tribute to our wartime nation that young men of the calibre required could be found, and would volunteer in their thousands.

As regards the boats, under the stimulus of war the British boat-building industry developed new designs, new materials and new equipment. Very many firms, large and small, were involved. It is fair to mention in particular Vosper Ltd – in fact the 'short' MTBs were often collectively known as 'Vospers'. But one astonishing shortcoming was that all Coastal Forces had petrol engines, whereas throughout the war the German E-boats ran on diesels.

Any overview of this story of MTBs must include a comparison with past naval history in the Mediterranean. During the Napoleonic wars Nelson's frigates sailed from Naples to harry the French, and the activities of Admiral William Hoste in the Adriatic were extraordinarily similar to those of Coastal Forces. The Island of Vis was occupied by the British – witness Fort Wellington and Fort St George and the old British Naval Cemetery.

It is good to record that this cemetery, which had become dilapidated, has now been restored to good order, largely thanks to the efforts of the Coastal Forces Veterans Association.

The achievements of all who fought in Coastal Forces created a proud new chapter in our long naval history in the Mediterranean. And those who gave their lives in doing so are remembered . . .

Here dead lie we because we did not choose
To live and shame the land from which we sprung
Life to be sure is nothing much to lose
But young men think it is – and we were young.

(From the inscription in the British War Cemetery on the Island of Vis.)

AUTHORS' NOTE

This history of the 'short' MTB flotillas in the Mediterranean is the second in what is intended to form a trilogy which will cover the operations of all the offensive arms of the Navy's Coastal Forces in the Second World War.

It differs from the first volume (*Dog Boats at War*) in that it has a joint authorship. H.F. Cooper, who himself served in two of the flotillas whose activities are described, joined L.C. Reynolds in 1987 in his Coastal Forces research, particularly concentrating on these Mediterranean flotillas. He made contact with all the surviving veterans who could be found after forty years, unearthing detail which does not appear in any official source, and thus breathing life into the history of this campaign. Indeed, he went further, and wrote separate histories for each flotilla, which form the basis for the content of this book, and which are now lodged with the Imperial War Museum and available for further study. The continuity and setting for the trilogy is supplied by his co-author, who has established the archive base into which dovetail all aspects of the research.

As in *Dog Boats at War* we jointly thank all those hundreds of veterans who have contributed in many ways, and who have been reached through the kindness of Douglas Hunt, Claude Holloway, and the CFVA Newsletter Editors, Harold Pickles and Pieter Jansen. And as before, we acknowledge the help of Geoffrey Hudson without whose encyclopaedic knowledge of the boats of Coastal Forces, errors would be inevitable.

Much of the early research was carried out in the Naval Historical Branch, with the help of Dr David Brown and Paul Melton, and at the Public Record Office. Particular support has come from the Imperial War Museum, where Dr Christopher Dowling first suggested a need for a definitive history, and where he, Roderick Suddaby, Janet Mihell, Elizabeth Bowers, Julia Mills and the Photographic Department have all made special contributions. Lord Lewin, Dr Knight and the Trustees of the Sir James Caird Trust at the National Maritime Museum generously gave the project their blessing. Rear Adm Sir M. Morgan-Giles has also maintained a constant interest in the progress of this work. Capt W. Chatterton Dickson RN (Rtd), the compiler of *Seedie's List of Coastal Force Awards*, kindly gave permission for the inclusion of the summary lists in Appendix 2.

It is proper to record thanks to officers and men of the Mediterranean MTBs who have read and confirmed factual detail in painstaking exchanges of correspondence to ensure accuracy, or supplied photographs. Some are acknowledged in the text or notes, but in particular the following deserve special mention even at risk of omitting others who helped: R. Aitchison DSC, Rear Adm C.C. Anderson CB, L.H. Blaxell OBE DSC, M.G. Bowyer, G. Bullwinkle DSC, R. Campbell DSC, W.J. Coals, Lt Cdr C. Coles OBE VRD RNR (Retd), Lt Cdr C.J. Collingwood RN (Retd), J.E.H. Collins MBE DSC*, Fred Coombes DSM, Miles Coverdale, Cdr C.W.S. Dreyer DSO DSC* RN (Retd), H. du Boulay DSC, R.G. Ellis, N.H. Evans, C.P. Evensen DSC*, F. Frenzel DSC, F.A. Gilpin, Cdr R.A.M. Hennessy LVO DSC

RN (Retd), M. Henzell, C.R. Holloway DSC, R.G.A. Hudson, P. Hyslop DSC, N. Ilett DSC, G.P.H. James DSC, Capt D. Jermain DSC* RN (Retd), C.J. Jerram DSO DSC*, A. Kennedy VRD, Lord Keyes, J. Lee DSM, L.P. Macey, J.T. Mannooch, Rear Adm Sir M. Morgan-Giles DSO OBE GM, P. Pidcock, Capt A.I.B. Quarrie CBE VRD RNR (Retd), P. Redhead, K. Rogers, C.S. Rundle, E. Scott, P. Shorer, R.R. Smith DSC, D. Souter VRD, L.V. Strong DSC, B. Syrett, R.P. Tonkin DSC, R. Varvill DSC, C. Wilkinson, Rt Hon Sir A.O. Woodhouse PC KBE DSC, E. Young.

We each have cause to be especially grateful for the support of our wives and families: neither of us has had to go outside the family for the task of typing and retyping manuscripts and drafts: in this Bert Cooper wishes to ensure that his enormous appreciation of the efforts of his daughter, Mrs Carol Scoble, is recorded, and Len Reynolds equally so for the continuing labours of his wife Win, together with the computer expertise of Roger Battye and Colin Daniel.

It is perhaps necessary to repeat here the explanations and justification of conventions used in the book, as in the earlier volume.

In an account which seeks to satisfy historians more accustomed to greater formality, there may be found unusual ways of referring to boats and individuals. First,

although RN, RNR, SANF(V) and officers from the Canadian, Australian and New Zealand Volunteer Reserves have the appropriate letters after their names (unless they are referred to frequently), because the great majority of officers were RNVR this has normally been omitted. And as all the Mediterranean 'short' boats of the Royal Navy were almost entirely Motor Torpedo Boats (there were no formally designated motor gun boats in this area), the prefix 'MTB' has normally been omitted before the boat number.

Similarly, as Coastal Forces had a particular 'small ship' camaraderie among its officers, and indeed the first names of COs were often used as R/T call signs, those names are often used, generally after a first formal reference, in an attempt to capture the appropriate atmosphere.

Notes from the text appear in two categories. In order to assist other researchers and readers wishing to see original texts, sources of information are usually marked in the text as footnotes. Longer and more complex notes are marked with a reference – e.g. (Note 1, Appendix 1), which signifies Note 1, which will be found in Appendix 1. Abbreviations commonly used are shown at the beginning of that section.

H.F. Cooper and L.C. Reynolds

INTRODUCTION

It is perhaps necessary to avoid one possible confusion in the title of this book. *Mediterranean MTBs at War* to the purist would of necessity cover not only the story of the 109 'short' MTBs which served in the region, but also that of the twenty-four 'long' MTBs which played their part from April 1943. These were the Fairmile D class MTBs, 115 ft in length, known as 'Dog Boats'. Their normally very separate operations have already been described in *Dog Boats at War*.

The separation is justified, as the whole concept of the operations of the 'short' boats was entirely different. Not only were they generally capable of greater speeds, but because of their size they presented a much smaller silhouette when attacking and could mostly approach an enemy more quietly. They were not as vulnerable to the threat of mines, and their function as a carrier of torpedoes as their main attack weapon was entirely different from the Dog Boat MTBs, which carried a heavy gun armament and could function well as gun boats.

There will be no need to continue to refer to our Mediterranean MTBs as 'short boats', because the term is only one of differentiation. In fact, the flotillas in this theatre were made up of a wide variety of classes, of lengths which varied from 40 ft to 78 ft. Such was the development in capability through the years from 1937 to 1945 that the primitive, poorly armed boats of the early days contrasted vividly with the powerful, sophisticated and well armed boats which finished the war; the introduction of radar and non-contact torpedoes alone makes it impossible to compare performance.

But in one respect there was an undoubted common factor – the resilience, the seamanship, and the aggressive will to engage the enemy displayed by the officers and men of these boats never flagged and proved in the end a decisive factor in their success.

The conditions in which they operated were totally different from those met by the flotillas in home waters. True, the climate was much kinder (even if the weather and sea conditions were not always as benign as imagined by the crews at home). But the operational demands were dictated, to a very large extent, by the progress of our armies in the various spheres, rather than being static as in the North Sea and Channel. The use of Advanced and Mobile Bases, or even of self-sufficient temporary camouflaged hiding-up places which became commonplace in the Aegean and Adriatic, were features of their war.

Almost everywhere crews lived aboard their own boats except when refitting in the major bases. Fuelling was often primitive and time-consuming, and spares for maintenance could never be taken for granted. But there were, of course, compensations. The crews found themselves in waters and harbours of great beauty steeped in centuries of historical grandeur, even if inadequate mail and shortage of fresh food often dimmed the appreciation! And for the lucky ones, there were very occasional all-too-brief sojourns in rest camps. To visit, for example, Taormina or Ischia, or Sassari in Sardinia, made up for a lack of shore leave and a realization that it was likely to be two years or more before any home leave could come their way.

It was a particular feature of Mediterranean operations that the flotilla was generally an all-important aspect of life. This was especially true when only one flotilla operated from a base, so that a feeling of isolation created a sense of interdependence. Of course, this was not the case when a major operation – such as the invasion of Sicily – drew all the flotillas together for a month or two: but they soon dispersed again and resumed what many regarded as the advantages of a separate identity.

The story of these flotillas moves from Malta to Alexandria, through disaster in Crete, to support of the Eighth Army along the coast of North Africa, to more reverses at Tobruk in the summer and autumn of 1942. Then with victory at El Alamein and the landings in Algeria, it describes new challenges, with increasing resources and success. It moves from Africa back to Malta and Sicily, then spreads out to Corsica and Italy, to the Dalmatian Islands and the Aegean, and finishes in a blaze of unsurpassed achievement in the Gulf of Lyons and the Northern Adriatic.

Many boats were lost, and many men. They served their country well, and their story, which deserves its place in the annals of the history of the Royal Navy, is dedicated to those who gave their lives in the Mediterranean MTBs.

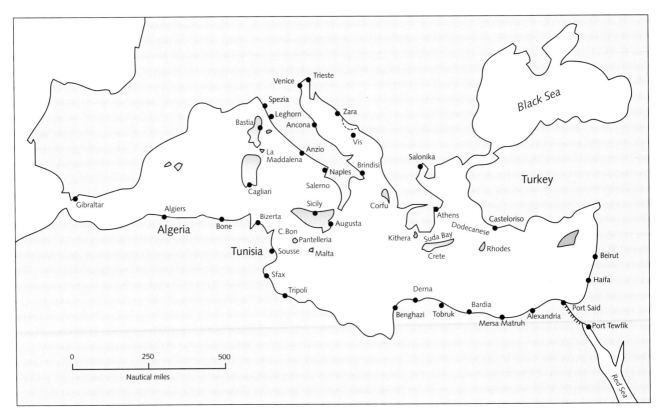

The Mediterranean – general.

CHAPTER 1

THE 1ST MTB FLOTILLA: MALTA AND THE RETURN TO HOME WATERS

(Note 1, Appendix 1)

1937–9

To begin a book which follows the operation of Motor Torpedo Boats in the Mediterranean in the Second World War by describing events in the mid-1930s may seem strange. But the fact that there were any MTBs in Malta when war broke out is explained by the culmination of a commercial and political struggle which had its origins in the heady peacetime pursuit of powerboat racing.

The Royal Navy had developed its First World War fleet of Coastal Motor Boats – CMBs – in 1916, and had seen them perform effectively in operations, particularly at Zeebrugge and in 1919 in the Baltic. Very soon after that war, for reasons which were both doctrinaire and economic, the programme was closed down and the hard-earned experience of the men who had pioneered the operational tactics of their new-concept boats was almost entirely allowed to waste away.

But in 1932 the first presages of another war began to loom menacingly with the emerging nationalism of Germany and Italy. Despite the 'big ship' mentality of the greater part of the Naval establishment, there were some who began to encourage the need for experiment in a new breed of high-speed boats for naval use.

Long before this, a larger-than-life character named Hubert Scott-Paine had attracted both public and official notice. He was a sailor, an engineer and an entrepreneur with a penchant for taking risks with early aircraft designs. He had founded the Supermarine Aviation Company in 1916, and employed a young designer named R.J. Mitchell, whose Spitfire much later brought everlasting fame to that name. Scott-Paine had sold Supermarine in 1924 and turned his attention to fast motor boats, founding the British Power Boat Company. Gathering around him a high-class team of designers and craftsmen, he began to produce a multitude of new-concept craft, and by 1928 his hard chine planing hull had put the company ahead of its competitors, and with it he produced *Miss England* in which the legendary Henry Segrave won the World Championship in the USA in 1929. One significant factor in this was that to power the boat Scott-Paine had used an aero engine, the Napier 'Lion'.

By 1932 Scott-Paine had developed a marinized version and obtained from Napier

1

the exclusive rights over this, which then became the 'Power-Napier Sea Lion'. As early as 1933, Scott-Paine realized that the time might be nigh for a successor to the CMBs of the First World War. His mind turned to a hard chine 60-ft hull to be powered by three Sea Lion engines, which could carry two 18-in torpedoes. He had already won RAF approval with a 37-ft seaplane tender for which Aircraftsman 1st Class T.E. Shaw – better known earlier as Lawrence of Arabia – had conducted the trials. Shaw became a great advocate of Scott-Paine boats, and with his many powerful contacts he added weight to the cause.

The ultimate conclusion, after two years of high profile marketing, was an order for two of the projected boats, placed on 27 September 1935. Secretly, Scott-Paine had begun work on one of the hulls even earlier. Fortuitously, following the invasion of Abyssinia by Mussolini in early October 1935, and with the knowledge that the Italian Navy had made great strides in producing its own version of an MTB, support came from the Commander-in-Chief Mediterranean for more boats to be ordered. By October 1935, four more 'offensive motor boats' of the Scott-Paine design were ordered, with the intention of making a flotilla ready for Malta as quickly as possible.

Until this time the Admiralty had retained the First World War name of 'Coastal Motor Boats' for these craft, but in January 1936 they announced that they were to be designated 'Motor Torpedo Boats'. In remarkably short time, MTBs 01 and 02 were handed over on 28 February to Lt Cdr G.B. Sayer RN who was later to be appointed Senior Officer of the 1st MTB Flotilla. Scott-Paine himself – a skilled racing helmsman – helped train the officers and coxswains to get the best out of their boats.

The torpedo firing mechanism was developed in conjunction with HMS *Vernon*, the Navy's School of Torpedoes and Mining. After experiments with forward firing discharge met problems, the decision was made to use a stern discharge system: the torpedoes were carried on overhead rails in the engine room, and a latticework girder (normally stowed on the upper deck) was hinged over the transom to form a continuation of the engine room rails. The boat aimed at the target, the torpedoes were fired and continued on track while the boat accelerated forward and veered away.

While MTBs 03 to 06 were still under construction, 01 and 02 were temporarily commissioned at HMS *Vernon* on 30 June 1936 and took part in a special demonstration for the new king – Edward VIII. MTB 01 was the first of HM ships in which the new king embarked after his accession.

By 27 April 1937, six boats had been commissioned, and the 1st Flotilla's first public appearance was another royal occasion. MTBs 03, 04, 05 and 06 escorted King George VI and Queen Elizabeth, together with Princess Elizabeth, down the Thames from Westminster to Greenwich for the opening of the new National Maritime Museum. For Hubert Scott-Paine it was a very proud event.

The flotilla finally sailed for the Mediterranean, with its depot ship HMS *Vulcan*, on 22 June 1937, making the passage under its own power. Calls were made at Brest, Corunna and Lisbon. By 17 July the boats had arrived at Malta, having proved their seaworthiness.

Despite the need of prolonged spells in the dockyard for repairs and refits, the Commander-in-Chief Mediterranean, Admiral Dudley Pound, was clearly impressed with their potential and did not hesitate to press the case for a great increase in the numbers of Scott-Paine MTBs in Malta, citing their value for attacking enemy harbours and submarines.

Hubert Scott-Paine (left) greets Capt Willis the CO of HMS *Vernon*, at the commissioning of MTBs 01 and 02 by King Edward VIII. Lt Cdr G.B. Sayer, the first SO of the 1st MTB Flotilla, looks on. (Courtesy, Southampton City Cultural Services)

MTBs 03, 04, 05, 06 of the 1st Flotilla escort the Royal Family (King George VI, Queen Elizabeth and Princess Elizabeth) down the Thames from Westminster to Greenwich for the opening of the National Maritime Museum, 27 April 1937. (Courtesy, Southampton City Cultural Services)

HMS *Vulcan*, support vessel of the 1st MTB Flotilla, on the Greek Cruise. (Courtesy, Capt D. Jermain RN)

1st MTB Flotilla on their Greek Cruise, Summer 1939. (Courtesy, Capt D. Jermain RN)

His estimate of the need was a further four flotillas at Malta, and yet another four at Gibraltar. This certainly did not gain Admiralty approval, but the 1937 Programme included a further nine boats, to add to the three already being built under the 1936 Programme.

Of these twelve boats, six were intended for Singapore (to be designated the 3rd Flotilla) and six for the 2nd Flotilla intended for Hong Kong. In the event, when the 3rd Flotilla entered the Mediterranean, it was decided to add the six boats to the 1st Flotilla to bring it up to twelve boats.

For the record, there was some renumbering of the boats: after the temporary commissioning of 01, she returned to Hythe, under the control of her builders until 1939. To bring the 1st Flotilla up to six for the passage to Malta, 07 completed in April 1937, was renumbered 01 and the original 01 was renumbered 07.

Then in 1938, before the 2nd Flotilla was shipped to Hong Kong to enable their MTB numbers to immediately follow on from those of the 1st Flotilla, 13 was renumbered as 07 and the original 07 (ex 01) became 13. And lastly, in June 1938, for superstitious reasons 13 (ex 07, ex 01) was renumbered 19.[1]

So from the operational point of view in pre-war Malta, Lt Cdr Sayer had twelve boats, 01 to 06 and 14 to 19.

The flotilla trained hard in peacetime Malta, getting to grips with the special demands of these unconventional boats and particularly with the stern discharge torpedo firing which needed much practice. Unquestionably at times the boats were driven too hard in sea conditions which, with the hard chine construction, led to 'pounding'

1   Rance, *Fast Boats and Flying Boats.*

5

and damaged frames. Scott-Paine had reduced weight by using an aluminium alloy for the decks of the boats, following the success of the material in his *Miss Britain III*, but in operational training conditions there were problems with corrosion, and later mahogany decks were fitted. All this led to long periods under repair in the dockyard at Malta.

During 1939, as is normal with Naval appointments, Sayer handed over the flotilla to a new SO – Lt Cdr C.M.(Monty) Donner RN – and by the fateful autumn of that year, a whole team of new COs was in place. It is right to record their names here, as the great majority went on to take a major part in the leadership of the flotillas that developed in the early years of the war.

MTB 01   Lt Cdr C.M. Donner RN
     02   Lt J.A. Eardley-Wilmot RN
     03   Lt A.A.T. Seymour-Hayden RN
     04   Lt A.J.R. Foster RN
     05   Lt W.J. Whitworth RN
     06   Lt H.J. Lloyd RN
     14   Lt D.H. Mason RN
     15   Lt L.J.H. Gamble RN
     16   Lt P.F.S. Gould RN
     17   Lt R.I.T. Faulkner RN
     18   Lt J.T. Mannooch RN
     19   Lt R.A. Ellis RN

Others whose names appear in various lists as earlier COs in the flotilla are Lt D. Jermain RN, Lt H.R.A. Kidston RN and Lt E.M. Thorpe RN. (Note 2, Appendix 1)

The boats were berthed in Msida Creek, Sliema, very close to what was to become HMS *Gregale* (Coastal Force Base, Malta) – the 'back base' for the next five years of all the Mediterranean flotillas. By June 1939, it seemed that war was imminent, and this gave additional urgency to the training routines, even though the peacetime pleasures of Malta, such as bathing picnics, tennis parties, and the races, were still there to be enjoyed.

In August, twelve young RNVR officers arrived to take over as First Lieutenants and Navigators of the boats. Among them were Ian Quarrie and Charles Coles, who were shortly to command boats themselves.

The CO of MTB 18, Lt J.T. Mannooch, known to all as 'Minnie' and later to serve as First Lieutenant of HMS *Midge*, the Coastal Forces base at Great Yarmouth, has supplied an excellent description of the atmosphere of the time, and indeed a full narrative of the extraordinary voyage of the flotilla through the rivers and canals of France when the boats were summoned home in November 1939. Although the full story, as he tells it, is somewhat beyond the scope of this history, there are parts which deserve to be recorded.[2]

On September 1st (1939) the boats prepared for war. Warheads were shipped on the torpedoes and loaded on board; the petrol tanks were topped up, the guns mounted, and the crews stood by for whatever might happen. The atmosphere was tense, as most of the COs expected Italy to come into the war and stage an immediate invasion of Malta. Clearly the task of the MTBs would be to sink the enemy transports.

On 3rd September, the COs were gathered in the wardroom of HMS *Vulcan*, the depot ship. The declaration of war came over the radio. Nobody said anything for a few seconds. Then Jock Guthrie, the Captain of *Vulcan*, said 'It'll all be over in eighteen months.'

Everyone was keyed up that night, and indeed for many nights afterwards, waiting for Italy to throw in her lot with Germany. Gradually things returned to normal. Training went on as before, but at a much higher tempo. The boats tried out new forms of attack: no one quite realised what differences would be found when the real thing presented itself.

2   An unpublished article, Mannooch, 'An account of the return of the 1st MTB Flotilla through the French Canals'.

Lts L.J.H. Gamble and A.T. Seymour-Hayden in 1939. (Courtesy, Capt D. Jermain RN)

MTB 14 in 1939. (Courtesy, Capt D. Jermain RN)

Lt P.F.S. Gould, CO MTB 16, in 1939. (Courtesy, Capt D. Jermain RN)

This state of increasing preparedness went on into November, when suddenly the orders came through that the flotilla was to return home to England. It was clearly thought that this – the only flotilla complete and ready for operations – would be more valuable in home waters where a real and menacing enemy threat already existed.

The decision to return through France was not altogether unexpected, but there was much discussion about the problems that might arise in an alien river/canal environment: sailors always want the certainty of enough water under the keel! But at least the threat of bad winter weather would be reduced by this route.

There was real concern about the seaworthiness of the older boats in particular. Some boats were despatched to Britain or Marseilles by freighter. The rest set out on 11 November, first to Bizerta and then via Ajaccio in Corsica to the mouth of the canal system near Marseilles. As luck would have it, they were caught on each leg by the most appalling weather, and all suffered to one degree or another with damage to frames and superstructure. These were the worst conditions any of them had ever experienced. Fortunately the flotilla was being escorted by the destroyer *Dainty*, and *Vulcan* waited in Ajaccio to help with repairs. But disaster was to strike as the boats laboured northward off Sardinia in a north-westerly gale.

During the night several boats developed serious leaks. The older boats were not in a condition to take this prolonged battering. In 06 in particular, the level of water in the engine room rose steadily despite constant pumping, until first one engine then another were completely covered. It became obvious that there was no hope of saving 06, and the CO ('Harpy' Lloyd) managed to get her alongside *Dainty* in order to transfer crew and gear and as much of the valuable gear as was possible. A fruitless attempt was made to tow 06, but in the end, 'Harpy' and his crew watched with distress as *Dainty* rammed her to make sure she sank.[3]

3 Mannooch, 'An account of the return of the 1st MTB Flotilla through the French Canals'.

Two of the boats enter a canal lock. (Courtesy, C.L. Coles)

A French pilot on the bridge. (Courtesy, C.L. Coles)

MTB 18 at speed. (Courtesy, the late J.T. Mannooch)

MTB 18, now at war (left, Sub Lt J.L. Fraser RNVR; right, Lt J.T. Mannooch). Note the quadruple Lewis gun mountings and the badge, which depicts a flying fish with a scorpion's tail. The motto is 'Caudae Spiculum Cave' (beware the sting in the tail). It was designed by the wife of the first SO of the flotilla, Lt Cdr G.B. Sayer. (Courtesy, the late J.T. Mannooch)

Two of the other boats sought shelter in a tiny harbour in northern Sardinia, and only escaped internment by the 'neutral' Italians through the kindness of a non-Fascist Italian port commander. Then with repairs at Ajaccio, the final leg was completed and the boats entered the canals on 24 November to make their historic passage. Their route took them up the Rhone through Avignon to Lyons, and then on northward up the River Saone to the start of the Burgundy canal system at St Jean de Losne, through Dijon to Ivigny where they joined the River Yonne and thence on past Paris, Meulun and Rouen to Le Havre, finally arriving in Portsmouth on 19 December.

There had been many adventures. Negotiating the bridges with the rivers running fast tested the skill of pilots and COs. Even more hazardous was the need to tow the boats through the canal system using military tractors, as even at minimum speed the wash would have reduced the water level drastically. The French tractor drivers would not slow down – however much beseeched – for the locks, and fenders and warps were much in evidence. Boats frequently went aground. Then they faced a 3-km tunnel, and because the towing craft broke down they had to go through under power, an ear-shattering and eerie experience with no head room or light.

And so the 1st MTB Flotilla passed out of the Mediterranean Command and within days, 14–18, the newer boats, were setting up the base at Felixstowe. They distinguished themselves at Zeebrugge, Ostend and Dunkirk, but most of all they provided the experience upon which to build the offensive force which developed during 1940 and 1941. In particular, Stewart Gould went on to become a legend in Coastal Forces, first in MGBs at Dover, and then leading the 32nd MTB Flotilla of Dog Boats in the Mediterranean until he was killed in April 1943 in a gallant daylight operation.[4]

4 Reynolds, *Dog Boats at War*.

CHAPTER 2

THE 10TH MTB FLOTILLA

(Note 3, Appendix 1)

1941

The year 1940 began without any Coastal Forces presence in the Mediterranean. The 'Phoney War' was just as evident there as in other areas. Italy had not declared war as had been expected, but remained a constant threat in view of her influence in the region and the existence of a sizeable Navy and Air Force, based in ports and on airfields which could at any time be the springboard for offensive action. The Royal Navy had the advantage of its well established bases at Gibraltar, Malta and Alexandria.

From the perspective of the 'small boat' protagonists in high places, it was well known that Italy had made greater strides than any other power in designing and building a fleet of small, fast boats. Their post-First World War commitment had begun as early as 1929, when first the SVAN yard in Venice and later the Baglietto yard at Varazze had begun to produce very effective Motor Torpedo Boats, so that by 1940 they had more than a hundred in commission.

These boats – known as MAS boats – which at first stood for 'Motoscafo Armato SVAN', and then later for 'Motoscafo Anti-sommergibile' (motor anti-submarine boats), always had the tremendous advantage of the Isotta Fraschini engines which were internationally regarded as the finest marine petrol engines available. The Italian MAS were generally smaller than the MTBs being built elsewhere, largely because the Mediterranean did not require boats which could operate in the far more demanding sea conditions of the North Sea. They varied in length from 48 ft to 60 ft, reached speeds of 42 knots and carried two 17.7-in torpedoes. Looking ahead, the Italian Navy was able by 1941 to develop a longer and more sea-worthy boat which incorporated some features of the early German Schnelleboot.[1]

Italy entered the war on 11 June 1940, at the height of the fateful summer when the German military machine drove the British Army out of the continental mainland of Europe and in one stroke left the Royal Navy the task of maintaining across the oceans the sea communications upon which our island nation depended. But now the approaches to our eastern and southern ports – the North Sea and the Channel – were bordered by an entirely hostile coastline from which attacks could be launched.

Despite these demands closer to home, the need for more small craft in the Mediterranean was constantly being pressed by the C-in-C, and by October 1940 it was decided to send a flotilla of MTBs to Alexandria. This was no small sacrifice, as resources were woefully inadequate, and despite strenuous efforts in Admiralty (albeit with hindsight,

---

1   Cooper, *The Battle of the Torpedo Boats*.

begun far later than required) the 1939 War Emergency Programme for Vosper, White and Thornycroft MTBs and British Power Boat MA/SBs (most later to become MGBs) was slow to materialize. Apart from the old 1st MTB Flotilla boats, a handful of Vospers, a few very early MA/SBs, and a number of craft being built for foreign navies and immediately requisitioned, the cupboard was bare and the demands increasing.

In fact, the scanty individual boat records of this time and one personal memoir reveal that only two MA/SBs (2 and 3) were shipped to the Mediterranean after January 1940, but only MA/SB 3 appears in reports.[2]

Motor Anti-submarine Boat (MA/SB) 3 was a 60-ft British Power Boat of 19 tons

displacement, built at Hythe and powered by two Napier Sea Lions. When MA/SB 3 was completed on 13 June 1939, she was equipped with an Asdic dome, ten depth charges and two twin 0.303 mountings aft of the bridge. The direct information about her comes from Fred Coombes, an 'active service' rating who was later to earn a DSM as Petty Officer Coxswain of a Dog Boat on the East Coast.

He joined the boat while it was being built, and was with her throughout her commission. The CO was Lt D.J. Ritchie RN. The first few weeks were spent at Portland on exercises, which continued when war was declared until, just after Christmas 1939, the boat was lifted aboard a merchant vessel and the crew despatched by rail across France to Marseilles, and thence by sea to Alexandria, where they rejoined the boat and found that

2   Personal memoir: the late Fred Coombes DSM, *Reminiscences of WW2*; copy at IWM.

MA/SB 03 was shipped to Alexandria in January 1940 and operated along the desert coast. (Courtesy, G.M. Hudson)

any removable fitting had been nefariously removed by the notorious dockyard workers there.

MA/SB 3 spent a lot of time at sea patrolling the desert coast westward and also eastward to Port Said and Haifa. Without any Base organization, they relied greatly on help from small Army units in garrisons along the coast. When Italy entered the war in the summer, they felt very vulnerable against Italian fighters, having only four 0.303s, and were greatly relieved when a 20-mm Breda cannon was mounted aft. They were despatched to Sollum on a special mission, and also to Bardia to support a raid; by the time they got there, Wavell had launched his counter-offensive, and the enemy had evacuated the port and was in full flight along the coast road. Coombes describes how Ritchie landed him and another rating to investigate and to bring back prisoners. His account is hilarious, but ends with the mission accomplished, one (Italian) officer and seven men having surrendered to two ratings in bathing costumes armed only with one rifle and one revolver (and clearly no reserve ammunition). The capitulation was encouraged by a burst of Lewis gun fire from Ritchie aboard MA/SB 3, a very short way offshore.

After this excitement, and a return to Alexandria, Coombes recalls a great increase in bombing attacks. In early 1941, the enemy attempted to block the all-important Suez Canal with the new acoustic mines, dropped by Italian aircraft. Just as in home waters, fast boats were called in to experiment with methods of detonating the mines safely. MA/SB 3 was pressed into service on 12 February 1941, with the urgent need to clear the canal for two vital convoys which were due. Coombes writes:

Being unable to sweep for these mines, the experts (miraculously shore-based) decided that a fast craft going over the known position of the mine (they had plotted the position of two) would explode the mine after the boat had gone by. A fast pilot boat did the first sweep, but wasn't quite fast enough, and went up with her nine-man crew. No. 3 was given the next chance for glory.

Lt Ritchie made his first run, but nothing happened – to our great relief. Nothing happened for the next five or six runs at speed, and things were beginning to get a bit boring. I was in sunbathing mode flat on the deck behind the bridge.

The skipper decided to call it a day, dropped our speed and headed for the experts on the bank. I must have dozed off, because I didn't know the exercise was over, when there was a terrific 'whump' and No. 3 was airborne. I don't know how high we went or at what point No. 3 left me, but I remember opening my eyes and seeing an Army tented camp on the far side of the high canal bank – and then I rejoined the boat with a jarring crash.

The skipper and all those on the bridge were badly hurt, the rest of us were in shock, and the boat was rapidly filling.

That was the end of MA/SB 3. Coombes saw her on the jetty when he got out of hospital, apparently being repaired; but the official record states, 'formally paid off 26 July 1941'. Lt Ritchie was later CO of SGB 4, and earned a DSC for an action in the Channel in July 1942.

This boat's short commission acts as a link in the Coastal Forces presence in the Mediterranean, as she arrived shortly after the departure of the 1st MTB Flotilla, and her demise occurred shortly before the arrival of the 10th MTB Flotilla in March 1941.

The story of the earliest days of the 10th Flotilla is typical of the 'hand-to-mouth' state of Coastal Forces at this time, as the struggle to meet the demands far exceeded the resources available. Because the 10th – in its various forms as will be seen – was the first operational flotilla in the Mediterranean,

Hull of MA/SB 03 after being mined in the Suez Canal. (Courtesy, G.M. Hudson)

and was ever present till the end of the war, it is fitting to trace its halting conception, gestation and birth, which began long before the boats arrived in the Command.

It was in April 1940 that two Thornycroft boats with extraordinarily chequered beginnings enter the saga.

They had originally been laid down for the Philippine Navy, but in 1939/40 when Finland was seeking arms, including MTBs, they were reallocated to that country. Before they were ready for despatch, Finland – by *force majeure* – had signed a peace treaty with Russia on 12 March 1940. The boats were actually loaded aboard a freighter at Blyth ready to sail when Lt C.C. Anderson RN was ordered to get there post-haste and by any means get them off-loaded. Courtney Anderson – destined ultimately to reach Flag rank – was to play a major part in the leadership of the flotilla until December 1941, and has been able to provide confirmatory information on these early days.

Norway had been invaded on 9 April 1940 and that had led to the decision to requisition these two boats.

Anderson managed, after some initial difficulty, to persuade the reluctant master of the freighter to off-load the two MTBs, and accepted a receipt for them on the back of a sheet torn from a signal pad.

The two boats became MTBs 67 and 68 and were commissioned on 19 April 1940 to form the 10th Flotilla. Anderson was CO of 67, and Senior Officer of the flotilla, and 68 was entrusted to Lt David Souter RNVR, one of the earliest RNVR officers to be given a command. Thornycrofts had built the CMBs (Coastal Motor Boats) of the First World War, and these two craft differed very little from the CMBs in construction. They were 55 ft long, and the one major improvement since 1919 had been to increase the power of each of the two Thornycroft RY12 engines to 650 b.h.p. Stern discharge troughs were used for housing and firing torpedoes.

Within three weeks, on 10 May, Hitler invaded the Low Countries, and the boats were sent down to Portsmouth. Courtney Anderson remembers being reprimanded for passing through the boom at about 50 knots – and being well satisfied at this initial performance. Awaiting their arrival was the newly appointed Flotilla Engineer Officer, Lt (E) C.W. Coverdale RN – known to all as 'Miles' – who was to perform miracles with the boats of the flotilla over the months to come.

In fact, his troubles began when the boats moved to Portland for torpedo trials. It soon became apparent that the weak link in the overall engine installation was the clutch mechanism which had not been improved since the First World War, and was to continue to cause considerable problems for Coverdale and the motor mechanics on each boat. Speed trials at Portland showed maximum speeds of 48 knots.

Shortly after, three more Thornycroft boats arrived to bring the numbers up to five. But these were smaller, less powerful boats and had not really been designed as MTBs. 104 was 45 ft in length and had been laid down and built in the hope that the Admiralty might accept her (an intelligent presumption). 106 and 107 were only 40 ft in length, and had been ordered as DCTBs (Distant Controlled Target Boats). All three were powered by a single RY12 engine. MTB 104 carried two 18-in torpedoes and MTBs 106 and 107 just one. They even varied in the maximum speed they could achieve due to different hull forms: 106 at 40 knots, 107 at 33 knots and 104 at 38 knots, and all three inherited the same clutch problems as the earlier two vessels. By 25 May, all were commissioned, and Courtney Anderson, no doubt reflecting on the problems ahead in station-keeping, led his 'job lot of a flotilla' to HMS *Beehive* at Felixstowe, where they were to be based.

All three of the new boats were commanded by RNVR officers: MTB 104 by Lt R.R. Smith who stayed with the 10th for three years before commanding a Dog Boat; 106 by Lt I. Quarrie who had been one of a small group of RNVR Sub Lieutenants appointed as a First Lieutenant in the 1st MTB Flotilla before the war, and went on to command boats to the very end, later becoming a Captain RNR; and 107 by Lt J. Cameron, who at forty years old, was probably the oldest serving MTB officer and was affectionately known as 'Grandpa'. After the war he became Lord Cameron, a distinguished Scottish judge.

These were stirring times, and it was no surprise when, as they approached Dover en route for Felixstowe, they were ordered into port, and Anderson in 67 found himself roaring across the Channel carrying three Belgian Cabinet Ministers back to their country, and with orders to return with King Leopold from Nieuport. But the King refused to leave his country, now being occupied by the Germans, so 67 brought back Admiral Sir Roger Keyes instead.

Next day the five boats moved on again to Felixstowe, but within 48 hours three of them were sent back to Dover. Thousands of British troops were trapped on the beaches of Dunkirk, and the operation to get as many of them as possible back to England began. The three boats became heavily involved in ferrying troops from the harbour and beaches to the larger ships offshore, and also operated a communications service between the larger naval units. 67, 68 and 107 all distinguished themselves, and Cameron in 107 and the temporary CO of 68 (Lt R.K.L. Walker) were each 'mentioned in despatches'. All three returned safely that first night without any casualties and with many passengers.

The night before the final surrender at Dunkirk, 107 is recorded as having escorted the destroyer *Vivacious* and three blockships into Dunkirk harbour. The following night 107 was back again with HMS *Shikari* and three more blockships, her role on each occasion being to take off the crews of the blockships as they abandoned them in position. Not content when this main task had been completed, Cameron was busy fishing individual soldiers out of the water, despite the fact that his boat with its single engine lacked astern gear and made manoeuvring extraordinarily difficult. He suddenly realized that all the guns ashore were firing at him: he was on his own as every other vessel had left. Then, and only then, did he leave and make his way back to the English coast – the last RN ship to leave Dunkirk.

To add insult to injury, he had to include in his report 'that he had become involved with the Goodwin Sands'! Some of the soldiers aboard, and his crew, lowered themselves over the side to push 107 clear and they returned safely to port.

Back they went again to Felixstowe, but when the Battle of Britain began in August 1940, all five were sent to Sheerness for air-sea rescue duties. There was such a shortage of fighter pilots at this time that it was absolutely vital that any who 'ditched' within reach should be picked up rapidly. They achieved a good deal of success.

By now, having obtained a reputation as 'maids of all work', they were detailed to accompany a raiding force for Operation Lucid. The object was to counter the build-up of German invasion barges in the French Channel ports by sending fire ships into Boulogne and Calais: the MTBs' task once again was to rescue the skeleton crews when their ships were in position. But the plan was dogged by ill fortune, and was cancelled three times. When it was finally ordered – on the last suitable night – the leading destroyer was damaged by an acoustic mine, and the operation aborted, never to be attempted again.

The gallantry of the RAF's fighter pilots having ensured that the Battle of Britain was won, a new phase of operations by the Luftwaffe began, with a campaign of night bombing of our cities and towns, and the laying of acoustic and magnetic mines in the swept channels used by our convoys. These, at first, caused losses among our merchant shipping and called for a rapid revision of sweeping techniques.

Many methods were tried, including – at first – the attempt to activate acoustic mines by sending high-speed boats over them, to explode them clear of their wakes. This was entirely an emergency and experimental measure, as at this time no scientific analysis had been made of these mines. There was some success with this (but failures too, as has been recorded in the case of MA/SB 3 in the Suez Canal in the following February).

At this time it led to the loss of MTB 106, commanded by Ian Quarrie. The 10th Flotilla had been pressed into this service in the Thames Estuary, and on 16 October 1940 106 was sent out at short notice in an emergency (a convoy was about to pass). Such was the urgency that permission to unload her torpedo was not granted, and when 106 slowed (from 35 to 28 knots) for a tight turn at the end of her eighth run she detonated the mine and blew up, scattering her crew over a wide area. There were no fatal casualties, but 106 was a total loss. Quarrie took the place of Jock Cameron in 107, and within two weeks orders came through that the 10th were to be sent to the Mediterranean.

It was clear that the two small one-engined Thornycrofts remaining – 104 and 107 – were not really suitable for flotilla operations, so 67 and 68 were joined by the five Thornycroft boats of similar design, MTB 213–217, which were originally laid down for the Philippines and were just completing. The only difference was a larger bridge structure, giving greater protection for the crew, but at least all seven boats now had the common capability of a maximum speed of about 42 knots, with two 18-in torpedoes and two twin Lewis machine guns.

MTBs 104 and 107, having been redeployed, were assigned to accompany the LSIs (Landing Ships Infantry) *Glengyle, Glenearn,* and *Glenroy* in a projected operation in the central Mediterranean: the capture of the heavily fortified and strategically important island of Pantelleria in the Sicilian Channel. The operation was cancelled before they left, although the Landing Ships – with 107 and 104 and the commandos aboard – still sailed, but were rerouted via the Cape to Egypt instead. Admiral Sir Roger Keyes, the Chief of Combined Operations was heard to comment: 'I expect they'll find you something to do out there.' And certainly 104 and 107 *were* used on many covert missions with such groups as the LRDG (Long Range Desert Group) but never as part of the 10th Flotilla.

The 55-ft boats were secured on trailers and driven by road to the Clyde (arriving in Scotland on New Year's Day 1941) and loaded aboard merchant ships to sail in convoy round the Cape to Port Said. Also in the convoy was SS *Salween* carrying all the crews of the seven boats and the flotilla staff.[3]

It was three months before they arrived in Alexandria, and the Mediterranean 10th Flotilla in its new form began its commission. Among the five new COs was Lt Cdr E.C. Peake RN, who, being senior to Courtney Anderson, became Senior Officer of the Flotilla in January 1941. The seven boats, and their COs, were:

MTB 67   Lt C.C. Anderson RN
      68   Lt R.R. Smith RNVR
     213   Lt W.T.K. Kemble RNVR

     214   Lt Cdr E.C. Peake RN
     215   Lt A. Fowler RNVR
     216   Lt C.L. Coles RNVR
     217   Lt R. Rickards RNVR

The arrival of the 10th Flotilla in Alexandria was greeted almost immediately by a total change in the strategic situation in the Eastern Mediterranean.

On 6 April 1941 the Germans and Italians had invaded the Balkan Peninsula, overrunning Yugoslavia, Albania and Greece in just eighteen days. The British Army personnel in Greece, with a high proportion of Australians and New Zealanders, were painfully evacuated to Crete and bases on the African coast. With no air cover to counter the might of the Luftwaffe, the Navy took a pounding, and several cruisers, destroyers and supply ships were lost and others crippled. But an incredible 51,000 men were brought out – 80 per cent of the forces originally deployed in Greece.

At the same time the desert war was taking another of its cyclical turns, and the Army, with its communications and supply routes stretched by the recent rapid advance westward, was pushed equally rapidly back, and it was decided to withdraw, leaving Tobruk as an isolated heavily defended garrison. The military resources were simply too thinly spread, and with the need to help first in Greece and then in Crete, there was disaster all round.[4]

It was into this situation that the boats of the 10th Flotilla – all of ancient design, and with constant engineering problems in the gearing systems, first discovered in 67 and 68 a year earlier – were thrust. They had hardly had time to work up together (a great drawback as only 67 and 68 had any previous operational experience) when the order came that they should proceed post-haste to Suda

---

3   Notes from R.W. Harlow, at the time L/MM of MTB 214.

4   Churchill, *The Second World War*, Vol. 3.

Bay on the north coast of Crete to assist in any way that might be required to repel the anticipated invasion of the island from Greece.

All seven boats left Alexandria at 0530 on 11 May, bound for their first stop at Mersa Matruh. Almost at once, 68 reported clutch trouble and returned to port to repair it. As soon as the other boats arrived at Mersa Matruh, they discovered that the 87-octane petrol which their engines required was not available. In view of the urgent need to press on to Crete, Lt Cdr Peake agreed to refuel with 70-octane, and this had just been completed when an RAF officer arrived with stores which the MTBs were to take to Crete. He brought, too, the alarming news that the 70-octane fuel was of such poor quality that even his lorries ran badly on it. Peake, realizing how serious this could be for his boats, sent 215 out for a test run, and the Engineer Officer warned that to use this fuel would wreck the engines. When the RAF generously offered 87-octane petrol from their meagre stocks, Peake decided that he had to accept the delay, and ordered the boats to defuel and then refuel with the higher quality fuel. It came in flimsy four-gallon cans, packed two to a wooden crate. The thin tin cans often leaked, and the work was dangerous, very slow and tedious, as the fuel all needed filtering: no high pressure hoses here!

At least the delay enabled 68 to rejoin – but all to no avail. Rushing from Alexandria she had fractured the fore bearer of the starboard engine and started a bad leak – so back she had to go.

It was at 1312 on 12 May that the flotilla eventually left Mersa Matruh for Tobruk. At approximately 1730, MTB 215 reported that

MTB 213 (55-ft Thornycroft) at Mersa Matruh, 1941. (Courtesy, G.M. Hudson)

The crew of MTB 67 at Mersa Matruh 1941. (Courtesy, E. Scott)

her starboard clutch was slipping badly, and the SO sent her back to Alexandria via Mersa Matruh. An hour later, 217 had the same trouble with her port clutch. Rather than send her back, Peake detailed 213 to stand by her and keep going at reduced speed to Tobruk, leaving just three boats to press on as fast as possible. They arrived there at 2300 and immediately commenced fuelling. 213 and 217 joined them at 0200 next morning.

The story from then on is a catalogue of disaster. It was a nightmare for the SO, the COs and the motor mechanics that very nearly every boat suffered from clutch trouble, and to compound it all, the weather deteriorated and the sea state reached a level at which the boats would not normally be able to operate. But they struggled on. 216's port clutch seized up and 213 stood by her;

Peake in 214 went on ahead, refuelled at Elaphonisi Bay from a tanker, and set out for Suda Bay. At least her next problem was the enemy, not engine trouble: she was attacked three times by a Dornier and replied as best she could, claiming to secure hits on the enemy aircraft.

214 secured alongside in Suda Bay at 1930 on 13 May, and Anderson in 67 joined her at 0630 the next morning having kept up her slower speed throughout.[5]

213 (Kemble) and 216 (Coles) meanwhile were having their own problems. The flotilla Engineering Officer, Miles Coverdale, transferred to 216 to assist with the seized clutch. In succession, Kemble towed 216, slipped,

5   ROP dated 15 May 1941 by Lt Cdr E.C. Peake, deposited by his family at IWM.

and then tried again; then his own boat's fuel pressure failed and was restored by hand pumping; and finally the towing pennant parted and was transferred, before one engine failed. At nightfall the two boats limped into the lee of Puli Island at Gavdo, each on one engine, only to find it was an unsafe anchorage. Three times they moved and tried again, and somehow saw the night out safely. Hungry, wet and cold, they secured to the shore, inflated their rubber dinghies, and landed to seek water and food. They were successful in both. They found a well and Charles Coles demonstrated his resourcefulness by shooting a wild goat which they cooked and ate.

Both W/T sets were out of action, and being urgently in need of fuel, they decided to limp on towards Sphakia, whence they hoped to be able to contact Suda Bay. This was eventually achieved, and on the morning of the 18th, the trawler *Syvern* entered harbour, refuelled both boats and set off with them towards Suda: 216 in tow, and 213 going on ahead; both arrived by noon.[6]

Meanwhile, the one remaining boat of those which had set off from Tobruk, 217 (Rickards), despite her port clutch problems, had been making her way independently and on one engine towards Crete, showing dogged determination. She arrived at Sphakia, where the locals thought they were Germans, and came to surrender the village! Rickards was unable to make himself understood, but his First Lieutenant could just remember one phrase of classical Greek from his school days (not so long before), which was 'Is there a soldier in the market place?' There was – a Private of the Royal Signals, with a landline over the mountains to Suda! And so it was that Peake learnt that 217 had reached Crete – if not Suda – safely.

6   ROP by Lt T.P.K. Kemble RNVR to SO
      10th Flotilla, 19 May 1941.

Of the five Thornycrofts that set out from Tobruk on the 13 May, only 67 and 214 had arrived in an operational state. 213 and 217 took some time to repair, but joined them before the invasion began; 216 remained out of action.

At first, 214 and 67 had carried out patrols in the Kithera Channel off the south coast of Greece, hoping to find a torpedo target but mainly to keep a lookout for the seaborne invasion which the Intelligence Services had predicted as imminent. As the tension mounted, and when four boats became serviceable, they alternated in pairs between the lookout patrols and a close defence position outside the boom.

The routine was that at dawn the boats would return, secure alongside, and the crews would go off to have breakfast in a tented camp some distance away in an olive grove. They returned to the base at 0900 with their officers to receive instructions for the day and the operational orders for the next night. The boats were too small for the crews to live aboard continuously, and when they returned to the camp to sleep, base staff took over to refuel the boats and carry out any maintenance. 216 being out of action, had her twin .303s mounted on their tripods in trenches in the dockyard, for use against the increasing air attacks by the enemy.

On 20 May the Germans launched their invasion force. Although it had been expected that both seaborne and airborne assaults would be employed, it had not been possible to anticipate the ferocity of the airborne attack.

In Volume 3 of his history of the Second World War, Churchill with all his experience of war expressed the opinion that the German assault on Crete was unique. Never before had an airborne attack on this scale been launched. Goering had clearly decided that after his failure to subdue the RAF in the Battle of Britain, he needed a prestigious victory here, and threw in all the resources he could. It was a reckless and ruthless attack, and a full regiment of four battalions of airborne troops was used on the morning of 20 May, and yet another in the afternoon. Their first target was the airfield at Maleme and the port of Canea, both only a few miles west of Suda Bay, and a fierce battle developed as the troops landed by parachute and glider. There were thousands of casualties on both sides, but still the enemy poured in, and attacks on Suda Bay itself were stepped up.[7]

On the night before the invasion (19/20 May), MTB 67 (Courtney Anderson) and one other boat had been operating from Canea, patrolling the Kithera Channel. When the two boats returned to Canea at dawn on 20 May, Anderson, having heard of a 'pension' where he could get a hot bath, went there and began to enjoy the luxury of immersing himself in the warm water. It was the first time he had had his clothes off since leaving Alexandria. He was actually in the bath when the window was blown in by a bomb, and when he looked through the hole he saw paratroops floating down outside. He rapidly dressed, ran back to the boats, crash started and set off for Suda Bay.

Despite the fact that the Allies – urged by Churchill to defend Crete to the death – had thrown in 40,000 troops, the situation deteriorated, even in face of gallant resistance by the New Zealanders led by Major General Freyberg VC. But it was in the air that the battle was being lost.

Courtney Anderson tells how he was sent on patrol in 67 on the night of 21/22 May off north-west Crete (the anticipated seaborne invasion having not yet materialized) when he encountered what he thought was another MTB. Both vessels stopped, cut engines, and

spoke to each other, but Anderson could not make out what the other was shouting, and eventually gave up and resumed patrol. Next morning – rather annoyed at an apparent lack of briefing – he made enquiries, and discovered that no other boat had been in his area at that time. He suddenly realised that he must have hailed a German patrol boat – possibly an E-boat.

67 was out again on the following night, and met the same boat. The German could have blasted the tiny Thornycroft out of the water but did not open fire, and so Courtney Anderson crept away until he reached the comparative safety of the darkness of the background mountains. As he did this, feeling very naked as he presented his unprotected rear to the enemy, he took a cursory glance over his shoulder and saw the German boat creeping off to seaward in the opposite direction. Our boats were under orders not to waste their precious torpedoes on small craft, saving them for enemy destroyers or transports. He assumed the German CO must have been under similar orders. Ships that pass in the night!

All the available boats of the 10th Flotilla had been out on patrol on the night of 22 May, leaving harbour at dusk and returning to pass the boom at first light. When they berthed, they were directed to avoid the main pier which had been the main target of dive-bombers, and to berth at the southern jetty. As already described, the crews were able to leave the boats to the base staff and go to the camp to get some sleep in order to be ready for the next night.

At 1150 on the 23rd, the normal considerable enemy air activity was in full swing, but there was no real indication that a specific attack was being made on the MTBs. The skeleton crews (one 'boat-keeper' from each crew, and the base staff) were manning the guns, when suddenly four ME 109 fighter aircraft peeled off and began an attack,

7   Churchill, *The Second World War*, Vol. 3.

Lt (later Rear Adm) C.C. Anderson RN (right) CO of MTB 67 with his First Lieutenant Sub Lt Kennedy. (Courtesy, E. Scott)

passing over the boats at 30 ft and sending heavy bursts of cannon and machine gun fire into the boats. Almost at once, the boat-keepers manning 213 and 217 were wounded, and the attack on 216 set both the boat and some petrol cans on the jetty on fire. Frantic efforts were made to extinguish the fires and save the boats, but the heat was too intense. A runner was despatched to the camp to fetch the rest of the crews, but when they arrived the jetty was impossible to reach owing to exploding torpedoes, ammunition and petrol tanks.[8]

At 1210, this initial attack was followed by another, and this time nine ME 109s, some carrying bombs, strafed all five boats for about half an hour. At the end of this second attack, all the boats were badly on fire. MTB 214 blew up at 1245, and at 1315 the next exploded. In doing so, it damaged and sank the remaining three boats. In fact Anderson's 67 was the last to sink, staying afloat for a time with her bows severely damaged. The whole dock area was then evacuated.

There was no doubt that the objective of this particular raid was to eliminate the five MTBs and to prevent them taking any further part in the operations around Crete. It was not perhaps untypical of the C-in-C (the redoubtable Adm A.B. Cunningham, who took a great deal of convincing that MTBs were of any real value), that he should, on receipt of the SO's report of the loss of his flotilla, send what appeared to be a heartless demand for more information. He wanted a plan of how the boats were berthed, and details of 'the action taken by you and the Commanding Officers of the MTBs to defend themselves against the enemy attacks'.

Fortunately, Capt (later Admiral) J.A.V. Morse, the NOIC Suda Bay, was staunch in support of the flotilla in his reply. He stated

MTB 67 severely damaged immediately after the air attack on 23 May 1941 in Suda Bay, Crete. (Courtesy, E. Scott)

that it was only through the tremendous efforts of the officers and men of the boats and the base staff that the difficulties experienced with engines and petrol supply were overcome and the boats kept service-able. He pointed out that there was a dire shortage of spares, that there really was no alternative to the berthing arrangements, and that wherever they had been berthed, as the bombing was frequent and comprehensive, any one part of the harbour was just as unhealthy as any other.

As to the morning of the actual attacks, he pointed out that as the boats were clearly the sole targets for the aircraft, they would in any case have been destroyed. His last paragraph reflected the reality of the situation:

---

8   ROP by Lt Cdr E.C. Peake RN, SO 10th MTB Flotilla.

The attacks developed so rapidly and the scale of the machine gunning was so heavy that it was quite impossible for any defensive action to be taken by MTB crews present at the time. What they were chiefly concerned with was the extinguishing of the fire which was started by the first burst of machine gun fire. They displayed great bravery and determination in their efforts, as throughout the whole time they were subjected to fierce fire from aircraft flying low over their heads. It is submitted that these efforts are worthy of commendation.[9]

This, then, was the sad end of these first boats of the 10th Flotilla within a very short time of the commencement of commission. There had been so many problems with engines and particularly the clutch assembly that, with a mixture of exasperation and affection for these fast and beautifully finished tiny boats, the COs and the Engineer Officer and his mechanics had nicknamed this 'The Wobbly Tenth'. But among the casualties and losses at Crete, the flotilla had displayed great resource and determination not only on passage to Suda Bay, but once there in operating nightly while experiencing continual hazard from the air by day.

The officers and crews of the boats were eventually evacuated on the very eve of the final surrender aboard the destroyer *Kandahar*, among the last men to leave Crete. The ship was continually attacked from the air all the way to Alexandria, and arrived there with just ten rounds of main armament ammunition remaining.

The last officer of the flotilla to return to Alexandria was Lt Charles Coles, the CO of 216. He was recruited as a beachmaster during the evacuation from Crete, aboard the Australian destroyer *Napier*. His knowledge

of the port of Sphakia on the south coast of the island, where with his boat he had been forced to stay en route to Suda Bay, was used to help guide vessels during the rescue of stranded troops.

There were, of course, big changes ahead for the officers of the five boats. Although there were plans to bring out a new generation of US-built MTBs to re-form the flotilla, they were not due until nearly the end of 1941, and therefore temporary (or in some cases more permanent) appointments had to be found. The SO, Lt Cdr Peake RN, left the flotilla, leaving Courtney Anderson to resume that appointment, albeit with only the rump of the flotilla to command – that is the two boats which had broken down and never reached Crete. MTBs 68 (R.R. Smith) and 215 (Alec Joy, a Canadian) were now available.

Lt W.T.K Kemble returned to the UK. Charles Coles was appointed Liaison Officer to a Royal Yugoslav Navy MTB, and was destined to return later to the flotilla. Lt Fowler was also given a similar appointment, but became seriously ill only a month later and died in hospital in Alexandria. Lt Wolfe, the spare CO of the flotilla, was sent to the Greek submarine *Papanicolas*, and Lt Rickards went to Malta to take command of the Italian MAS 452, which had been captured during a raid on the island and subsequently renamed wittily as HMS *Xmas*. He was killed in an air raid on Malta later in the year.

The crews of the five boats were kept together as much as possible, and held to join the new boats when they arrived.

Courtney Anderson and his two boats had a colourful and varied time over the next few months. Their first assignment was to help in the blockade of the Lebanon from a base in Kyrenia in Cyprus, during the Syrian campaign. Their task was to prevent caiques from penetrating the blockade, and they patrolled off the Turkish coast. In this, the SO had the unique experience – as a young RN lieutenant

9   ROP by Lt Cdr E.C. Peake RN and by Capt J.A.V. Morse DSO RN, Naval Officer in Charge, Suda Bay, at the time.

Italian MAS boat 452 captured in a raid on Malta, and later renamed HMS *Xmas*, when her CO was Lt R.M. Rickards RNVR, previously a CO of a boat in the 10th Flotilla. (Courtesy, E. Scott)

MTBs 68 and 215 – 'the rump of the 10th Flotilla' – at Kyrenia in Cyprus, 1941. (Courtesy, E. Scott)

– of taking under his command two Swordfish aircraft based in Nicosia to add to the depleted strength of his flotilla. The aircraft even sank a French destroyer – a first 'kill' for the 10th Flotilla.

When the caique traffic had been halted, the two boats were moved across to Haifa, with a main operational object of patrolling off Beirut. Maintenance was still a huge problem with a shortage of supplies calling for improvisation, particularly on the part of their highly regarded Engineer Officer Miles Coverdale. Anderson remembers one of his remarkable feats typical of this period. A new propeller shaft was required for one of the boats, and using the workshops of the Palestine Railways, Coverdale took up a length of the jetty railway line and machined a new shaft from it.

Torpedo targets off Beirut were very scarce, and Richard Smith in 68 became very

frustated, and decided that if the only targets were to be found inside the harbour, he would go in and tackle them there. Not only did he drop a depth charge under each of two merchantmen, but on his way out he torpedoed two more. It was a daring and highly successful raid – the greatest success so far of the 10th Flotilla – and Courtney Anderson in reporting it recommended Richard Smith for a DSC he so clearly deserved. But by a stroke of ill fortune he had chosen to make his attack the night before Beirut fell, and the ships he had sunk were blocking off jetties and piers required by Allied shipping moving into the port. So instead of a decoration, both Smith and Anderson were admonished for not realizing that the fall of the port was imminent.

When the Lebanon surrendered, the two boats returned to Alexandria, and from there were sent to operate along the desert coast from Mersa Matruh. They laid mines off

MTB 68, taken from 215, on passage to Alexandria. (Courtesy, E. Scott)

An Italian Breda gun mounting captured at Tobruk, later used aboard MTB 61. (Courtesy, G.M. Hudson)

Bardia and Derna, and searched in vain for enemy shipping to torpedo.

It was not until February 1942 that the much needed Coastal Force Base at Alexandria was commissioned and named HMS *Mosquito*. It was at Mahroussa Jetty, and from then on it became the home for an ever increasing number of MTBs, MLs, and HDMLs. The first CO was Commander R.H. Macbean RN, and Miles Coverdale was appointed as Senior Engineer Officer.

The enclave of Tobruk, so long isolated, was relieved on 10 December 1941 as Rommel was forced back – largely because his supply routes had been so strangled at sea by the Royal Navy.

Almost at once MTBs 68 and 215 moved up to Tobruk from Mersa Matruh. Their task was clearly to join the continuing blockade which sought to prevent Rommel's army from refitting and regrouping before it could attack again.

But within three days – on 14 December – while returning from night patrol, the two boats collided. 68 sank and 215, after picking up all the ship's company, struggled back to Tobruk with a large hole in her bow. She was patched up at Tobruk, and the Senior Officer, with great misgivings, attempted to get her back to Alexandria. His fears were justified when 215 foundered off the desert coast and he and his crew were rescued by some New Zealanders. The hull was later salvaged, but was beyond repair.[10]

The original 10th Flotilla was no more. The seven boats which had arrived in the Mediterranean in March had all been lost by December. They had entered the fray with tremendous spirit, but, quite apart from the ferocity of the Luftwaffe at Crete, had always had to fight against problems beyond their control. With no properly organized base, no certainty of spares and repair facilities, and with no reliable source of fuel of the quality

and grade they required, they had been battling against the odds. Most of all, their small and rather frail boats had proved to be vulnerable in winds over Force 3, and very 'wet' too, taking in water most of the time when at sea. The constant problems with the gearboxes had been the last straw, and despite tremendous efforts by Miles Coverdale and his engineering team – both base staff and boat motor mechanics – they had never really been solved.

But the 'spirit of the Tenth' was not allowed to die. Even before the loss of 68 and 215 in mid-December had closed one chapter, a new one was about to start. A new generation of boats was on its way to Alexandria from the USA.

---

10   Account by Rear Adm C.C. Anderson CB, SO 10th MTB Flotilla at the time.

CHAPTER 3

THE 10TH AND 15TH FLOTILLAS

Plans to reinforce the MTBs in the Mediterranean were made shortly after the disaster in Crete in May 1941 made it an obvious necessity. Clearly there was a realization in high places that the particular needs of the desert campaign in the Eastern Mediterranean called for increased numbers of small boats capable of operations close inshore in support of the Army, minelaying, and with the potential to torpedo large targets. The problem had been to find them from the very limited pool of boats available when a similar urgent need was acknowledged in home waters.

The solution in the first place was to seek aid from the USA where Churchill's close relationship with President Roosevelt was unlocking untold supplies and resources under the beneficence of the 'Lease-Lend' agreement. The US Navy was now concentrating on a new design for their PT boats, and was able to consider handing over a flotilla (they called it a squadron) of their 70-ft PT boats. In so doing, they created a link with the story of Hubert Scott-Paine in Chapter 1 of this history.

When the British Power Boat Company completed the building of the Admiralty's 1938 order for 60-ft MTBs, Scott-Paine began to plan secretly and, at his own expense, to design a 70-ft MTB, using his gifted Chief Designer, George Selman. The 70-ft private venture boat became known as PV70. Knowing that he was in competition with Vosper for orders for future MTBs, Scott-Paine had first negotiated with Rolls-Royce and based his concept on the use of their Merlin engines, in marinized form.

Trials in November 1938 were very encouraging, and a public demonstration was staged in February 1939 in which PV70 reached 47 knots and displayed her manoeuvrability and seaworthiness. Among the foreign parties attracted, the President and Chief Designer of the Electric Boat Company (ELCO) of Bayonne, New Jersey – with a long history including supplying 580 Motor Launches for the Royal Navy in the First World War – attended and were very impressed. By March they had funded the building of a 70-ft MTB for ELCO and secured an option from Scott-Paine to have a licence for exclusive rights to manufacture the boat in USA.

When war was declared in September 1939, the boat for ELCO was already on board the SS *President Roosevelt* en route to New York, and Scott-Paine arrived in the USA shortly afterwards. He was by now aware that Rolls-Royce might not be able to produce Merlin engines in sufficient quantity for the orders he anticipated in view of demands on them by the Air Ministry for aircraft engines, and he was anxious to investigate the possibility of an American alternative which it might well be possible to link with an ELCO contract if one was secured.

In an extraordinary round of negotiations, he demonstrated PT9 (as the 70-ft became), and then in succession met with the ELCO management, the President of the Packard Corporation of Detroit concerning engines, the Secretary to the Navy, and President Roosevelt himself, all in the space of four weeks. By 3 October, Packard had agreed to supply engines, and the US Navy had provisionally ordered twenty-three boats from ELCO. By 1 December he had signed the agreement with ELCO for the exclusive rights to manufacture the Scott-Paine MTB which was to become the basis of the US Navy's PT fleet (PT was their term for MTB, from 'patrol torpedo boat').

A week later, ELCO received the contract to start building PTs 10–20, which were to form the MTB Squadron 2 of the USN. Although these 70-ft Elco boats and the lengthened 77-ft version were indeed derived from Scott-Paine's hull, the later Elco PT boats were of ELCO's own new 80-ft design and he was given little credit for the fact that these became the basis of the US PT fleet.[1]

However, the Packard engine was to turn out to be the salvation of the whole problem of the power unit in British boats for the rest of the war, and the nation had now to thank Scott-Paine for yet another major contribution to the war effort.

This was the background to the way in which the USA provided the Royal Navy's Coastal Forces with a much needed injection of new boats at a crucial time.

In March 1941 the Lend-Lease Bill was passed, and immediately the decision that Elco PT boats could be handed over (actually made in principle a year earlier) was able to be implemented.

So it was that a few days later the Senior Officer of the USN's MTB Squadron 2 was ordered to bring his ten boats – PTs 10 to 19 – from Cuba to New York, so that they could be prepared for handover at Bayonne.

They were splendid boats each with three 1250 b.h.p. Packard engines which gave them a maximum speed of well over 40 knots. At 20 ft they were beamy for their length, and they displaced 32 tons. They had been driven hard by their American crews when they had set off for a cruise in the West Indies, meeting exceptionally heavy weather. Several of the boats had suffered broken frames, which was similar to the experience of the Royal Navy's 70-ft British Power Boats in home waters.

In the autumn of 1941, the 10th Flotilla's new SO, Lt Cdr C.D. Noakes RN, together with Lt R.A. Allan and Lt (E) M. Henzell RN, travelled to Bayonne to supervise, check and approve the alterations, and were very impressed with the performance and equipment of their new boats. They realized that they had received rough handling by the previous 'owners', but such deficiences as lack of any armour plate and of self-sealing fuel tanks (as they had been built in peacetime) were disregarded at the time.

There were frustrations and delays when Admiralty officials raised problems by demanding modifications, some of which necessitated removal of equipment of quality. One change which *was* greatly appreciated was the installation of two standard RN 21-in torpedo tubes in place of the four 18-in tubes fitted originally.

There was urgency to get at least some of the boats out to the Mediterranean, along with the realization that they faced the slow passage round the Cape as the Gibraltar route was at this time simply not possible. By the end of October 1941 the first two boats (259 and 260, previously PTs 10 and 11) were ready for shipment to Egypt, and they left New York as deck cargo on a merchantman bound for Port Tewfik at the southern end of the Suez Canal. Max Henzell, the

1   Rance, *Fast Boats and Flying Boats*.

PT 12 which became MTB 261 in the 10th Flotilla against the background of the New York waterfront. (Courtesy, Southampton City Cultural Services)

PT 10, a 70-ft Elco of the US Navy's MTB Squadron 2 before being handed over to the RN. She became MTB 259. (Courtesy, D. Currie)

flotilla's Engineer Officer, accompanied them, and the voyage took sixty-five days. They were still en route when the Japanese attacked Pearl Harbor and the USA declared war on Japan, Germany and Italy.

At Port Tewfik they were off-loaded, and joined by their officers and crews who had eagerly awaited their arrival.

The Senior Officer, Lt Cdr Noakes (known to his COs as 'Daddy' as he was considerably older than the others), took command of 260. Before being appointed to the 10th Flotilla as SO he had come back from retirement and had served as First Lieutenant at HMS *Hornet*, the new Coastal Force Base at Gosport. His half-leader, Lt R.A. Allan, was a pre-war RNVR officer and had served in MTBs from April 1940 in the experimental and requisitioned boats which, with the 1st Flotilla, represented the Navy's meagre force of MTBs.

He was appointed to 259, and together the boats set out through the lakes and entered the Suez Canal. There were strict restrictions on speed in the Canal to prevent damage to the banks, but, claiming urgency, they received permission to exceed the normal speed limit and as a result the usual 12-hour passage of 90 miles took only 3 hours 23 minutes!

The remaining eight boats followed at regular intervals over the next four weeks, were each commissioned on arrival, and had all arrived at Alexandria to the new Coastal Force Base HMS *Mosquito* by the end of February 1942. The details are as follows:

Boat	Commis-sioned	CO
MTB 259	23.01.42	Lt R.A. Allan RNVR
MTB 260	23.01.42	Lt Cdr C.D. Noakes RN
		Lt M.H.B. Solomon RNVR
MTB 261	09.02.42	Lt C.C. Anderson RN
MTB 262	09.02.42	Lt C. Coles RNVR

MTB 263	16.02.42	Lt I.A. Quarrie RNVR
MTB 264	16.02.42	Lt D. Austin RNVR
MTB 265	24.02.42	Lt J.A. Wolfe RNVR
MTB 266	22.02.42	Lt R.R. Smith RNVR
MTB 267	24.02.42	Lt A. Joy RCNVR
MTB 268	22.02.42	Lt D.C. Souter RNVR

Of these COs, Anderson, Coles, Quarrie, Smith, Joy and Souter were survivors from the early days of the 10th Flotilla and were delighted to receive boats which promised to be far more reliable than those of the old 'Wobbly Tenth'.

Lt Courtney Anderson RN – who had handed over once again as SO to his more senior successor – recounts one experience which, being typical of the young MTB commanders, catches the atmosphere of the time.

On passage through the Suez Canal, knowing that there were different Egyptian pilots for each of the three sections of the Canal, Anderson managed to persuade the first pilot (as Noakes had, before him) to waive the 8-knot restriction. He claimed there would be less wake if the boat planed at a much higher speed. The second pilot – in the Bitter Lakes section – tried once again to impose restrictions, until he heard of the speed the boat was capable of reaching. It then transpired that among the pilots there were three privately recognized (and illegal) canal records: first, the highest speed ever; then the highest average between two stations; and lastly the fastest complete transit. The second pilot established that his rival must already have collared the first two, and urged Anderson to go flat out. He did, and filmed 261 overtaking a motor cycle policeman driving at speed on the road alongside the Canal. With the cooperation of the third pilot, all three records were broken: highest speed 47 knots, highest average between stations 32 knots, and shortest ever transit in 2 hours 18 minutes.

MTB 263 of the 10th Flotilla, previously PT 14. (Courtesy, D. Currie)

Rather naturally, the Canal Company reacted angrily next day and insisted on all its pilots obeying the 8-knot rule. But Rear Adm Anderson wonders if these 'records' are still intact, and suspects they are![2]

At Alexandria the boats had a short period in which the crews could get used to them, and generally working up. But Noakes had a sense of urgency, and by mid-February had led the first four arrivals westward to Tobruk for a short period. He had very quickly decided, with ten boats to command, to hand over 260 to Lt M.H.B. Solomon RNVR and travelled in different boats according to circumstances. Almost at once the unit of four was carrying out night patrols 100 miles west of Tobruk off Derna, hoping to find an

enemy transport seeking to reinforce the German Army as it prepared itself for another drive eastward: but the flotilla had no immediate success.

After a few days they were joined in Tobruk by HMS *Vulcan* which had been the depot ship for the 1st MTB Flotilla in Malta pre-war. They were clustered around her when five or six Stuka dive-bombers launched a fierce attack. They were fortunate to escape without damage or casualties. *Vulcan* left rapidly for Alexandria, no doubt feeling rather vulnerable. From then on the boats tied up to wrecks in the harbour, using camouflage netting and being careful to shift after a German reconnaissance plane had flown over. Air cover was patchy, and boats suffered from occasional hits from machine gun fire.

The first unit, having had a gruelling time patrolling at night and enduring air raids by

2   Notes from Rear Adm C.C. Anderson CB, in 1942 CO of MTB 261.

day, was replaced by later arrivals after ten days. They had had the additional strains of having to filter all the petrol – which tended to be water-contaminated – through chamois leather, which was a very long, tedious process.

The system of replacing units to allow for slipping and maintenance back at Alexandria continued through March and April. It was punctuated by one unfortunate incident in mid-March when 263 (Quarrie) was fourth in line as the unit ploughed westward from Mersa Matruh towards Tobruk. Their sailing orders had warned them to look out for a U-boat which had been seen patrolling off Mersa Luk not far from Tobruk. Soon after turning towards the port, a wake was sighted, and Quarrie brought his crew to action

stations and closed to investigate. Depth charges were set and speed increased to 30 knots. Unfortunately the 'wake' proved to be surf breaking on a beach with outlying rocks, and 263 struck one of the rocks, damaged a propeller, and was then lifted by the swell on to the reef. The engines spluttered to a stop, and in the silence which followed, a loud clear voice challenged: 'Halt! who goes there?' Quarrie responded: 'Don't shoot, Sarn't Major – I'm a friend!'

The boat had run aground right in the middle of a rest camp occupied by a South African unit. It took some time to get 263 off the reef, with the combined efforts of the Flotilla Engineer Officer and working parties from the RAF and Pioneer Corps, and she was then towed back by an HDML to Alex-

MTB 263 off Tobruk. (Courtesy, P. Pidcock)

andria where she remained on the jetty for some months before resuming operations.[3]

For four months the boats of the 10th maintained patrols, withstood long passages and air raids in Tobruk, and yet were unable to find targets for their torpedoes. However far west they probed, they could not reach the Axis supply lines from Italy to North Africa, and with the enemy holding mastery of the skies, daylight patrols were not undertaken.

Throughout this period, the boats on standby or 'resting' in Alexandria were called upon for clandestine work (Coastal Forces tended to call them 'cloak and dagger' or 'false nose' operations). They landed or picked up Greek agents or small Army reconnaissance units on Crete. A typical example was Operation Leader on 15 April, when 259 (Allan) and 264 (Austin) sailed from Bardia to Crete to land four agents, and brought back eight men for return to Egypt.

In May, 264 was sent out from Alexandria in an emergency in bad weather to assist a hospital ship which had been bombed by the Luftwaffe. Ploughing into short steep seas, she broke her back, and joined 263 out of the water on Mahroussa jetty. When Rommel broke through the Allied lines towards El Alamein in June 1942, orders were received to demolish the two boats if the enemy approached Alexandria; fortunately it was an order that never had to be carried out.

In mid-April, the 10th Flotilla was reinforced in Alexandria by the first four boats of the 15th Flotilla, which arrived from the USA in exactly the same way as the 10th itself had travelled three months earlier. They too were Elco boats, but benefited in several ways from the fact that they were built to an improved specification agreed by the US Navy Department. The main difference was an

Lt R.A. Allan RNVR, CO of MTB 259 in 1942. By 1944, he was Cdr R.A. Allan DSO OBE, and later Baron Allan of Kilmahew. (Courtesy, E. Young)

additional 7 ft in length added aft, making them 77 ft. Their three Packard engines were of the latest design and layout. The fuel tanks were self-sealing, and their armament was one hand-operated 20-mm Oerlikon, one twin 0.5-in power-operated turret on the centreline, amidships, two 21-in torpedo tubes and four depth charges. This first group of four boats were numbered 309 to 312, and six more were to follow in June (they were already on the way) numbered 307, 308 and 313 to 316.

The Senior Officer, Lt D. Jermain DSC RN, had already distinguished himself in two of the earliest Coastal Forces actions of the war. He won his DSC when he pioneered a method of attack by dropping a depth charge

3   Notes from Capt I.A.B. Quarrie CBE VRD RNR (Retd), in 1942 CO of MTB 263.

MTB 264 in Alexandria. (Courtesy, P. Pidcock)

under the bow of the target, damaging a merchant ship off Flushing in November 1940.

In the previous month, he had torpedoed two trawlers in the Dover Strait. He had spent several months at Bayonne, the Elco Yard, keeping a watchful eye on the modifications to each boat, together with the Flotilla Engineer Officer, Lt (E) Purser RN.

The ten boats of the 15th Flotilla were:

BOAT	COMPLETED	COMMISSIONED	CO
First Batch			
MTB 309	11.02.42	22.04.42	Lt D. Jermain DSC RN
MTB 310	20.02.42	22.04.42	Lt S. Lane RCNVR
MTB 311	17.02.42	29.04.42	Lt J.D. Lancaster RNVR
MTB 312	21.02.42	29.04.42	Lt I.A. Quarrie RNVR
Second Batch			
MTB 307	04.02.42	23.06.42	Lt J. Muir RNVR
MTB 308	31.01.42	23.06.42	Lt C.P. Evensen RNVR
			(Lt R. Yates RNVR)
MTB 313	28.02.42	14.06.42	Lt A.D. Foster RNVR
MTB 314	28.02.42	14.06.42	Lt H.W. Sheldrick RNVR
MTB 315	07.03.42	05.06.42	Lt O.B. Mabee RCNVR
MTB 316	14.03.42	05.06.42	Lt R.B. Adams RNVR

It was natural that from the start the two flotillas should work closely together, especially since they were all of the same build. Early in May, when the first four boats of the 15th had worked up, they joined the Tobruk force, reinforcing the 'duty watch' of the 10th and then relieving them.

Throughout May and June 1942, the boats of the 10th and 15th worked together, sharing the night patrols off the enemy-held ports to the west of Tobruk, and landing small army units behind Rommel's lines. Similarly, occasional missions to Crete broke the pattern: on 22 and 23 May, Denis Jermain carried out two of these landings on successive nights.

Not long after, on 26 May, Jermain in 309 and Quarrie in 312 were on patrol off Bomba, not far west of Tobruk, when they sighted an F-lighter (a rare occurrence at this time). Having been starved of targets, they set their torpedoes to run at the shallowest possible depth and fired all four. They all passed either beneath or close to bow and stern, an experience which was to become all too common in attacks on F-lighters in the months ahead. But Jermain had pioneered the 'gunboat' technique of dropping depth charges under the bow, used very successfully by Robert Hichens' flotilla at this time in home waters. He roared in, planted two depth charges very close and was sure that one exploded right beneath the target. But although they searched, they could find neither the F-lighter nor any evidence of wreckage, so could claim no success.

Early in June, there was a call for five of the 10th to prepare themselves for Operation Vigorous, planned to get supplies through to the besieged island fortress of Malta, which was being pounded daily by the Luftwaffe. Operation Vigorous from the east was timed to coincide with Operation Harpoon from the west.

Convoy MW11 of ten merchant ships formed up in Alexandria, and by 14 June was off Tobruk. It had a very heavy escort of 7 cruisers, 1 anti-aircraft cruiser, 26 destroyers, 4 corvettes and 2 mine-sweepers – a clear indication of the importance of getting this convoy through.

One unusual element in the large escorting force was HMS *Centurion*, a First World War battleship converted pre-war into a target ship, and recently adapted for this operation to resemble the battleship HMS *King George V*, by the use of much canvas and wood.

The plan was that five of the merchant ships would each tow an MTB. If the convoy was attacked by surface vessels during passage, the tows would be slipped and the MTBs would attempt to attack the enemy vessels with torpedoes.

The five MTBs available were 259 (Allan, acting as SO), 262 (Coles), 264 (Austin), 266 (Smith), and 268 (Souter). Each was heavily loaded with supplies, making them less stable and therefore more vulnerable.

It was not long before things began to go wrong. On the first night, the weather deteriorated to such an extent that the tows had to be slipped to avoid further damage to the lightly constructed MTBs. But for 259 the decision came too late. Soon after release, she was badly awash and sinking, and had to be abandoned by her crew. They were eventually picked up by 268, which had had her own problems. The towing gear had been designed in a very clumsy fashion, with the intention of preventing damage if the tow became difficult – as it did! A heavy wire towing warp ran right round the boat to a bridle ahead of the bows. It was all too heavy to heave in, and to clear it 268's First Lieutenant Sub Lt Newall, a New Zealander, went overboard to cut it free with a hacksaw. The remaining boats got back to base eventually but it had all been an unhappy experience.

Even the major units had their difficulties, and were constantly attacked from the air having been sighted by reconnaissance aircraft almost as soon as they left port. And to add insult to injury for the MTBs, the larger, more robust E-boats of the 3rd Flotilla, led by Lt Wupperman in S-56 and operating from Derna, attacked the escorts and torpedoed and damaged the cruiser HMS *Newcastle* and severely damaged the destroyer *Hasty*. Eventually, Adm Vian, delayed and running short of fuel, and cut off by the battleships of the Italian fleet, had to turn back, losing HMS *Hermione* and two of the merchant ships.

From the start, the towing operation had been fraught with danger for the MTBs, and only the urgency of the operation's objective had overcome the COs' misgivings. (Note 4, Appendix 1)

These operations at the end of May coincided with momentous events ashore. Rommel, having rested his army and replenished and strengthened his forces, began an offensive against the Eighth Army's Gazala line west of Tobruk. He met determined resistance from the British and Free French troops, but by 11 June he had outflanked the French line at Bir Hacheim and broken through, advancing rapidly and inflicting heavy casualties as he closed on Tobruk.

The boats of the 10th and 15th (at this time there were six of them) continued to operate nightly from Tobruk, watching the battle raging ashore, with the awesome artillery fire continuous in each direction.

On the morning of 20 June four of the boats returned from patrol aware that Rommel's advance had come very close to the port. They refuelled and had breakfast, and discovered that the naval authorities had little information on the enemy's progress and were refusing at first to accept the urgency of the situation. When German tanks and artillery appeared close to the harbour, the boats dispersed to seek shelter behind the numerous wrecks and then prepared to leave.

During the afternoon, after dive-bombing by Stukas and shelling, they were at last ordered to evacuate, taking as many of the Coastal Force base staff as possible with them. 260 (Solomon) and 262 (Coles) laid a smokescreen between the enemy ashore and the anchorage, and soon ships of all shapes and sizes – the slow and the speedy – were passing through the boom and turning east towards Mersa Matruh and Alexandria. The MTBs worked prodigiously to take on board as many men as possible, both naval and military, before they began their next task of forming a screen around the retreating convoy, which Jermain organized. Solomon in 260 went back into the harbour to attempt the rescue of 120 soldiers from a blazing wreck; Coles with a large number of Indian troops aboard was sent on to alert Mersa Matruh of the evacuation. But it proved impossible to protect the straggling cavalcade of mainly helpless craft from a raid by E-boats, and several were sunk.

When Coles arrived at Mersa Matruh he discovered that land communications from Tobruk had been severed, and the port authorities were unaware that Tobruk had fallen. The news came as a great shock, and as there was no time nor resources to set up any sort of basis for defence of the town and harbour, the task of demolishing the harbour installations – such as they were – and evacuating port personnel, began again. The sour smell of defeat was everywhere. (Note 5, Appendix 1)

All the operational boats of the 10th and 15th reached Alexandria, and at once began the next phase of operations. With Tobruk and Mersa Matruh in enemy hands, there was hope that there would be targets to attack, and nightly patrols were immediately organized. But the enemy were able to reinforce their reserves further west to avoid air and MTB attacks, and the boats found no targets. Some boats were used to land small parties behind the enemy lines, cutting communications by blowing up roads, railway lines and bridges, and by ambushing supplies.

By this time, all ten of the 77-ft Elcos of the 15th Flotilla had arrived at Alexandria, and joined the eight sound boats of the 10th. There was a change of leadership for the 10th Flotilla. Lt Cdr Noakes was appointed elsewhere (he actually went to India where he set up a Coastal Forces Base, and returned to the Mediterranean three years later, as Captain Coastal Forces). In his place, Lt R.A.(Bobby) Allan became SO, being senior to Courtney Anderson, one of the few occasions when 'Qualified Officer, Coastal Forces' (QOCF) outranked an experienced RN officer. But future events were to demonstrate that both went on to very distinguished careers. Anderson went back to General Service and Lt M. Yeatman took over 261.

In addition to the eighteen Elco boats of the 10th and 15th, yet another flotilla was arriving at Alexandria at this time. The 7th MTB Flotilla was composed of Vosper boats built at that company's new yard at Portchester under the 1939 War Programme. They were therefore of very early design, 71 ft in length, and 19 ft 3 in in beam, displacing about 35 tons. They had been laid down at the end of 1940, and their building process had suffered many problems from this circumstance of time.

Not only was this the period of very heavy air raids on Portsmouth, particularly aimed at the Naval Base, but also Vospers had enormous difficulty recruiting skilled staff and obtaining the quantity and quality of raw materials required. The rapid expansion in demand for all types of small boats had created shortages of both craftsmen and particularly of well-seasoned timber.

The boats were given the numbers from 57 to 65 inclusive, and their completion and commissioning extended over five months from October 1941 to March 1942. The first SO was Lt R.A.M. Hennessy RN, and while his boats gathered as each one completed, the Admiralty process of decision on where the 7th Flotilla would be deployed was delayed. Suddenly in December 1941 the die was cast – they were to be sent to Alexandria. Robert Hennessy was not even given time to work up the boats which were ready. The first three were loaded up during January in Glasgow and Liverpool, and despatched on the long voyage round the Cape to Port Tewfik and the Suez Canal in exactly the same way as the 10th and 15th had travelled during the previous eight months. All but one (MTB 65) of the rest followed during March and April, and for various reasons these first seven boats all arrived at Alexandria, Suez or Port Said over a very short period early in June 1942.

Unfortunately, with the exception of MTB 61, they were not ready to begin operations for several weeks. Each boat had been housed in a cradle on the upper deck of a merchantman, and they had experienced very bad weather in the South Atlantic. MTBs 58 and 59, badly stowed aboard SS *Collegian*, were extensively damaged, and several others needed minor repairs. When they undertook sea trials, there was a succession of problems as they broke down, and a programme of repairs, including a complete change of steering gear, was drawn up. The 7th in fact monopolized the time of the base staff in Alexandria.

MTB 61 was commanded by Lt T.J. Bligh, who was destined to become a legend in Mediterranean Coastal Forces in the three years which followed. 61 is recorded as joining the 10th and 15th at Mersa Matruh and Tobruk before the withdrawal from Tobruk on 20 June 1942.

With all the boats back in Alexandria at the end of June, and Rommel advancing remorsely eastward and threatening to break

MTB 61 (Lt T.J. Bligh), armed as a gunboat in 1942. (Courtesy, Alec Foster)

through to Cairo, the naval authorities decided to disperse many naval units to the Levant. The 15th was retained in Alexandria to continue patrolling the desert coast, and with another more specific task. If Rommel did reach the port, the ships of the immobilized French fleet moored just inside the boom were to be torpedoed to prevent them falling into German hands.

On the night of 31 August, four boats of the 15th – 307 (Muir), 310 (Lane), 311 (Lancaster) and 315 (Mabee) – were sent on a mission to attempt the interception of a major German convoy bound from Greece to Tobruk. Its importance was unquestioned: it carried fuel for Rommel's tanks and transport, and other vital supplies.

The boats set out from Alexandria, and the intended interception point south of Crete involved a round trip of some 700 miles, far

beyond normal range. Each boat carried 1,000 gallons of fuel in four-gallon cans on the upper deck, and a stop was made as they approached their attack area to refuel, and to throw the cans overboard. The unit was found by the Luftwaffe and subjected to wave after wave of low level bombing attacks. They used every evasive tactic and maintained constant anti-aircraft fire with their light guns, expending almost all their ammunition. Such was the intensity of the attacks that they were forced to abandon their interception and they turned back to Alexandria, fortunately without casualties or losses.

But, unknown to them, their presence *had* led the Germans to alter the convoy's course and it in turn had been intercepted by the RAF and successfully attacked.

The majority of the 10th Flotilla were sent to Haifa and Beirut, and the 7th Flotilla to Famagusta in Cyprus, where the opportunity was taken to effect improvements to the boats. There began a period of enormous tension and apprehension as the outcome of the defensive battle at El Alamein was awaited, and there was great relief when the news came through that in five days at the beginning of September, Rommel's attempt finally to break through to Cairo had been repelled. The new command headed by Alexander and Montgomery had won its first battle, and was able to begin planning its offensive to regain all the territory lost and push westward along the coast. Alexandria was no longer under threat, and the flotillas all returned there.

Once again normal operational duties were resumed, and nightly patrols moved along the desert coast, together with the landings of Army units behind Rommel's lines.

In mid-September, in a bid to draw away some of Rommel's forces ranged against the Eighth Army at El Alamein, an operation was proposed to attack Tobruk. It was given the codename 'Agreement', and the plan in out-line was to synchronize an assault from the sea with a sudden lunge by a mobile land column from the desert, behind the German lines. The objective was to seize, if only temporarily, the harbour at Tobruk and to destroy shipping, fuel stocks and port facilities there. The RAF was to play a part, with a diversion, a bombing raid and the provision of fighter protection. (Note 6, Appendix 1)

The four forces involved were:

Force A
The two Tribal class destroyers *Sikh* and *Zulu*, with 350 Royal Marines embarked, escorted by four Hunt class destroyers *Aldenham*, *Hurworth*, *Beaufort* and *Exmoor*.

Force B
Military units including men of the Long Range Desert Group, specially trained in long-range operations behind the enemy lines.

Force C
Sixteen MTBs – the available boats of the 10th and 15th Flotillas – with three MLs. Each MTB was to carry ten Army personnel; the MLs carried demolition parties and stood by to take over the troops of any MTB which broke down.

Force D
The supporting force: the cruiser *Coventry*, and the destroyers *Belvoir*, *Croome*, *Hursley* and *Dulverton*.

The original plan had apparently first been conceived as a purely military operation, overland, by experienced troops with a record of success in clandestine sabotage operations. But the planners in Cairo, 'short of experience but full of grand ideas' according to one participant, produced a far more complex plan. From the MTBs' point of view, there seemed to be little understanding of the operating methods of the boats, developed painstakingly from their past experience.

The misgivings of the COs throughout the two weeks or so of the preparation period increased day by day. Security seemed non-existent, with landing rehearsals directed to be carried out in full view of the Yacht Club, 'watched by members of the Egyptian royal family and anyone else who might be curious'. Soldiers were marched onto the jetty and embarked with no attempt at secrecy. Talk of an impending 'behind the lines' landing in strength seemed to be rife in the clubs and bars of Alexandria.

Sub Lt Norman Ilett, the First Lieutenant of 313 who wrote an account of this period soon afterwards, remembers the arrival of a 'genial and somewhat middle-aged Lieutenant Commander RN' to be the base's SOO (Staff Officer, Operations) at this time. He gave the first information on 'Agreement'. Among other things he gave orders that the boats should be painted in a wavy green and black camouflage pattern. He claimed, as a fisherman, that these colours were those of sea bass, which were notoriously hard to catch! He also gave details of various items of escape equipment to be issued, such as fly button compasses, which would be handy for those who might have to find their way home from Tobruk by land. All calculated to inspire confidence!

The SO of the 15th Flotilla, Lt Denis Jermain DSC RN, had been the representative of the MTBs at the early briefing meetings, although the new SO of the 10th, 'Bobby' Allan had recently been promoted to Lieutenant Commander RNVR, and was senior to him. But despite the fact that both had been operating in MTBs at home and in the Mediterranean since 1939, they were deemed to be too inexperienced and the powers-that-be decided to appoint a Commander RN as SO MTBs for Operation Agreement.

The Commander was a gallant officer who had done fine work in command of a heavily armed but slow river gunboat (HMS *Ladybird*) in support of the Eighth Army, and he certainly knew Tobruk well. But he had never operated in MTBs, and strangely did not join Jermain's boat (309) until Force C left Alexandria on the evening of 12 October. Jermain had been left in the dark on the final details of the operation.

The actual passage westward began quite smoothly. The boats were in two columns – the 10th led by Bobby Allan (260, 261, 262, 265, 266, 267 and 268) and the 15th with Cdr Blackburn RN (with Denis Jermain) in 309, followed by 307, 308, 310, 311, 312, 313, 314 and 315. Despite a very low cruising speed of 7 knots (very uncomfortable for these powerful boats) only one of the sixteen boats experienced any problems. 268 had to return to Alexandria with engine trouble, her military personnel transferring to ML 353.

Until the evening of the 13th, all seemed to be going well: the supporting Force D, further out to sea, had not been detected, and the MTBs of Force C were prepared for the turn in towards their objective. It was here that things began to go wrong. The SO MTBs gave the order to increase speed to 24 knots. Interpreting the order, and conscious of the two long lines of boats astern, Jermain began to use the standard MTB drill of signalling the increase in steps of 5 knots, both to give time for each boat to maintain contact, and to enable the engines to 'clear their throats' after the long period of slow running. Cdr Blackburn was anxious to reach 24 knots more rapidly, and ordered Jermain to abandon the 'stepped' increases. Inevitably this led to problems: such a violent speeding up, given the difficulty small boats have at night with forward vision, and no experience or training in such a manoeuvre with so many boats, led to the break up of the unit into small groups of three or four. Thus confused, they struggled westward independently. At

least they were assisted by the gun flashes indicating air activity over Tobruk. But the large-scale air raid seemed to have put the defending troops into full alertness – and it also seemed to end thirty minutes earlier than expected.

The objective for the MTBs was a very small inlet named Mersa es Sciausc just to the east of Tobruk harbour, and outside the booms protecting it. Here they were to land their troops from the Northumberland Fusiliers, when signalled to enter and given leading lights by the overland troops of Force B.

But there were by now two separate problems. SO MTBs suddenly found he only had seven boats in company rather than fifteen, and the first boats to approach the mouth of Mersa es Sciausc could not see any signal nor any leading lights. In the early stages of planning, Jermain had seen how difficult the approach would be, and discussed with his COs the best way of negotiating it safely. In very dark conditions with none of the expected marker lights and no signal to tell them to proceed, there was confusion. Most of the boats had by now arrived, but could not act together. They were milling around waiting for orders and convinced that they had sailed into a trap, the plan having gone radically wrong and possibly been abandoned. They were fired at from shore and picked up by searchlights.

In fact, Force B, although they had reached the vicinity of Mersa es Sciausc, had had a rough time. Their CO, Colonel Haselden, had been killed, and the young officer deputed to arrange the signals for the MTBs was late, delayed by enemy patrols. His signals were underpowered and could not be effectively placed. [4]

As a result, only two of the MTBs, acting independently, got into the cove and

---

4 ROP in CB04272; additional detail in Smith, *Massacre at Tobruk*.

disembarked their troops. They were 314 (Lt H.W. Sheldrick with the Divisional leader Lt C.P. Evensen aboard) and 261 (Lt M. Yeatman). Unfortunately, 314 grounded on rocks and it proved impossible to get her off. The crew were taken off by 261, and the demolition charge was set: it never activated. She was captured by the Germans, put into service as RA 10 and sunk on 30 April 1943 at Augusta in an air attack. She served with the 6th R-boat Flotilla. 261 left the inlet and rejoined a group of boats lying off the coast.

There were several more attempts to get into the cove, but none was successful. Both SO MTBs and Bobby Allan sought to be aggressive and helpful but the defence of Tobruk was determined and – in the view of the COs who were sure the raid was compromised by poor security – thoroughly prepared for the attack. Help was offered to the destroyer *Sikh* of Force A which had run into trouble attempting to land her Royal Marine force to the north and west of Tobruk town. *Sikh* was sunk by shore batteries, and *Zulu* later by air attack.

So, under continuing fire from shore at first light, the MTBs were ordered to return to Alexandria, and a new and even more hazardous period began. The raid had clearly been a failure all round, as the separate sections had each been unable to achieve their objectives. Now it was a question of getting ships and boats and men back over the 360 miles to Alexandria despite the constant attention of German aircraft.

Jermain gathered several boats together and began to shepherd them into the diamond formation which had proved an effective defensive technique under air attack, allowing each boat to take evasive action and yet have some advantages of combined anti-aircraft fire. Unfortunately some boats were still isolated and also still had petrol in canisters on the upper deck. This was probably a major factor in the loss of three

boats at this stage. Once hit, the petrol cans went up like torches.

Sub Lt Norman Ilett, the First Lieutenant of 313 (Alec Foster), tells how his boat's Old Etonian motor mechanic (known as Claude to the crew) performed miracles in dealing with engine room and upper deck fires after one attack. The burning cans on deck were thrown or kicked overboard, and Claude first evacuated the engine room, dowsed the fire by activating the sprinklers from the upper deck, and then returned below to get the boat under way again.

312 (Ian Quarrie) was the first to be lost. She was hit by fire from the Macchi fighters early on and was soon burning fiercely. The survivors got away in a collapsible boat and by a remarkable coincidence were mostly picked up by 266 (Richard Smith). As Quarrie was helped aboard, Smith welcomed him, calling out 'We mustn't make too much of a habit of this!' – and Quarrie realized that

MTB 313, a 77-ft Elco of the 15th Flotilla, in Benghazi. (Courtesy, Alec Foster)

Sub Lt N.B.G. Gray, First Lieutenant of MTB 310, taken prisoner off Tobruk after aircraft attack. (Courtesy, D. Souter)

two years earlier, on 16 October 1940, Smith had performed the same rescue act when MTB 106 was blown up by a mine in the Thames Estuary. Soon after, 266 was near-missed by bombs from Stukas, and damaged by bomb-splinters. Smith got her back safely to Alexandria.

The fate of 308 (Roy Yates) which came next, was not known until much later. 310 was nearby when she was destroyed, and her crew witnessed it, but could not report as she too was sunk shortly after. 308 had already been slowed down by hits from the fighters, but when a Ju88 attacked, she sent up such a hail of fire that the bomber, in a shallow dive, was hit and crashed into 308. Both were completely destroyed with no survivors.

310 (Stewart Lane, a Canadian) had herself been dive-bombed by a Stuka and hit on the bow. The boat began to go down by

the head, and the survivors launched the small assault craft carried for the raid and nine or ten set out for the desert coast. It was fully a week later when they were found by German soldiers near the coast, carried ashore and into captivity. By then, only three were still alive including the First Lieutenant, Sub Lt Nigel Grey. They were themselves near to death with thirst, burned and dehydrated. All the rest including the CO had died one by one. Several months later, Charles Coles was taken prisoner, and met Nigel Grey in the prison camp, and heard his account of the end of both 308 and 310 for the first time.[5]

Jermain and Allan did well to get the remaining eleven boats, several of them

5 Smith, *Massacre at Tobruk*; additional detail from Charles Coles OBE VRD.

damaged, back to Alexandria in the face of frequent dive-bombing (and high level) attacks. By organizing the defensive patterns and using their speed and ability to alter course rapidly to evade bombs as each attack began, it was possible to get through unscathed.

Together with 314, aground in Mersa es Sciausc, four of the ten 77-ft Elcos of the 15th Flotilla had been lost in the operation. The officers and men deeply resented implications which reached their ears of 'lack of dash' and 'inexperience and incompetence'. The lessons of Crete seemed not to have been learned. The boats were too vulnerable to withstand attack from the air in daylight when the enemy had air superiority: the RAF's fighter cover, despite gallant attempts from distant airfields, could not be sustained. But there was one positive outcome. The fact that all but one of the boats had run the 700 miles of the operation without engine trouble had finally dispelled all memory of 'The Wobbly Tenth' and the COs knew they had fine boats with which to carry on the battle.

It was not only the MTBs which had suffered. Reports now revealed that the cruiser *Coventry* and the destroyers *Zulu* and *Sikh* had been sunk in addition to two of the three MLs. The human toll was even more grievous: 280 naval officers and men, 300 Royal Marines, and 160 Army personnel had died. No wonder one historian described Operation Agreement as 'the result of wishful dreams and ambitions which had far outrun practicality'.

There is an interesting comparison to be made between this operation and the St Nazaire Raid of March 1942, six months earlier. Both raids had a similar main objective – the destruction of port installations – and heavy casualties were sustained in both, but St Nazaire was deemed a success, and Tobruk a failure. Those involved felt that the differences at Tobruk lay in the lack of attention to security during the preparations, bad planning, and bad decision-making throughout.

The situation in Alexandria by the end of September 1942 was therefore that the 10th Flotilla now had nine boats, two of them temporarily paid off with serious damage; the 15th had six, and the 7th Flotilla was about to become operational as the necessary repairs were completed.

Immediate decisions were made to re-organize the flotillas. The SO of the 10th, Lt Cdr R.A. Allan was selected to take command of a Mobile Coastal Force Base which was in process of formation. Together, Bobby Allan and his CFMB were to make an enormous contribution over the next two years to the effectiveness of the Mediterranean flotillas, as will become clear in the succeeding chapters.

This made it possible to merge all the surviving boats of the two flotillas into one, to be known as the 10th. It had an immediate effective strength of thirteen, under the command of Denis Jermain.

Although it was not possible to predict it at the time, the disaster at Tobruk was later to be seen as a turning point, not only for the fortunes of the MTBs, but also in the whole progress of the Mediterranean war.

The Eighth Army under its new commander, General Bernard Montgomery, was about to be unleashed. It was to be, as Churchill dubbed it, the turning of the 'Hinge of Fate'.[6]

6   Churchill, *The Second World War*, Vol. 4.

CHAPTER 4

THE 10TH AND 7TH FLOTILLAS

In the aftermath of the Tobruk raid, having lost four of the fine 77-ft Elco boats, morale among the officers and men of the MTBs at Alexandria was understandably at a low ebb. Fortunately, the newly appointed Captain Coastal Forces Mediterranean, Captain Hubback RN, was alert to their needs, and in a sensitive move to restore their enthusiasm sent four of the boats on an operation to attack shipping in Rhodes. The chosen boats were MTBs 307, 311, 316 and 309, commanded temporarily by T.J. Bligh of the 7th Flotilla whose 61 was under repair. They left Alexandria on 30 September and the first leg was to Paphos where they refuelled.

Next day they moved on to Rhodes, moved close in without being sighted, and fired their torpedoes into the inner harbour where ships were alongside the quays and at anchor. There were loud explosions as they withdrew, but without proof they could make no claims of successful hits. Jermain later commented that whatever material results accrued, there was satisfaction in making an incursion deep into hostile waters without intervention from the air, which had been far from their recent experience. (Note 7, Appendix 1)

On return to Alexandria, the patrols westward were resumed, along the coast behind which the two armies were preparing for a major battle: Rommel intending to break through to Cairo and beyond, and Montgomery determined to drive back the German Army. The MTBs sought to ensure that Rommel's troops could not be supplied by sea within the range of their patrols: but Mersa Matruh was too small anyway for any sizeable ship to enter, and the more westerly ports were well covered by aircraft and submarines, which sank many supply ships.

Meanwhile, with the battle at El Alamein about to begin, boats of the 10th Flotilla were being fitted with equipment designed to simulate a landing force behind enemy lines, to act as a feint diversion. On the night of 23/24 October, the artillery barrage heralded the start of this famous and significant battle. Earlier that day, a strange convoy sailed from Alexandria: 3 destroyers escorting 12 LCTs, followed by 10 MTBs and 2 MLs, and 4 merchant ships from Port Said. It was confidently expected that their passage would be reported to the enemy. In fact, as soon as darkness fell, the MTBs alone carried on and the rest returned to Alexandria: Operation Rumble Bumble had begun. Its name derived from the noise made when the Elcos' silencers deflected exhaust gases under water. However, on this occasion the intention was the opposite of secrecy and silence. When they reached Ras-el-Kanais, where there was a beach about 60 miles behind Rommel's lines, they turned in and began to set up a cacophony of noises appropriate to a landing, using loudspeakers, anchor chains, mortars, demolition charges on floats and flashes to simulate bombardment. It was a technique which was used in future landings as a diversion, and in retrospect the High Command was delighted with its success, with reports that German forces had been despatched to deal with this threat to the rear of the line. There was some fire from the shore, and 313 was damaged below the water line, began taking water and had to be sent back to Alexandria. As was so often the case, the motor mechanic was able to improvise and used the main engine circulating pump to lower the level in the bilges.

As the main force returned to base, they had a grandstand view of one of the greatest artillery battles in history. They also saw the success of another diversionary ruse – a group of anchored dummy boats which were attracting heavy fire from shore. Among congratulatory messages for the success of Rumble Bumble was one report from the pilot of a Wellington bomber who described 'an enormous battle taking place off one of the beaches between guns ashore and boats some distance off'. The feint obviously looked realistic from the sky.[1]

Similar operations took place on the next two nights to keep the pressure on the Afrika Korps, who could not afford to ignore the ruse entirely, in case one such episode was the real thing. After one of these, the 10th created a stir in Alexandria by a most unusual form of entry. It was normal when returning at night to anchor off the channel until daylight. On this morning, German minelaying aircraft dropped mines around the MTBs. As it would have been suicidal to start engines, they broke out awnings and rigged them as sails, and entered harbour under sail for all the world like Nelsonian brigs.

The battle of Alamein raged for eleven days, and by 3 November, Rommel's army was in rapid retreat westward: 60 miles on

the first day, and as far as Mersa Matruh on the second. In rapid succession, Sidi Barrani, Tobruk and Benghazi all fell by 18 November. The 10th were kept busy acting as sea raiders, occasionally shooting up lorries on the coast road, staging fake (and actual) landings and generally causing confusion among the retreating troops. Sadly, their prime purpose of torpedoing enemy ships was never achieved at this stage, since no targets presented themselves.[2]

MTBs of the 10th Flotilla were the first vessels to re-enter Tobruk, having been the last to leave on 20 June. On they went to Benghazi, to find a harbour strewn with wrecked vessels, creating hazards for pilotage: 309 (Ross Campbell) fell foul of an underwater object and damaged a shaft and propeller, which were repaired in Tobruk.

The CF Mobile Base, commanded by Lt Cdr R.A. Allan, now began to come into its own with its fleet of lorry workshops. Pausing at Mersa Matruh and Tobruk, it moved on to Benghazi and then further west to Ras Helal beyond Derna, where the 10th established itself for a short while late in November. It was at this stage that the decision was made to send an 'advance guard' of the flotilla to Malta, where patrols could more readily assist a blockade of the major ports further west such as Tripoli and Bizerta.

But the Eighth Army was by now not the only Allied force in North Africa. The First Army of US and Commonwealth troops had landed in Morocco and Algeria; Oran and then Algiers had been taken, and the western arm of the pincer movement began to advance eastward towards Tunisia. Very quickly, the ports of Bougie and Bone were in Allied hands and the next objective would clearly be the major port of Bizerta, which

---

1 ROP at PRO in ADM199/567; and notes from Capt Denis Jermain.

2 Churchill, *The Second World War*, Vol. 4.

10th Flotilla at anti-aircraft practice in Eastern
Mediterranean, 1942. (Courtesy, IWM – A 11896)

was receiving the supplies and reinforcements the beleaguered German and Italian armies so sorely required.

C-in-C Mediterranean was now faced with a new problem – the fruit of success on land – of redistribution of his naval forces, including the MTBs, along a coast and in ports which had only just become available to him.

The first group of the 10th Flotilla to reach Malta arrived there on 9 December 1942, and as a Coastal Force Base had not yet been established, they were welcomed, as a temporary measure, at the renowned Submarine Base at Manoel Island. Within a few weeks, a private house and garage buildings at TaxBiex – only a short distance further up Marsamaxett harbour – were requisitioned,

and HMS *Gregale* was commissioned as CFB Malta. Its first CO was Lt Cdr Marshall, a veteran of the CMBs (Coastal Motor Boats), the MTBs of the First World War.

Gradually the other boats of the 10th Flotilla made their way to Malta, while those already there began patrolling, sometimes off the coast of Sicily and at others in the 'Sicilian Narrows' around the island of Pantelleria.

One of the boats which had a more adventurous passage to Malta than most was 309, commanded by Ross Campbell, a Canadian. It was a feature of the 10th Flotilla that Jermain had welcomed Commonwealth officers.

Of the other Canadians, Stewart Lane had given his life off Tobruk, Alec Joy had joined

MTBs berthed temporarily at the submarine base in Malta, early 1943. (Courtesy, IWM – A 14545)

the flotilla in its early days and Ollie Mabee was to prove an outstanding CO for years to come in home waters. Norman Broad and Leonard Newall were New Zealanders, Harry Wadds was Australian, and Hannington and Whipp South Africans.[3]

When Ross Campbell sailed for Malta in January 1943, he was puzzled when the 'dead-reckoning' navigation did not bring Malta into sight at the appropriate time, and believing his repairs may have reduced the speed his engine revolutions normally gave, he maintained the same course. A surprisingly long time later, breathing a sigh of relief, he and his navigator sighted an island. They closed and were about to enter harbour with the crew 'fallen in' on the fo'c'sle, but they found that the signals emanating from shore made no sense. Someone drew attention to a flag flying at the masthead of a heavily armed vessel also entering harbour. Rapid consultation of the signal manual revealed that it was in fact the Italian mercantile ensign. It suddenly dawned on Campbell that he had not found Malta, but Pantelleria, the Italian fortress island (which was to take so long to subdue a few months later). He slowed, allowed the Italian vessel to pass into harbour, and carried on past the entrance. He knew he was getting short of fuel, but in making his quiet escape was able to note the positions of shore defences, which were impressive but fortunately silent.

For a few minutes all three engines stopped for lack of fuel, and while the motor mechanic was feverishly reconnecting fuel lines to draw on the residue in each tank, Italian aircraft flew over but did not open fire. Eventually 309 limped back to Malta on one engine to conserve fuel, and Campbell had to face an irate Vice Admiral Malta who had despatched ships and aircraft to search for the missing boat. When Campbell, a

future ambassador, was informed of the cost of that search, he is reputed to have suggested that it should be reimbursed out of his pay. The Admiral's reply was that as he was on Canadian rates 'that is probably possible!'[4]

January 1943 was notable for the 10th Flotilla, as at last contact began to be made with enemy ships which in all their patrols off the desert had been so scarce. And it also brought yet another move for this most itinerant flotilla, as Jermain was ordered to take a small group of his boats to Bone, where targets were expected to be more extensive, since Bizerta, 120 miles to the east, was the major port for German reinforcements. He expected this to be a short-term deployment and took with him only a minimum number of base staff: but his boats had to transport Commando units which were urgently needed in North Africa.

In fact, on 13/14 January, three of the flotilla en route from Malta to Bone met an enemy merchant vessel on its way to Bizerta. In bad weather conditions they fired their torpedoes but failed to hit.

The half-leader of the flotilla, Lt Peter Evensen DSC, was left in Malta with the other boats, and their patrols alternated between the south-east coast of Sicily and the North African coast, particularly off Tripoli which the Allied Eighth Army was rapidly approaching from the east.

On the night of 19/20 January, the 10th Flotilla notched up its first successful torpedo attack, off Tripoli. As Evensen, with 264 (Sheldrick), 260 (Wadds) and 313 (Foster) were searching for targets just to the north of the port, to their delight they came across three tugs attempting to tow an Italian submarine which had gone aground while approaching the harbour. They first drove off the tugs with gunfire, setting one of them on

---

3 Note from Capt Denis Jermain.

4 Note from Ross Campbell, at this time CO MTB 309.

North Africa, Sicily and West Coast, Italy.

fire. The submarine (later identified as the *Santorre Santarosa*) was then hit by a torpedo from 260.[5]

On the following night the same three boats returned to Tripoli with orders to attack the harbour mole of the port with gunfire in an attempt to encourage the enemy to abandon the port. In fact when the Army entered Tripoli on 23 January, they found the harbour installations intact and gave the MTBs credit for their help.

It was at this stage that the Vosper boats of the 7th Flotilla began to make their first impact on operations. In Chapter 3 the arrival of the early boats of that flotilla at Alexandria in June 1942 (MTBs 57 to 65) was described, and also the fact that these nine Vospers proved in need of major overhaul before they could operate. Only 61 (Bligh) was able to join the 10th that autumn in patrols along the desert coast. These early arrivals had been reinforced by a second group of Vospers of later design (nine boats with numbers from MTBs 73 to 95) which had originally been designated the 8th Flotilla, but were incorporated into the 7th on their arrival at Alexandria.

The boats of the 7th Flotilla, with their COs were:

MTB 57 Lt M.H.B. Solomon – later Lt D. Scott RN

58 Lt L.F. Ramseyer, also succeeded by Scott

59 Lt R.A.M. Hennessy RN, the SO, who handed over the command to Lt D. Owen-Pawson

60 Lt C.P. Evensen – later Lt R. Keyes RN

61 Lt T.J. Bligh

62 Lt C.T. Finch

63 Lt R. Keyes RN

64 Lt P. Ridyard

65 Lt D. Owen-Pawson – later Lt R.W. Cordery

Those which began as the 8th Flotilla were:

73 (Lt F.L. Tomlinson, later Lt G. Aimers)

75 (Lt L.M. Bulling RCNVR)

76 (Lt W. Keefer RCNVR)

77 (Lt J.B. Sturgeon)

78 (Lt R. Varvill)

79 (Lt E.S. Good)

82 (Lt P.R.A. Taylor RNR, later Lt C.A. Rees)

84 (Lt G.R. Smith)

95 (Lt P. Redhead RNR)

Their SO, Lt R.A.M. (Robert) Hennessy RN, was an experienced Coastal Forces officer. He had, when war broke out, been the CO of MTB 07 in the 2nd MTB Flotilla in Hong Kong. He had returned to Britain in March 1940 and in May had taken command of MTB 69 of the 11th Flotilla, based at Dover. In October 1941 he had been appointed to 57 and to be SO of the 7th Flotilla. He had had a frustrating time through the second half of 1942, trying to get his boats ready for operations, but at last they were almost there, and were now required in Malta. 61, 77 and 82 were the first to be sent, and arrived in Malta on 25 January. By March most of the others had joined the 10th at HMS *Gregale*, sharing in the patrols. Hennessy, in common with Jermain and Evensen, no longer commanded his own boat, but on operations travelled in a boat of his choice. In practice, most commonly he used 77 (J.B. Sturgeon) whenever it was available.

It was not long before boats of the flotilla had their first chance of an attack on the enemy. Hennessy with 77 (Sturgeon), 61 (Bligh) and 82 (Taylor), was patrolling off

---

5 ROP at PRO in ADM 199/541; MO3231.

MTB 59 of the 7th Flotilla (CO Lt R.A.M. Hennessy RN) showing SO's stripe on bow. (Courtesy, N. Hughes)

Maritimo, a small island off the south-west coast of Sicily, on 16/17 February, when he first received a sighting report of a merchant ship and two destroyers, which was later increased to four merchantmen. 61, now operating as a gunboat since her torpedoes had been removed and her gun armament increased by the addition of three Italian Breda 20-mm guns, was sent down the port side of the convoy to create a diversion while 77 and 82 made their torpedo attack on the starboard side. They saw no positive result from their attack, and Sturgeon in 77 decided to attempt a depth charge attack under the bow of the merchantmen. 77 came under heavy fire, and just as the First Lieutenant, S/Lt D.M.W. Napier, was about to release one from its rack, he was hit and killed instantly. It was a harsh beginning to the 7th Flotilla's operations. Two of the faster Elcos of the

10th had left Malta an hour later than the Vospers with orders to rendezvous with them, but because of that unit's change of position they missed them and so went in search of targets. They found an escorted merchant ship and were preparing to fire their torpedoes when a torpedo-carrying Wellington appeared, promptly released its missile, blew up the target and left the MTBs thwarted.[6]

Meanwhile, Jermain's section of the 10th in Bone were settling in and beginning patrols along the coast to Bizerta. At first they found that their old SO Bobby Allan, now commanding the Mobile Base, had only just arrived and was in the early stages of setting up more permanent services, but they were astonished at the speed with which facilities

6 ROP printed in *London Gazette* dated 15 October 1948.

were provided. Lorries were commandeered, and supplies begged and borrowed from other service units. The fast minelayer HMS *Manxman* arrived with equipment, including cradles to enable boats to be slipped, and wide areas of concrete were laid to take their weight. A large shed provided engineering facilities. Unfortunately, as the Allied Air Forces were not yet fully established with airfields, the port was subjected to very heavy air raids, particularly by Stuka dive-bombers. They had, at this stage, the advantage of airfields in Tunisia, Pantelleria and Sicily. These were to continue for several months, but were rendered less effective by strong anti-aircraft defences.

C-in-C was determined to forestall both major seaborne enemy reinforcement into Tunisia, and evacuation from it, and established a tight ring of cruisers and destroyers

at sea by night. The MTBs began to patrol, also at night, close in off Bizerta, but it seemed from the lack of any enemy shipping that they were well aware of the stranglehold, and chose to reinforce by day. This denied the MTBs any targets, but made supply ships more vulnerable to aircraft attack. Three MTBs did meet a group of E-boats off Bone on the night of 30/31 January, and fought an inconclusive action.

In an intelligent reaction to the frustration bred by a lack of targets, the MTBs were fitted, early in February, with minelaying chutes which enabled the 77-ft boats to carry six mines, and the 70-ft boats four. Initially the officers and crews resented the change in their role, but when reports began to come in of enemy sinkings in areas where they had laid mines, they realized the wisdom of the change and were converted.

MTB 82, a Vosper of the 8th MTB Flotilla (which joined the 7th). (Courtesy, G.M. Hudson)

It was natural that the crews became very attached to their boats and proud of the availability and performance records of each, leading to a fierce loyalty. If a boat suffered damage – a natural occasional occurrence in high-speed boats in winter, even in the Mediterranean – they sought to ensure that the repair was as speedy as possible so that there was no question of the crew being moved to other boats, which happened when a boat was temporarily paid off. They would turn to and help with repairs. A good example was that of 266 which was considered irreparable at Bone after the hull was damaged in heavy seas. Her First Lieutenant, Norman Broad, a resourceful New Zealander, obtained some lengths of heavy angle-iron and shaped them to fit the port and starboard chines. When these were bolted in place to strengthen the middle third of the hull, 266 was pronounced seaworthy again. Shortly after, he was appointed in command, and remained so until he was killed in action in March 1944 in the Aegean.

The 10th continued their minelaying activities off Tunisia for two months, in which time they laid 108 mines off Plane Island, Cape Zebib, Galita Island, Zembra and Bizerta. Towards the end of March they resumed their normal role as MTBs, but not before a brush with Italian MAS boats while actually on a minelaying sortie off Zambretta. Three MAS boats appeared and were immediately engaged by 316 (Adams) and 265 (Oxley) whose combined fire set one on fire and left·her stopped when they had perforce to return to their minelaying.[7]

It was a feature of German ingenuity in the face of a grave shortage of escort vessels and indeed of cargo-carrying ships that they developed both the F-lighter (based on the equivalent of the British TLC) and the Siebel ferry. Both could be used either to carry cargo or, in a more heavily armed version, to make valuable additions to convoy escorts or in a coast defence role. The Siebel ferry was constructed of two independently powered barges about 80 ft long joined – like a catamaran – by a bridge or deck of variable width, often making a total beam of 50 ft. They were only capable of about 8 knots and had a very shallow draught, so were very difficult to attack with torpedoes. When they carried three 88-mm and two 37-mm guns, they could beat off attacking MTBs unless they could be surprised.[8]

It was four of these Siebel ferries that Lancaster in 311 and 265 (Oxley) sighted when on patrol off Plane Island on 22/23 March. It was not for nothing that Lancaster was known to his flotilla colleagues as 'Butch': he was aggressive, and determined to get among the enemy despite the disparity in numbers. Even so he took time to assess the speed and the identity of these targets, and decided on a silent approach with his port torpedo set at a mere 2 ft. He fired at the third Siebel at 700 yds, and immediately heavy fire was opened by all four of the targets. The two MTBs switched to a gun attack and hit the fourth in line at very close range, making smoke as they disengaged. The extent of the enemy's fire – seemingly all tracer shells – had blinded them, and 311 therefore could not see the result of the torpedo attack, but Oxley in 265 reported an orange glow followed by a black column of smoke. 311 had a fortunate escape on the 35-knot return to base when a mine exploded in her wake, causing no damage.[9]

Lancaster in 311 and Oxley in 265 were out again on 27/28 March, this time carrying Cdr Oliver, the Senior Officer Inshore Squadron (SOIS) who loved to get away from

7 ROP at PRO in ADM 199/537.

8 Pope, *Flag 4*.
9 MO5755; ROP at PRO in ADM 199/541.

his desk to see some action. Lancaster discovered a supply ship off Bizerta, and promptly torpedoed and sank it, with an E-boat looking on which never got involved. As the Commodore had commanded a light cruiser sunk by a torpedo on a Malta convoy a year earlier, he was delighted to be present.

The next operation, on 31 March, continued the run of success, and was certainly the most telling blow the 10th had struck so far. It began badly when two of the boats were forced to drop out, one with a man overboard to be searched for, and the other with engine trouble. To Jermain's dismay, this latter was the boat he was travelling in, and with a heavy sea running he was unable to transfer to one of the other boats. He ordered R.R. Smith in 266 to carry on as SO, accompanied by 315 (Newall).

Their objective was the interception of a heavily escorted convoy of merchantmen approaching Bizerta which would pass through the channel between Cape Zebib and Cani Rocks. German records later revealed that there were three sizeable 'steamers' escorted by four Italian Torpedo Boats (small destroyers), a corvette and three German submarine-chasers.

Smith and Newall waited a mile off Cape Zebib for the destroyers and submarine chasers (which they thought were E-boats) to pass, and remained unseen. They were then able to set their sights on the second and third merchantmen in line, and fired when ready. Smith hit the second and Newall the third: each blew up and sank rapidly. As they withdrew at top speed, they came under heavy fire, but got away without damage. It had been a brilliant unobserved attack despite a strong escort and very heavy seas. German records reveal that the two ships they had destroyed totalled 6,912 tons, and that the first merchant ship in line had also been sunk – by a torpedo from aircraft – a great blow at a crucial time for the hard-pressed German

Army. Unfortunately, the weather on the return got even worse, with gale force winds, and 266 suffered severe hull damage, breaking her back. With speed reduced to 8 knots they both got back to Bone – but it took until 1100 next day.

Three months later came announcements of awards of the DSC to both Smith and Newall, DSMs for their coxswains, and other awards for their crews.[10]

These successes were dimmed by the sad news that 262 had been lost, reportedly on 24 February in a strange incident. It is not surprising that detail of date and indeed of all the circumstances could only be estimated, as it was later revealed that two of the crew had died, three were missing, and seven had been taken prisoner. The seven who became POWs included the CO, Charles Coles, two temporary officers, and the coxswain, Petty Officer Percy Ward.

It was not until PO Ward escaped and got back to England later in the year that the story was first recounted; and only when Charles Coles arrived home at the end of the war that his report could be filed, over two years later. Ward had taken advantage of the confusion caused by Italy's armistice in September to make his break for freedom, and was awarded the BEM for his exploit. Charles Coles' account reveals successive strokes of ill fortune.

MTB 262 was operating independently off Galita Island, having been sent there in lieu of a 'work up' after major repairs. She was laying mines, when to the CO's horror she experienced a total battery failure with apparently no chance of repair, and drifted away from the island. Coles was a resourceful man, but all efforts to get under way by any means were unsuccessful, so he decided to

10 MO5893; ROP by CO MTB 266, held by authors; Rohwer and Hummelchen, *Chronology of the War at Sea*.

sink his boat to prevent her from falling into enemy hands, and attempt to row or paddle the 30 miles to the African coast. The two assault boats were launched and the crew manned them. Demolition charges were activated and the depth charges set to detonate when the boat settled to 20 ft. Very quickly it became obvious that the rough sea running made the assault boats totally unsuitable for the long haul ahead, and they began to take in water and first one sank and then the other.

The only course open to them was to attempt to reboard 262, which was settling very slowly some 300 yds away. Coles first sent Sub Lt Piper, a strong swimmer, to reboard and attempt to remove the detonators from the depth charges. He did a

MTB 267 of the 10th Flotilla at Malta, February 1943. (Courtesy, G.M. Hudson)

wonderful job and threw the detonators over the side. Surprisingly the positive buoyancy of the boat was keeping her afloat.

Those who were still in the water struggled to get back aboard, but the water was still very cold in February and three of the weaker swimmers failed to make it. The rest scrambled aboard and kept the boat afloat by blocking the holes made by the demolition charges and bailing and pumping by hand. A Luftwaffe patrol spotted the plight of 262, and Coles, reasoning that this would probably lead to the capture of the boat, decided to rope the remaining men together and swim to the island, first making sure that the boat would sink more quickly.

Two more of the crew died at this time, and the rest were picked up by a rescue boat from the island, manned by French fishermen but carrying two armed Italian NCOs. All the survivors were too weak to offer any resistance, and became prisoners of war. The MTB sank. It was a very sad end to a fine boat and stalwart crew, and the long experience Charles Coles had brought from the very start of the flotilla's operations since 1941 was no longer available and deeply missed.

April began with news that 267 (Joy) had also been lost, but to the sea rather than to the enemy. On 2 April she was en route from Benghazi to Malta and encountered very heavy weather. She was another boat to break her back and had to be sunk by gunfire after all her crew had been taken off.

But also in April came reinforcements to the MTB fleet. The first two flotillas of Dog Boats (the D class Fairmiles) began arriving at Bone having made the passage from Milford Haven to Gibraltar at 10 knots through U-boat infested waters. Two more flotillas were due in May and June. Admiralty announced that the 20th Flotilla of American-built Vospers and the 24th Flotilla of older Vospers which had been operating in home waters would also be despatched shortly. And with the involvement of US troops in the First Army now in the Mediterranean, the first American PT boats of Higgins construction arrived at Bone under the command of Lt Cdr S. Barnes USN, who was quickly to gain the respect of all. This was the 15th PT Squadron (known as 'Ron 15') and to British eyes their greatest asset was an advanced radar system with PPI (plan, position indicator) which gave a wonderful picture of land and ships with ranges of 10 or more miles clearly displayed on a circular plot in the charthouse. This was a far cry from the primitive radar of very limited scale and definition available at this time to the British MTBs.

Meanwhile, on land, the fierce battle to trap the German Army into a smaller and smaller portion of Tunisia and ultimately to drive it out of Africa was proceeding apace. The German Army was hemmed in around Bizerta and Tunis, fighting a vigorous rearguard action. Montgomery had broken through the Mareth Line on 29 March and the First Army was pressing on the western flank. On 7 April troops from the two armies made contact. By 12 April both Sfax and Sousse on the eastern coast of Tunisia had fallen, and were being prepared as bases from which the boats could operate. All available boats, and many ships of the Mediterranean fleet, were ready to prevent the evacuation of German troops from the Cap Bon area.

The 7th Flotilla, anxious to get properly into the fray after weeks of largely fruitless patrols off Sicily, was despatched to Sousse within days of its fall, and found no support group there, nor any facilities such as fuel and water, or stores of food and ammunition. The men of the flotilla worked hard to set up their own base and had to initiate all the necessary services before they could begin operations. But from 24 April patrols were sent out on almost every night, covering the

coast of Tunisia. MTBs 77 (Sturgeon), 75 (Bulling), 61 (Bligh) and 82 (Rees) carried the main brunt of these, but five other boats took a share.

With Dog Boats now also operating out of Sfax, the 10th Flotilla from Bone, and destroyers further off shore, a system of 'boxes' – square grids on a control chart each carrying an identifying symbol – was introduced, to indicate clearly delineated areas for patrols.

The boats of the 10th Flotilla were as busy as the 7th, and it was not surprising that these operations close inshore among the rocks and shoals and minefields should bring casualties. On 2 May, 311 (Lancaster) was on patrol with 316 (Adams) between Cani Rocks and Zembra Island on the approach to Bizerta, when 311 was badly damaged by an exploding mine and had to be abandoned. 316 picked up all her crew, three of whom were injured, and then sank 311 by gunfire.

On 5 May, 264 was allocated to operate with the 7th Flotilla, and was near-missed by a mine off Cap Bon. By 7 May, with the German troops compressed into a very small area around Cap Bon, the end was clearly very near, and the C-in-C, Admiral Cunningham, determined to prevent any evacuation by sea, brought in sixteen destroyers behind the MTB patrols, and next day issued his famous signal for Operation Retribution: 'Sink, burn and destroy. Let nothing pass!'

It was on 8 May that Bligh's 61 met her fate. The 7th were patrolling off Kelibia and there was no movement, so Bligh requested permission to enter Kelibia harbour and use his 20-mm cannons to destroy any targets inside. Unfortunately, the charts were old and inaccurate, and 61 fell foul of a shoal and struck hard. Bligh tried everything to get her off, ditching depth charges and ammunition and reversing at full speed. He even organized a human tow column as the water all around was so shallow, but she would not budge. Hennessy reluctantly ordered him to destroy his boat.

Bligh's description of the last rites of MTB 61, written for the author of *Flag 4* in 1954, was characteristically colourful. He had been expecting far greater hostility from the occupants of the harbour, who seemed puzzled by all that had been going on for the past two hours. All the activities to this point had been conducted in whispers. The First Lieutenant waded round the boat to find the deepest point to ditch the weighted confidential books canvas bag. The motor mechanic pumped petrol into the bilges and poured it everywhere he could in the other spaces below decks. Bligh pocketed the loaded two-star cartridge pistol and as PT 209, sent in to pick up the crew, approached he sent the crew wading and swimming towards her. The enemy at last opened fire, and Bligh took a deep breath and fired the signal pistol into the mess deck. 'There was a great roar of flame and the whole foredeck lifted away from the sides like a giant crocodile snapping at a bird'. Bligh was blown off the bridge, hit the deck and then, miraculously only slightly hurt, splashed his way to the PT and was carried off to safety. He went on to command a Dog Boat and the 57th Flotilla with great distinction.[11]

264 was mined two nights later and, although beached, was irreparable and was therefore paid off.

From then on both flotillas at last began intercepting small craft carrying German troops, and many prisoners were taken. The 10th Flotilla collected 36 men on 9 May and 117 on the 11th, and the boats of the 7th found 13 on 10 May and 5 on the 11th.

The operation by 316 (Adams, with Jermain aboard), 265 (Oxley) and 309

(Campbell) on 11 May was the most notable of these. They picked up prisoners from rafts, a boatload from Kelibia, a battleship's motor launch, a motor cruiser and three very small boats. The 117 prisoners included a group of German paratroopers. In the midst of all this activity a partly submerged hull was seen and thought to be a large supply submarine. Two torpedoes were fired but no hit recorded, and when the target was closed it was found to be the partly submerged wreck of a destroyer.

The return to Bone with 117 prisoners aboard three small boats, each with a crew of nine, presented problems. Ross Campbell in 309 reported that he had almost five times as many prisoners aboard as his total crew complement. But the captives proved to be very docile and appeared to be glad that their part in the war was over. One amusing aspect was that the sailors guarding them used machine guns taken from the prisoners and had to receive some instruction from a German soldier on the firing procedure, who finished his demonstration with a short sharp burst into the sea.

On 13 May, General von Arnim surrendered his forces to the Allies, and Operation Retribution came to a successful conclusion. One hundred and fifty thousand German and Italian troops were captured, and a very large quantity of tanks, artillery pieces, ammunition and transport were left behind.

Thus ended the North African campaign, with the 7th and 10th Flotillas playing their small but significant parts in the successful outcome.[12]

The C-in-C, on 13 May, signalled to his ships:

The campaign in North Africa has concluded with the surrender or destruction of all Axis forces. It is

---

11 Sir Timothy Bligh, then CO of MTB 61, in Pope, *Flag 4*; Summary of ROP at NHB.

12 ROP in BSR 199; Dorling (Taffrail), *Western Mediterranean 1942–1945*.

MTB 84, returning from Sousse, Tunisia, May 1943. (Courtesy, H.F. Cooper)

a tribute to the work of our light forces that even in the desperate circumstances in which the enemy found themselves, no real attempt was made to evacuate by sea, and that such few as made the attempt were speedily rounded up by ships on patrol. I have watched with satisfaction the progressively good work performed in harassing the enemy during the last weeks and in particular in the last phase which has enabled a large number of craft of different types to work by day and by night in close proximity to an enemy coast without confusion and with a high degree of success. I congratulate you all on a difficult and arduous job well performed.

The boats were also complimented by Vice Admiral, Malta, who made sure C-in-C was aware of their work by signalling to him: 'Reliability of MTBs exceeded all expect-

ations. They were very useful in completing the Tunisian blockade.'

But the 10th particularly had suffered severely, having lost MTBs 262, 264, 267 and 311, and the damage to many of the remaining eleven boats meant that a period of refitting, repair, maintenance and engine changes was essential before the next phase of the Mediterranean war. The crews, too, deserved some rest after months of constant operations, living aboard their tiny craft in cramped conditions. To this end, 265, 309 and 316 were sent to Bone, 268 and 313 to Malta, and 260, 261, 263, 266, 307 and 315 to Bizerta where HMS *Vienna*, the Coastal Force Depot ship, had arrived.

The 7th Flotilla left Sousse and returned to Malta, where they found HMS *Gregale* the new Coastal Force Base to be well established, and both Grand and Marsamaxett harbours becoming daily more crowded. Lt Hennessy was promoted to Lieutenant Commander and appointed in command of the base.

The new SO for the 7th was Lt A.C.B. Blomfield DSC RN, who was to lead the flotilla with distinction for the next eighteen months. The flotilla, which had begun with eighteen boats after the initial amalgamation with the 8th, was by now effectively down to eleven as 57, 58, 59, 60, 61, 63 and 64 of the early Vospers had either been under repair, paid off, converted for other use or sunk.

There was little respite for one unit of the 7th, which received orders to return to Sousse on 6 June. Lt Sturgeon led the three boats in his own 77, accompanied by 73 (Lt F.L. Tomlinson) and 84 (Lt G.R. Smith). On arrival they were told to fuel and prepare to join Force K, a group of cruisers and destroyers charged with an attack on Pantelleria. The island – together with two others, Lampedusa and Linosa – held strategically important positions in the 'Sicilian Narrows' and it was clear that they had to be taken. At Sousse, fuelling was by hand-pumping and was a lengthy procedure – it took all the next day.

On 8 June the three boats left Sousse with HMS *Whaddon* to rendezvous with Force K. At 1120 the cruisers began their bombardment of the island's defences, with little response from the shore batteries. Then it was the turn of the destroyers from much closer range, and finally the MTBs closed right in to attack visible points as directed. They came under machine-gun fire from the shore and 77 suffered hits but no real damage.

In view of the intensive bombing of the island, and the heavy bombardment by the cruisers and destroyers, it was difficult to see the purpose of the MTBs' attack, unless it was simply to draw fire and give markers for further bombardment. Later it became

clear that after many days of bombing and bombardment, this operation on 8 June was indeed designed as a test of reactions before a land assault on a heavily defended mountainous island fortress could be mounted.

The unit returned to Sousse in company with HMS *Whaddon*. The days of 9 and 10 June and were spent refuelling, repairing an engine defect in 77, and taking ammunition aboard. On 11 June they reported to the Admiral's headquarters ship, HMS *Largs*, at 1000, and 73 and 84 were sent on air-sea rescue duties. It became clear that the seaborne landing was taking place and that only sporadic resistance was being offered. 77 remained with *Largs* and in due course took the Chief of Staff and his party ashore into Pantelleria harbour to arrange the surrender of the island, and stood off to return them when required. 84 brought another party in at 1400. 73 was still engaged on air-sea rescue duties, and was returning from one when she was attacked by two enemy aircraft. Her bridge was shattered by cannon fire, killing the First Lieutenant (Sub Lt R.K. Druce) and wounding the CO, Lt Tomlinson, so badly that he later died of his wounds. The coxswain, L/Sea A.L. Harrison, took over and brought 73 back to HMS *Royal Ulsterman* to hand over the wounded. Sturgeon, when he rejoined, put the First Lieutenant of 84 (Sub Lt R. Aitchison) in command of 73. He rapidly reported that she had been holed in the port wing petrol tank and also below the water line, so 84 was sent to escort her back to Malta, taking her in tow when it became obvious that petrol was leaking into the bilges.

When 77 was released, she returned ahead of the other two. It was considered later that the Pantelleria operation was the first occasion on which bombing from the air truly led to the capitulation of an invasion objective. An amusing story circulating at the time suggested that the only casualty in the whole naval operation was a torpedo gunner bitten by a donkey!

77 later returned to the area to join the forces liberating Lampedusa (which had a garrison of 5,000 Italians) and Linosa. By 13 June all this was accomplished and the seaways through the Mediterranean were at last clear, and the Allies had use of an important airfield on Pantelleria to supplement those on Malta.[13]

13 ROP by Unit SO Lt J.M. Sturgeon in BSR 207; account by Ronald Aitchison; Dorling, *Western Mediterranean.*

Quite naturally, the enormous build-up of ships in Malta led to the obvious conclusion that an assault on occupied Europe was imminent: the speculation at the end of June simply concerned where and when it would be launched.

Joining the 7th in Malta, apart from the newly arrived Dog Boats of the 20th MGB and 33rd MTB Flotillas, were two new flotillas of 'short' MTBs. The 24th Flotilla of 71-ft Vospers commanded by Lt C.W.S. Dreyer DSC RN had in fact been operating in home waters in the Channel from Newhaven since early 1943; Dreyer had been one of the early group of RN officers to become MTB specialists. He had won his first DSC at

The officers of the 24th MTB Flotilla with their SO, Lt C.W.S. Dreyer DSC RN (centre) in Malta, 1943. (Courtesy, E. Young)

MTB 86 of the 24th Flotilla (CO E. Young). (Courtesy, E. Young)

Dunkirk when he commanded MTB 102 (a 1937 experimental Vosper) and a Bar to that DSC in August 1942 when he was SO MTBs in Dover.

In summary, the eight boats of the flotilla were:

MTBs   81 Lt L.V. Strong
          85 Lt P.H. Hyslop
          86 Lt E. Young
          89 Lt W.J. Archer
          97 Lt M.G. Bowyer
        226 Lt W.O.J. Bate
        242 Lt C.R. Holloway
        243 Lt H. du Boulay

The other flotilla, only just commissioned,

was the 20th, whose boats were of Vosper 71-ft design but built in the USA. They had been shipped across the Atlantic to Oran in LSTs (Landing Ships, Tank), had sailed on to Algiers and Bizerta, and were arriving in batches at Malta at this time. Their SO was Lt H.A. Barbary RN, and the boats were:

MTBs 287 Lt J.D. Lancaster DSC
        288 Lt P.A. Taylor DSC
        289 Lt Barnsdale RNZNVR
        290 Lt D. Austin
        295 Lt F. Frenzel
        296 Lt W. Rickard
        297 Lt J.R. Woods   RCNVR
        298 Lt The Hon F. Shore

During this period of uncertainty all the boats were used for patrols on the south-east coast of Sicily, which for many of the newly arrived MTBs acted as valuable working-up patrols. Indeed this was very necessary because the majority of them had largely untried crews and had had little time for exercising together since commissioning at Algiers.

As June ended and July began, tension mounted. The numbers of boats in Malta increased daily (some had to use an 'overflow' anchorage in St Pauls Bay), and the state of readiness reached an even higher level.

Captain Hubback, Captain Coastal Forces, Mediterranean (CCF Med), was due to be succeeded within a few weeks by Capt J.F. Stevens RN who was destined to oversee this powerful force of MTBs, MGBs, MLs and HDMLs for the next two years. His staff was greatly strengthened with experienced officers, and in particular by his newly appointed SOO (Staff Officer Operations), Lt Cdr Morgan-Giles RN, another whose impact on Mediterranean Coastal Forces was to be of the greatest significance.

There was not much longer to wait. On 5 July the COs were summoned to a highly secret meeting, and were given a first briefing on Operation Husky – the invasion of Sicily. Among the hundreds of ships that would be taking part were the smallest of all: the eight flotillas of MTBs and MGBs. And this time, they would have a function which, because of the geographical features, meant that they alone would be bearing the brunt of operations in the narrow confines of the Strait of Messina between Sicily and the toe of Italy.

CHAPTER 5

OPERATION HUSKY – THE SICILIAN CAMPAIGN: THE 7TH, 10TH, 20TH AND 24TH MTB FLOTILLAS

JULY TO SEPTEMBER 1943

This history of 'The Mediterranean MTBs' very largely concerns individual flotillas, usually operating independently, and frequently in isolation from the other flotillas. Their operations also tended to be separate from those of the 'long' boats – the D class Fairmiles or Dog Boats described in *Dog Boats at War*. But the demands of the invasion of Sicily brought together the four 'short' boat flotillas (the 7th, 10th, 20th and 24th) more closely than at any other time. It also ensured that they worked in harmony with the four Dog Boat flotillas (the 19th and 20th MGBs, and 32nd and 33rd MTBs).

However, it was still the general rule that units detailed for specific patrols were provided from one flotilla, rather than mixed. It was an arrangement which made tactical sense, as each of the different types of boats which made up the flotillas had its own characteristics, particularly of attainable speeds.

It is not easy to piece together the complex interweaving pattern of the highlights of the MTB operations in Operation Husky. There was so much continuous activity that the ultimate reports were lacking in detail, and have to be put together by individual accounts which support and link the Reports of Proceedings of direct contacts with enemy forces.

But if the activities of the MTBs are described as 'a complex pattern', they pale into insignificance when compared with the complexity of the huge logistical problem of delivering a very large invasion force off the shores of Sicily at H-hour on D-Day: 0245 on 10 July 1943. Heavily escorted convoys of troop transports and supply vessels had been converging on the approaches to the landing beaches for days. Some had come from the USA and Britain without any staging point. Others had gathered first in North African ports, and had the benefit of additional preparation time. It was miraculous that this, the largest invasion fleet in history at this time, had suffered very little interference from the enemy.[1]

The actual landing beaches were located on the south-east coast of the island, where British and Canadian troops made the assault, and on the south-west coast, the area allotted to the United States forces. All had

1 Roskill, *The History of the Second War, The War at Sea*, Vol. 3, pt 1; Dorling, *Western Mediterranean*.

significant immediate objectives – to get ashore and capture the main airfields in order to reduce the threat of heavy air attacks on the densely packed fleet just off shore.

The MTBs involved in the protection of that fleet on the morning of the invasion left Malta during the early afternoon of 9 July and immediately met adverse sea conditions. They found themselves butting into a short steep sea whipped up by a gale force headwind. It was wet – very wet – and just the sort of conditions which led to broken frames and broken backs in the older boats. But there was no holding back on the day of an invasion, and miraculously the weather eased after midnight and allowed time to be caught up.

The Dog Boats were to provide close support off the actual landing area, but the 'short' boats had much further to go: they headed up the east coast to patrol the northern area of the Strait of Messina. Their task was to intercept any German E-boats, U-boats, larger units of the Italian Navy or any other surface craft which might menace the invasion fleet.

Two boats of the 7th Flotilla were fitted with the 'rumble-bumble' apparatus previously described when a feint landing was simulated during the Battle of El Alamein. They made their noises well north of the invasion area in the hope of confusing enemy response. As cruisers were also bombarding Catania with the same intention, and there were reports of enemy troop movements in the 'wrong' direction, the efforts of the MTBs may well have been effective.

In common with all the other ships of the huge naval force, they met no enemy, and after a long tense night they returned to Malta to prepare for the continuing round of patrols which would go on relentlessly for five weeks.[2]

The MTBs had clear orders. By operating in the narrowest section of the Strait – only 3 or 4 miles wide between Sicily and the Calabrian coast of Italy – they had a good chance of interception should the enemy appear. Their first duty was to inform the HQ ship of any enemy intrusion, and then to attack any target. It was necessary to arrive on patrol by dusk and remain till dawn, and because their patrol area was 150 miles from Malta this meant a very long total operational period, especially since the daylight return left them vulnerable to aircraft attack, and alertness had to be maintained. It was normally 24 hours before they got back to Malta.

This was not the only hazard on these northerly patrols. The shore batteries and searchlights on both coasts were on constant alert, and frequently lobbed shells in their direction, necessitating rapid changes of course and speed.

After the initial landing these patrols continued, as the troops ashore were still being supplied by a stream of merchant vessels which required protection. The Dog Boats provided units to the south, where the Strait was far wider, and communication between the two groups enabled them to work together as required.

The first enemy contact came to four boats of the 7th Flotilla on the night of 11/12 July. They were led by their new SO, Lt A.C. Blomfield DSC RN, whose boats were passing Catania on their way north to the patrol area when they came across an Italian minesweeper. Curiously, she had been abandoned by her crew and left adrift. They searched her, removed documents and then sank her before moving on.[3]

Meanwhile, the Army was making rapid headway and had taken the nearest airfields.

2   Pope, *Flag 4*; Dorling, *Western Mediterranean.*

3   Summary of recorded actions, NHB.

The ancient port of Syracuse fell on 11 July and they were closing in on Augusta with its huge enclosed harbour, which was essential for the next phase of supply and reinforcement. The 10th and units of the 20th Flotilla were held in reserve in Bone and Bizerta. They were moved to Malta on 13 July, poised ready to join in with the patrols.

Records indicate that soon after this a possible double tragedy was averted as MTBs from the 7th and the Dog Boat 32nd Flotillas fired torpedoes at the cruisers and destroyers of Force Q off the Sicilian coast. The cruisers *Euryalus* and *Cleopatra*, after obtaining no response to a challenge, opened fire. Just in time, recognition was achieved. A possibly apocryphal account of subsequent signals circulated: 'Force Q to MTBs: you are very lucky – we were about to blow you out of the water.' Reply: 'You are even luckier – we've fired four torpedoes and missed'.[4]

On the night of 12/13 July came, at last, some real success. Christopher Dreyer led a patrol to the very neck of the Messina Strait, north of Reggio. His boats were 81 (L.V. Strong) of his 24th Flotilla, and 77 (J.B. Sturgeon) and 84 (G.R. Smith) of the 7th – all Vospers of similar vintage. The unit stopped off Raineri Point and lay still with engines cut. Suddenly a U-boat was sighted entering the Strait from the north, on the surface. It was hugging the coast and steering very close to 81, and Strong went astern to try to get into a firing position. Dreyer got off an enemy report 'Nuts Starboard' ('enemy in sight to starboard'). As the U-boat passed, they both sighted a second U-boat following astern. Strong continued in astern, was sure his firing line was right, so sent off one torpedo. It hit, and the U-boat blew up scattering debris all over 81. In the meantime, 77 and 84 chased after the first submarine.

77 fired but tragically suffered two misfires when in an ideal position, and 84 missed as the U-boat dived. They both followed up with depth charges. No result could then be claimed, but the destroyed U-boat was established as U-561 and it was later learned that the one which had escaped was U-375. After this attack by the MTBs she had to put into the Adriatic port of Valona for urgent repairs. She did eventually sail to return to her home base at Toulon, but never arrived and was posted as missing and presumed lost at sea with all hands.

While the boats were searching for survivors, 81 sighted two more vessels moving south along the Italian shore, and it was thought that they were also U-boats. Strong fired his remaining torpedo at 800 yds, but when he clearly missed astern it was realized that these were possibly E-boats cruising at 25 knots. They were followed to the southern limit of their patrol area, where a unit of Dog Boats of the 33rd Flotilla was alerted. In fact, they were subsequently intercepted and sunk – a very satisfactory night for Coastal Forces. (Note 8, Appendix 1)

On the previous day Augusta had fallen to the Allies, and after clearing of mines and jetties it became available as a major port and, more significantly for the MTBs, as a Coastal Force Base which would cut the length of patrols by many hours. Lt Cdr Allan had moved his CF Mobile Base from Bone to Syracuse on the 12th, and by the 15th had begun to receive MTBs at Augusta. Throughout the rest of the campaign, boats were able to operate from this base and only needed to return to Malta for engine changes, refits, and rest periods.

There was no let-up in the activity, since on the night of 15/16 July Tony Blomfield with four of his 7th Flotilla – 77 (Lassen in temporary command), 57 (Aimers), 62 (Finch) and 82 (Rees) – again sighted enemy vessels. His unit was lying 'cut' (i.e. stopped with

4   Pope, *Flag 4*.

engines cut) in a central position between Messina and Reggio, when he sighted an enemy unit moving south, hugging the Italian shore. He identified them as six E-boats (later to be confirmed, by sheer coincidence, as belonging to the German 7th Flotilla). Blomfield ordered a crash start, and headed point-blank for the enemy. The E-boats, realizing they had been spotted, turned 180 degrees and shot northward pursued by the MTBs. As they closed, 77 fired torpedoes at a very shallow depth setting at the leading boat, and followed up, attacking the last in line with guns. All six E-boats responded with heavy fire at 77, but the other Vospers were able to join in and soon two or three of the E-boats were in trouble with fires breaking out and one stopped dead. The leading boat blew up and sank, having presumably been hit by at least one of 77's torpedoes.

By this time the shore batteries on the Sicilian coast had been roused, and heavy and sustained gunfire sent shells close to the boats. 77 was repeatedly hit by shell fragments. Blomfield, now under heavy pressure, made smoke and disengaged to the south followed by the rest of his boats; they were tracked by searchlights and continuing coastal battery fire. A near-miss on 82 severely wounded C.A. Rees, the CO, and killed one of the crew. She was sent back to Augusta.

Blomfield would not retreat entirely from the scene, and remained till 0500. Suddenly a group of E-boats being chased northward by the Dog Boats on the more southerly patrol appeared. He attacked again, received more damage, but the other two boats of his unit continued to chase the enemy until they reached the shelter of the shore batteries. All the boats of the 7th had been damaged, but all could be repaired. 77 had been hit below the waterline, and as the auxiliary engine which worked the pumps had been put out of

action the crew had to bail by hand to get her back to Augusta.

German records confirm that five boats of the 7th E-boat Flotilla, led by their SO Cdr Trummer, had been severely damaged, but do not state that any were sunk. Several months later, Lt Blomfield was awarded a Bar to his DSC for this action and Lassen (a New Zealander) a DSC. Deservedly, too, members of the crews of 82, 57 and 77 received DSMs and three were mentioned in despatches. In Coastal Forces, where a small number of officers and men worked and lived together in close proximity, there was perhaps a stronger bond of team spirit than in larger ships. Certainly the officers knew only too well that in close action the fate of their boat (and their lives) depended more than anything else on the efficiency of the gun teams and of the engine room crew.[5]

From this time on, with the shorter run from Augusta proving a great boon, boats from all four of the flotillas provided units each night to keep their vigilant watch, normally from the centre of the narrowest section of the Strait, with all its hazards. The Dog Boats, too, were similarly deployed in the 'boxes' further south than the 'short' boats.

The 10th Flotilla did not have long to wait before they were back in action. On the afternoon of 16 July, Jermain led a patrol of four of his boats, 315 (Newall), 260 (Wadds), 313 (Foster) and 316 (Adams), northward from Augusta to the patrol area. They stopped 2 miles short of Messina. They were expecting – if they saw anything – to be lucky enough to intercept landing craft or E-boats, but to their intense surprise their first sighting was a large Italian cruiser steaming at full speed through the narrow channel straight for them. There was hardly time to do

---

5   MO10054; ROP at PRO in ADM 199/541; Rohwer and Hummelchen, *Chronology of the War at Sea*.

Lt Alec Foster, CO MTB 313, with A/B Jan Lurcher the Seaman Torpedoman. (Courtesy, N. Hughes)

316 blow up only a short distance to star-board. She had been almost alongside while the boats had been stopped, exchanging calm shouted conversation only minutes earlier. He was just thinking that very shortly 313 might go the same way, when he was summoned to the bridge and found Alec Foster sitting on the deck with a leg wound. The coxswain told him what had happened, in richly descriptive, highly flavoured Liverpudlian. The CO had been hit and knocked over as the coxswain was sighting before firing the torpedoes at a range of about 300 yds. He'd put the wheel over to disengage, but Alec Foster – probably not clear what was happening – had scrambled to his feet and pulled the firing levers. As Ilett put it, the torpedoes were doubtless on their way towards the toe of Italy.

There was no sign of 316, nor of wreckage or survivors. Nothing could be done for her. Ilett found the spare officer of the 10th Flotilla, Sub Lt John McKim, lying on his back in the wheelhouse under a blanket; he was conscious but obviously badly wounded. He died about half an hour later. 313 had clearly been hit by a number of close-range weapon shells, but everything that was needed seemed to be working, and Ilett set off for Augusta. He transferred the CO to a cruiser at first light for medical attention.

Meanwhile Jermain with 315 and 260 was chasing the cruiser down the Strait and watched her as she turned to port and made eastward for Taranto, incidentally being attacked by an Italian plane.

The next morning Sub Lt McKim was buried at sea off the seaward end of Augusta's swept channel with full naval honours, and the flotilla mourned the loss of 316 and her crew.

The cruiser was identified as the *Scipione Africano* of 3,362 tons and 444 ft in length. She had eight 5.3-in guns, eight 37-mm and eight 20-mm cannons, fourteen machine guns

anything more than attempt to get into an attack position. 315 and 316 shot across to the eastern side, presumably hoping to find a firing angle on the cruiser's port beam, and the cruiser turned slightly towards them leaving her starboard side vulnerable to an attack. She was pouring out shells of every calibre on both sides, and almost at once 316 (to port) was hit at very close range and blew up in a sheet of flame. 260 and 313, both on the cruiser's starboard bow, scrambled to fire their torpedoes. Harry Wadds in 260 got his away, and although he thought one had hit, the cruiser did not check its speed. Alec Foster in 313 was not as fortunate. His First Lieutenant, Sub Lt Norman Ilett, described later what he saw of the action. He was aft by the Oerlikon when he saw Dick Adams'

and a claimed speed of 41 knots. Alec Foster, the CO of 313, after a spell in hospital, returned to Britain. He was one of the longest-serving COs in the 10th Flotilla but was not lost to Coastal Forces, as he continued to give distinguished service in home waters till the end of the war. He was succeeded in command of 313 by Lt T.G. Fuller DSC RCNVR who had come out to the Mediterranean in command of a Dog Boat which had been paid off after an explosion.[6]

Patrols were continuing every night, but there was very little enemy movement. The allocation of patrols fell into a pattern. Each flotilla in Augusta would provide a unit on alternate nights, with the result that two or three units would normally be employed. The air raids on Augusta, which had started as soon as the port began to receive a very large amount of shipping, intensified: this meant that a non-patrol night in Augusta provided very little rest.

On patrol on 18 July, the inevitable search-lights and fire from shore batteries claimed their first victim among the 'short' boats, although 641, a D class MGB, had already been sunk off the toe of Italy after a direct hit four nights earlier. MTB 75 (Bulling) of the 7th Flotilla received a hit and was badly damaged, her crew sustaining severe casualties. Initially her survival was in doubt, but she was taken in tow and managed to get back to Augusta.[7]

On the following night, boats of the 10th Flotilla, still smarting after their encounter with the *Scipione Africano* two nights earlier, were on the Messina patrol when they sighted a submarine off Reggio and attacked it with depth charges. They were immediately picked up by searchlights and heavily engaged by the shore batteries at close range, and were forced to withdraw.

Roskill in *The War at Sea* Volume 3, reveals that the Strait was covered by as many as 150 shore batteries, some of them as big as 280 mm (11.2 in) with others of 170 mm (6.8 in) and 152 mm (6 in), together with a large number of 3 to 4-in mobile guns. Bearing in mind the narrowness of the northern end of the Strait, it was small wonder that hits were being secured on the MTBs which penetrated nightly into the area.[8]

There then came a period when these patrols had only the unpleasantness of the shore batteries but with no contacts at all to make them seem worthwhile. Night after night the boats would carry out their allotted tasks but no enemy ships attempted to break through, nor was there any sign of passage between the Sicilian and Italian shores. And there was no letting up on the air raids on Augusta, where on the night of 21 July a bomb which detonated close to her stern sank 288 of the 20th Flotilla. Despite their constant patrolling, the boats of this flotilla had not yet sighted the enemy, and it was a cruel irony to suffer their first loss in an air raid. The crew were all rescued by 290 and drafted to other boats after a short break. This came at a time when Lt Barbary's flotilla of US-built Vospers had only just been made up to full strength by the arrival of the last four boats from Malta.

In the 10th Flotilla, there was a welcome change of scene for one unit. The US Army had taken Palermo on the north coast of Sicily on 22 July. Soon after, the US PT boats of 'Ron 15' which had worked with the 10th from Bone in April and May, and which had been supporting the western section of the invasion, moved in to make Palermo their base. There was a call for some British boats

6 MO9579; Notes from Capt Denis Jermain and Norman Ilett.
7 Summary of actions at NHB.

8 Summary of actions at NHB; Roskill, *History of the Second War, The War at Sea*, Vol. 3.

to join them, and Jermain sent his half-leader Evensen there with half his flotilla. They found it a welcome change to be able to approach the Strait of Messina from its northern end without first having to run the gauntlet of the approach from the south.

The hazards of the air raids on Syracuse and Augusta continued, and several Coastal Force boats were damaged and sunk.

In the land war, the Eighth Army had been held up. Unable to force a way through along the coast past Catania and the seaward side of the great mass of Mount Etna, despite a landing by commandos and an attack on the Catania bridges by airborne troops, Montgomery was forced to regroup. It took until the end of July to bring his army round west of the Etna massif, and the first two weeks of August before progress northward towards Messina speeded up.

While all this was going on, and with little change to the MTB operations on the east coast, two events which were to have lasting effects on Coastal Forces were taking place. First, Capt John Felgate Stevens RN took up his post as Captain Coastal Forces Mediterranean, and immediately showed his style of command by visiting the boats in Augusta. He was very rapidly destined to earn the respect and affection of those with whom he came in contact over the next two years.

And in the political background to the war – something which did not usually bother the officers and men of Coastal Forces at all – the news broke that Mussolini had fallen from power, and it was generally expected that the new Italian government would not have the stomach to continue to fight alongside their German allies. The question being asked was whether this was going to speed up the end of the Sicilian campaign, and if so would the evacuation of German troops from the Messina area into Italy bring fresh challenges to the Navy, and in particular to Coastal Forces.

It was known later that this had been anticipated by the German High Command, and plans had been drawn up for this evacuation. The execution of these plans was delayed by the acceleration of the advance of both the American and Commonwealth offensives by early August. In the end, the Germans carried out a highly efficient withdrawal across the narrowest section of the Strait well north of Messina by day and night over a period of six days. In fact, most of the passages were by day and were not severely disrupted by Allied air attack; by night, when heavy bombing raids were also mounted which kept the MTBs out of this most northerly area, the traffic reduced.[9]

It was not until the night of 9 August that there is any further report of MTB incidents, and that was another blow to the 10th Flotilla when during a patrol 265 was hit in the bow by a heavy shell which blew out all the section forward of the bridge, and left the bridge itself wrecked. Sadly, the CO, Lt G.D. Oxley RNVR, was severely wounded and died of his wounds. The boat was towed stern first to Augusta, where the shipwrights did a complex repair job using plywood and concrete, to enable her to return to Alexandria, via Malta, for more permanent repairs.[10]

The 20th Flotilla were able, at last, to fire their torpedoes in anger when on 11/12 August they sighted three merchant vessels about to enter Messina. 289 (Barnsdale), 295 (Frenzel) and 290 (Austin) fired all their six torpedoes in a 'zone attack' at long range, which was all they had time for, and although there was a considerable explosion, there was no basis on which any claim could be made.[11]

Yet another sinking by a shore battery occurred off Messina on 15/16 August. This

9   Roskill, *History of the Second War, The War at Sea*, Vol. 3.
10 MO11089; ROP at PRO in ADM 199/541.
11 MO10726; ROP at PRO in ADM 199/541.

MTB 265 of the 10th Flotilla, hit by shore battery in the Strait of Messina. (Courtesy, L.C. Reynolds)

time it was a Dog Boat, MTB 665, which was hit. She was commanded by Lt Peter Thompson DSC RCNVR, and it was not possible for his patrol companions to get close enough to take off her crew. Each time they tried, they were forced to retire under heavy and accurate fire. MTB 76 of the 7th Flotilla (commanded by Lt Keefer, himself a Canadian) was in the vicinity, and offered the help of his smaller Vosper with its lower silhouette. The SO of the Dog Boat patrol accepted his offer and transferred to 76 to help in any way. She headed north, hugging the coast, and made her way towards the burning hull of 665. As she got close to 665, she came under intensive fire, and 76 was forced to withdraw after a courageous attempt to rescue the crew of 665. Other reports

indicate that several attempts to approach 665 were also made by other 'short' boats that night: both 315 (Newall) of the 10th and 85 (Hyslop) of the 24th tried but were forced away. Some of 665's crew, including the CO and the navigator, were eventually picked up by a German patrol boat and taken prisoner.[12]

On the following night, 16/17 August, came the last action of the Sicilian campaign. It involved three boats of the 24th Flotilla led by Lt L.V. Strong in 81, with 242 (Holloway) and 243 (du Boulay). It was a very dark night, and the unit proceeded to within half a mile of Messina, where they stopped and cut engines. Soon after, Strong heard heavy

12 MO12026; Reynolds, *Dog Boats at War*.

engine noise and thought it might be the Reggio–Messina ferry. However, when the 'vessel' appeared, it was in fact two German R-boats. Strong had orders not to waste torpedoes on small targets, so ordered a gun attack, opening fire from 81 as he gave the order. The R-boats replied with far heavier fire-power, and 81 received their concentrated broadside. 243 had stopped with one engine out of action, and 242 had been blocked and lost sight of 81 briefly. As Strong, realizing he was on his own, turned away for support, a fire started on his bridge and demanded immediate attention. Simultaneously the starboard engine was hit and put out of action. The engine room hatch had been blown off and clearly 81 was in a bad way. Action was broken off, and on return to Augusta all three boats were found to have

taken hits and been damaged, with a number of casualties.[13]

On 18 August, General Patton entered Messina from the west two hours before General Montgomery arrived from the south, and the campaign was over. From a naval point of view, the huge assault armada had been delivered on time, the landings had been swiftly achieved, and the only losses had been three MTBs, one MGB, and three submarines. But these, and other battles, had taken their toll: ninety-six officers and men of Coastal Forces had been killed or wounded or were posted as missing.

Now was the time for C-in-C and CCF to evaluate the effectiveness of the Coastal Force

13 MO11089; ROP at PRO in ADM 199/541.

MTB 85 of the 24th Flotilla (CO P. Hyslop) in the Strait of Messina. (Courtesy, N. Hughes)

contribution to the campaign, in blocking the narrow Strait of Messina. Because of the formidable network of searchlights and coastal batteries on both sides of the Strait, it would have been impossible for larger naval units to have undertaken the night patrols without the probability of heavy losses. In the circumstances, the MTBs sailed up and down the channel night after night, and carried out their orders relentlessly. Although some boats were lost, and in the event the enemy did not attempt to breach the blockade in any strength, they performed their task well and played their full part in the success of the Sicilian campaign.

There came a lull of some two weeks before the victory was followed up by a landing in Calabria – the first thrust into mainland Europe. For Coastal Forces, whose boats had notched up thousands of engine hours, there was a good deal of maintenance and repair work to be done, but before the end of September some boats were once again to be heavily involved in operations.

Some were used to land small parties of clandestine troops behind the enemy lines in order to identify dispositions and strength of units. A group of 20th Flotilla boats was moved to Palermo where they joined the 10th and the US PT boats, ready to operate off the Italian coast.

Action began again on 2 September, when the battleships *Valiant* and *Warspite* bombarded targets south of Reggio, and at 0430 on the 3rd, artillery gave support to the ferrying of the invasion army to landings on three beaches to the north of Reggio. Opposition was not very strong, as the Germans were clearly retreating from the toe of Italy to establish new defensive positions further north. Operation Baytown was over quickly, and attention was then given to an attempt to cut off the retreating German Army at Vibo Valentia, about 40 miles to the north.

This landing was code-named Operation Ferdy and was timed for 0430 on 8 September. Forty-four landing craft were used to take the 231st Brigade ashore, covered only by one monitor *Erebus* and an assortment of river gun boats, LCGs and LCFs (Landing Craft 'Gun' and 'Flak') and by some Coastal Force craft.

There was more opposition than expected, and German air activity was heavy. MTB 77 (Sturgeon) of the 7th Flotilla had been chosen to carry the Flag Officer Sicily, Rear Adm R.R. McGrigor, to conduct the sea operation. Shortly after 0800, a bomb landed 2 ft from 77's starboard quarter and threw her into the air, ripping off her bottom. She sank, but everyone on board was taken off by ML 1128. The indomitable Admiral, who had been blown off the bridge and landed on the deck aft having injured his leg, hauled down his flag and hoisted it immediately in the HDML.[14]

The loss of MTB 77 was a sad blow for the 7th Flotilla. Under her CO, Lt J.B. Sturgeon DSC, she had been on thirty-three operations, had fought a number of successful actions and, although damaged on seven occasions, had never had to abandon an operation because of defects. Brian Sturgeon later became SO of the 24th Flotilla, but was killed in action in the Dalmatian islands in April 1944.

MTB 84, also of the 7th and now commanded by Sub Lt N.L. Ilett, was detailed to remain in Messina as a despatch boat for the NOIC. Mostly she was given dull jobs, but on the day of the landing at Vibo Valentia, 84 was sent urgently to take a medical officer to the hard-pressed landing force there which was suffering many casualties. She ran the gauntlet of heavy fire from shore and delivered the doctor safely. Ilett's command

14 MO11406; ROP at PRO in ADM 119/541; Pope, *Flag 4*.

MTBs of the 24th Flotilla escort the surrendering Italian fleet off Malta, September 1943. (Courtesy, G.M. Hudson)

did not last long, as soon after this 84 was sent to Malta but arrived there in a sinking condition through a leaking stern gland. She was temporarily paid off and Ilett was given command of 57.

The Italian government had surrendered formally to the Allies on 8 September, and honoured its undertaking to hand over Italy's major ships. One group was sailed to Malta where six MTBs of the 20th and 24th Flotillas escorted them to an anchorage off St Paul's Bay on 11 September. Admiral Sir Andrew Cunningham signalled to the Admiralty: 'Be pleased to inform their Lordships that the Italian battle fleet now lies at anchor under the guns of the fortress of Malta.'[15]

15 Roskill, *History of the Second War, The War at Sea*, Vol. 3.

Among the boats which had escorted the Italian fleet to St Paul's Bay was MTB 86 (Young), with both Lt Cdr R.A.M. Hennessy RN, the CO of HMS *Gregale*, and Lt C.W.S. Dreyer DSC RN who had been SO of the 24th Flotilla, on board. Christopher Dreyer had been very ill for some weeks, and he was shortly to be invalided home to Britain. In December, the award of the DSO was promulgated for his leadership during Operation Husky. He handed over the 24th to Lt David Scott RN, who had been a CO in the 7th Flotilla. Dreyer's great experience in the Channel and during the Sicilian campaign was later to be put to good use in the planning of the Coastal Forces' contribution to the Normandy invasion.

The Eighth Army, allocated the eastern side of the Apennines for the advance northward through Italy, broke out very quickly after the initial landings at Reggio and reached and took Taranto on 10 September, and Brindisi on the 11th. They now had two large ports at their disposal.

The last significant assignments for the MTBs in this period were all connected to the major landing at Salerno – Operation Avalanche. By this time, the 10th and 20th were based at Palermo, and were used in support of the landings in various ways. The main objective of the assault was to secure the port of Naples, and its planning had, of necessity, been hasty because the date and the priority for the operation were not decided until late in August. The surrender of the Italian government as the invasion fleets were heading for the beaches led to some minor confusion.

But it all began as planned. After initial bombardments, the assault forces went in early in the morning of 9 September. The land forces then met dogged resistance, and those at sea were subject to air and artillery attack of a severity not entirely expected. A new weapon – the radio-controlled bomb – for which there was no immediate antidote, sank and damaged several ships. In the end, Naples fell; but the operation had taken far longer than expected.

A much less hazardous set of operations, largely carried out by the Dog Boats but joined by some boats of the 20th Flotilla, was the surrender of the off-shore islands in the Bay of Naples – Capri, Ischia, Procida and Ventotene.

It was after the surrender of Ventotene on 8/9 September that two boats of 20th Flotilla, 298 (Lt The Hon F. Shore) with 289 (Barnsdale), were sent to attempt a landing of agents on the mainland in the Gulf of Gaeta. During the passage they encountered an enemy convoy consisting of several F-lighters, Siebel ferries and R-boats moving along the coast. Shore immediately attacked the largest F-lighter, and both his torpedoes hit and

destroyed the target, which blew up with the ammunition it was carrying. It was the first torpedo sinking by a boat from the 20th Flotilla, and a very rare success for a torpedo attack on F-lighters by any of the flotillas at this time.[16]

Shortly after this, Shore was given another task, being sent to the island of Ponza where Intelligence reported that Mussolini was being held, and if possible to bring him off and hand him over to the Allies. Unfortunately he had already been moved to Sardinia.

Meanwhile, the boats of the 10th at Palermo had been assigned to air-sea rescue duties off the Salerno beachhead. One particular reason for this was the large number of Seafire fighters, carried by the RN escort carriers, which were having to 'ditch'. This problem was caused by the slow speed of the escort carriers (17–18 knots), the flimsiness of the Seafire's undercarriage, and the light winds which prevailed throughout the operation. Additionally, many of their pilots had received insufficient training to cope with such conditions.

The boats were kept very busy indeed, and had a punishing schedule. A unit of three would leave Palermo at midnight and arrive off the landing area at first light. There they joined Force V (the invasion fleet) for their duties, until dusk when aerial activity generally ceased and they set off back to Palermo, arriving at midnight just as the next unit of three was leaving. These operations lasted until the land airfields became available. In this period, the 10th saved twenty-two airmen from the sea, including some Germans and Italians.

A new phase of operations was about to begin for the four flotillas, and it coincided with the loss of Lt Denis Jermain DSC and Bar RN, the longest-serving SO of the Med-

16 Summary of actions at NHB; Pope, *Flag 4*.

iterranean flotillas. He was appointed to command an escort destroyer in the Atlantic, and went on to reach the rank of Captain before he retired. His successor in command of the 10th Flotilla was his divisional leader, Peter Evensen, who was promoted to Lieutenant Commander.

Now that the concentrated requirements of the Sicilian campaign were over, Captain Coastal Forces had to allocate his flotillas to cover the requirements of the whole of his command.

He decided to send the 7th Flotilla to operate off the west coast of Italy, and the 10th Flotilla to cover the Aegean. The 20th and 24th were to prepare themselves for work in the Adriatic, where the east coast of Italy was now the right flank of the Eighth Army's advance up the Italian peninsula, and political developments were indicating that the Dalmatian coast would become increasingly significant.

These dispositions set the scene for a great deal of the story of the Mediterranean MTBs still to unfold, as the flotillas once again began to operate independently. But now they had a background of experience which was to stand them in good stead.

CHAPTER 6

THE 7TH, 10TH, 20TH AND 24TH MTB FLOTILLAS

SEPTEMBER TO DECEMBER 1943

The heavy toll on all the flotillas by the end of the Sicilian campaign in lost and damaged boats had first to be assessed. Equally important was attention to the maintenance state of those that had come through unscathed, and consideration for their crews after an unusually high density of operational calls.

The base and the dockyard at Malta were both very busily engaged in an intensive period of docking, slipping, engine changes and attention to lists of minor repairs, as were the bases at Bizerta, Bone and Augusta. Each flotilla gathered itself for the next phase and then set off to their new field of operations. For clarity, the operations in each region are described consecutively.

THE 7TH MTB FLOTILLA

During September, the huge island of Sardinia, politically ready to capitulate since the change of government in Italy and the handover of many naval ships, had meekly surrendered. The two Dog Boats of the 20th MGB Flotilla sent with Brig Gen Theodore Roosevelt and an Italian colonel to 'absorb' Sardinia, arrived at Cagliari on 18 September and without ceremony the deed was done. The 'family' nature of Coastal Forces was emphasized by this operation. In command of MGB 662 was Lt T.J. Bligh, late

of the 7th Flotilla, last mentioned when he destroyed MTB 61, aground in Kelibia harbour in May; the CO of MGB 660 was Lt A.H. Moore, who was shortly to leave his Dog Boat and join the 7th Flotilla, and eventually to become its Senior Officer.[1]

The fall of Sardinia left available the major Italian naval port of La Maddalena, situated in the Strait of Bonifacio between Sardinia and Corsica. Maddalena was one of a group of islands in this windswept channel, and was as unwelcoming in many respects as Scapa Flow in the Orkney Islands. But it provided a good sheltered harbour with ready-made facilities, about 90 miles from a suitable central patrol area on the Italian west coast.

It was immediately decided that this would be the next location for the Coastal Forces Advanced Base, because Augusta, and to a large extent Messina, had already been left behind in the tide of war. Bobby Allan – as everyone in the Mediterranean called him – had been promoted to Commander, and he lost no time in laying his plans for the transfer of the base. He went for a reconnaissance of the facilities at Maddalena, satisfied himself that it had the necessary basic requirements (in fact, there were far

1 Description by the late Sir Timothy Bligh in Pope, *Flag 4.*

more facilities already in place than he had had at Bone), and returned to Messina to despatch the convoy which had been prepared. All the base's lorries and equipment had been loaded aboard three LCTs, and the convoy was completed by the tanker *Empire Damsel* and an escort of six Dog Boats and two minesweeping MLs.

Although the convoy was delayed by bad weather which caused a halt at Milazzo, it went safely through the minefields swept by the MLs, reached Maddalena before the end of September and the base was rapidly established. Within a few days, more Dog Boats and eight boats of the 7th Flotilla had arrived and almost at once operations began.

Lt Blomfield, the SO, had left five boats of the flotilla still under repair at Malta, and the eight at his disposal – all now showing signs of increasing age and unreliability – did their best to maintain patrols. The main area to which the boats were despatched was that section of the Italian coast north and south of the island of Elba. They sighted an F-lighter escorted by a heavily armed trawler on their first patrol on 10/11 October, close to Elba. As 76 (Cochran) and 79 (Good) went into attack, they came under heavy fire. Three torpedoes were fired but missed and they were beaten off and could not get close for another attack.[2]

There followed weeks of constant patrolling with no enemy sightings, and frustration grew, especially since the PTs of Ron 15, which had moved up at much the same time from Bizerta, did find targets with their superior SO radar.

On one of the rare occasions when they met the enemy, the exchange of fire was inconclusive, and 79 (Good) received damage to the hull from shells which penetrated the petrol tanks. She was sent back to Malta for repairs.

There followed two more blows to flotilla morale. First 73 was alongside in Maddalena on 24 November during a rare air raid, and was sunk with two of the crew killed. Sub Lt Aitchison, now the 'spare CO' in the flotilla, was in temporary command.

Shortly after, Sub Lt Ilett arrived from Malta in 57, which had had a structural defect ever since she entered the Mediterranean eighteen months earlier. The first task allotted to her was to take the Senior Officer Inshore Squadron (SOIS), Capt Dickinson, to Ajaccio on the west coast of Corsica. They met heavy weather – not unusual in the Strait of Bonifacio – and SOIS saw for himself that 57 bent alarmingly in the middle, took water constantly on the bridge, and was just as wet below where water leaked freely through the deckhead. They had to return to Maddalena, and Capt Dickinson ordered that 57 should be paid off as a liability to the crew. (It is said that he gave instructions that she should be scuttled, but records suggest that this fate was delayed.) Ilett was given command of MTB 78.

The frustration continued, with the PT boats detecting targets, but being let down by their old (US) Mark VIII torpedoes which often denied them the success they deserved.

As November merged into December, a major decision was made, which came as no surprise to the men of the 7th and which delighted most of them, despite their affection for their old boats. The flotilla was to be re-equipped with a new set of boats, all built in the USA and due to arrive shortly at Algiers as deck cargo.

The plan was that as the old boats were paid off, the crews were to be transported to Algiers, where they would take over the new boats and sail them to Malta for a working-up period.

The change was to lead to a new and highly successful phase of operations, but as it had to be preceded by a lengthy period of prepara-

2   Summary of recorded actions at NHB.

tion, this is best described after returning first to the boats of the 10th Flotilla, bound in September 1943 for a completely different experience in the Aegean.

THE 10TH MTB FLOTILLA

During the period after the fall of Sicily, the 10th had gathered at Palermo, joining the division led by Lt Evensen which had been there for several weeks. Working with the PT boats of Ron 15, they had carried out mainly air-sea rescue duties off the beaches of the Salerno landings in early September, and then moved to Messina.

With the newly promoted Lt Cdr Peter Evensen DSC now in command, the orders arrived directing the 10th to proceed to Malta and then immediately on to Alexandria as they were urgently needed in the Aegean. Many of the officers and men of the flotilla knew the area very well and welcomed their return to the Eastern Mediterranean. They left Messina where they had had a very short period to regroup, effect repairs and maintenance and snatch some relaxation, on 21 September.

The 10th Flotilla, with its long history of operations at Crete, off the desert coast, at Tobruk and more recently in Operations Retribution and Husky, had once again lost several boats in action. The group which Evensen took to Alexandria was only six strong out of the twenty which had originally made up the 15th and 10th before their amalgamation.

The survivors were 260 (Sub Lt M. Beaumont), 266 (Lt J.N. Broad RNZNVR), 307 (Lt J. Muir), 309 (Lt R. Campbell RCNVR), 313 (Lt T. Fuller DSC RCNVR), and 315 (Lt L.E. Newall RNZNVR). 265 was still under repair and could not join until later in the year.

Responding to the urgency of the orders, the boats arrived in Alexandria five days after

leaving Messina, having covered over 1,000 miles and staged at Malta, Benghazi and Tobruk, at each of which they had refuelled.

At Alexandria they were fully briefed on the new and ever-changing pattern of war which now faced them in the Aegean.

The story of the High Command's indecision over the need to commit forces to influence the military situation in the area was complex, and had been made even more so by Italy's surrender early in September. There was a realization that the Aegean was strategically very important for the future situation in the Balkans, and that Rhodes specifically was the key to the Aegean. But there was an unwillingness to mount a major campaign which would make demands on the resources of all three services at this time.

The Germans had clearly decided that *they* considered this a vital area, and had reinforced both naval and air strength even at the expense of weakening other fronts. On 26 September, they demonstrated this by a major air raid on Leros harbour in which the British destroyer *Intrepid* and the Greek *Queen Olga* were sunk.

With total control of the air (the Allies only had six fighters at Kos and most of the region was out of the range of aircraft from Cyprus or Egypt), the Germans were determined to take the islands one by one, and it was into this situation that the 10th was now plunged. A high-level decision was made to try to hold Leros and Samos for as long as possible. How this was to be achieved against total German domination in the air was a worrying aspect for the men of the 10th Flotilla. Kos fell on 3 October to make the position even worse, followed by Kalimnos and Symi by the 11th, and Naxos and Lavitha on the 12th.[3]

The British MLs had been active, and had used the most easterly of the Dodecanese

---

3   Churchill, *The Second World War*, Vol. 5, Chap. 12.

islands, Casteloriso, as a base. It was a tiny island lying very close to the coast of southern Turkey. The 10th Flotilla arrived there early in October having used an overnight stop in the Lebanon to gain experience in the use of camouflage netting: a very necessary addition to their expertise at this time.

An early success of a minor nature took place on 7/8 October when 313 (Fuller) and 309 (Campbell) – both Canadians – were patrolling between Rhodes and Symi. They came across a seaplane moored in the roadstead off Symi harbour, and destroyed it rapidly with gunfire and shot up a caique. There was some firing from the shore, but it was ineffective.[4]

It soon became obvious that the local Greek population (mostly old people) on the island of Casteloriso were very unhappy about the arrival of the 10th Flotilla. The Germans were strengthening their garrisons on the islands they had taken, and the Greeks feared they would suffer when it became known that it was being used as an advanced base for the MTBs. It was not long before their fears proved to be justified.

On 17 October Stuka dive-bombers mounted an attack on Casteloriso harbour and heavily damaged the area used by the flotilla. Unfortunately, 313 (Fuller) was alongside at a point where a building on the jetty received a direct hit, and the collapsing masonry seriously damaged 313's hull. So much masonry fell on her that the only tow point available to 309 (Campbell) when she attempted to drag her away was high on the after Oerlikon. Nevertheless, the tow out of the harbour was accomplished and temporary repairs by her own crew sufficed to enable her to reach Alexandria under her own power. She was paid off on 27 October and

spent over three months in a local shipyard under repair. Tom Fuller left the flotilla and, returning to the Dog Boats in which he had originally entered the Mediterranean, was promoted to Lieutenant Commander and made SO of the 61st MTB/MGB Flotilla, where he added to his aggressive reputation and incidentally added a second Bar to his DSC.[5]

Facilities in the harbour were so badly damaged that it was necessary to find another operating base, and one was found, surprisingly, in a sheltered area at Vathris, near Bruden, in neutral Turkey. Only a few base staff were left at Casteloriso as an emergency repair and maintenance base. But operating from Turkish waters brought its own problems, as some Turkish authorities were hostile from the start. At first the officers and men were not permitted to set foot on Turkish soil, or even to obtain water from shore sources. A ring of artillery was set up opposite the MTBs' anchorage to make sure that no attempt to do so was successful. By day the boats lay under camouflage nets, with the crews sweltering in the heat. By night, they folded up the nets and crept out, in company, to carry out patrols looking for enemy targets among the islands.

Now and again the patrols over-reached themselves by operating too deeply into enemy territory, only to pay the penalty of being attacked by fighter aircraft. In daylight, ME 109 and Macchi fighters from Rhodes were the main threat, and the flotilla strategy was to fight them off in open water rather than to give away the location of their hiding place.

The problem of supplies was solved by the regular arrival of the caique *Ragea* from Cyprus, whose visits kept the flotilla going for long periods. She was 60 ft long, and if she

---

4   MO54956; Summary of actions at NHB.

5   Eye witness account by Ross Campbell.

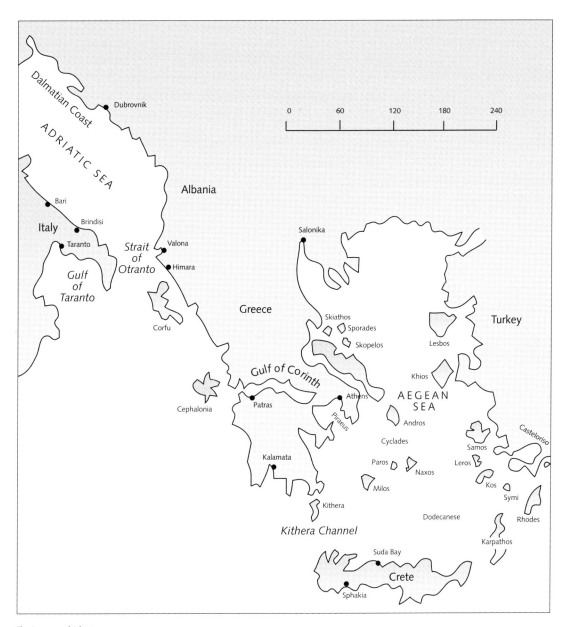

The Aegean and Adriatic.

had been sunk by enemy aircraft it would have been a crippling loss. The crews soon became adept at supplementing the food supplies with fish. The favourite method was to attract fish around a line baited with corned beef, and then throw in a hand grenade to stun the shoal and scoop them on board.

The first major success for the 10th Flotilla from its covert base came on 19/20 October. Peter Evensen in 315 (Newall) with 309 (Campbell) and 307 (Muir) set out for a patrol off the north coast of Kos. Taking advantage of moon conditions, he led the unit at 12 knots to a position one mile offshore by

85

0045. They then quietly moved eastward to the west coast of Kalimno which was the extreme limit of their patrol. On the return run at 0235, a sharp lookout reported a vessel close to the shore, and 'Ns' were flashed down the line (signifying 'enemy in sight'). As they closed, the target was revealed to be an F-lighter with its bow down, apparently ashore; and then suddenly another vessel was seen about half a mile to the east.

Evensen began to deploy his boats, sending 309 to attack the F-lighter, and ordering Muir in 307 to stand by. Aboard 315 he told the CO (Newall) to head for the second target, now identified as a coaster of about 500–600 tons. As soon as his sights were on, he fired two torpedoes: the first missed ahead and was seen to explode on the beach, but the second ran true, passed under the coaster, and hit a previously hidden F-lighter unloading on her far side. The vessel disintegrated with a massive explosion and caught fire.

Immediately, Evensen sent Muir in to make a second attack on the coaster, and his starboard torpedo struck home on her bow.

Meanwhile, Ross Campbell had got 309 into position and fired both his torpedoes at the originally sighted F-lighter. Once more there was the frustration of seeing a torpedo run true but pass beneath the shallow lighter. This time there was no explosion.[6]

This early success for the 10th came at a time when the German offensive in the Aegean was being intensified by the introduction of more and more aircraft, troops and naval units, and the major British ships in the area began to suffer losses from air attack and from an extensive mining programme. Leros was under heavy pressure and the British garrison was running short of supplies.

Despite these generally adverse factors, the boats at Casteloriso continued to operate, and were required on 12 November to join a

relief run to Leros which got some supplies ashore. Next day, the Germans invaded Leros, and although the garrison repelled this first attempt, some units ashore were trapped. All available ships and boats were sent to help in the defence, and 309 and 307 were among the vessels attempting to take off some of these troops. They did succeed to a limited extent, and miraculously suffered no damage or casualties when subjected to fierce small-arms fire at very close range.

On 14/15 November, Newall in 315 led a unit of three boats from Casteloriso to patrol off Leros once again. 266 (Broad) and 307 (Muir) joined him, but 307 developed a bad leak and had to return to base, leaving the other two to continue towards Leros.

They had been on patrol for many hours when at 0513, Newall sighted two craft he thought were R-boats. They were about 300 yds away, and were laying a smoke screen. He quickly made an enemy report on W/T while closing, and suddenly searchlights from the shore revealed the whole scene: behind the smoke screen, an assault by about a dozen German landing craft, each packed with troops, was in progress. The nearest, by this time only 100 yds away, was very similar to a British LCI (Landing Craft, Infantry).

315 and 266 moved in to 50 yds range and then began an attack on this target with every gun that could be brought to bear. Fire spurted from her, she came to a standstill and became a blazing wreck. The R-boats opened fire from long range – fortunately not very effectively. Newall had sighted a large powered barge and was just preparing to attack it when in the glare of the searchlights appeared a destroyer. His first thought was that this was an enemy warship and an excellent target, and he shifted aim to make a torpedo attack on the destroyer, instructing 266 to attack the barge.

Broad chose to make that attack with his two depth charges, and timed their release so

6   MO13230; Summary of actions at NHB.

accurately that they exploded under the barge, sinking it and throwing its numerous troops into the sea.

Newall fortunately decided to challenge the destroyer before attacking, and discovered that it was HMS *Echo*, which had landed British troops on besieged Leros and was just leaving the island. *Echo* joined the two MTBs in attacking the German landing craft and continued to wreak havoc among them until all three withdrew in time to avoid an air attack on the return to Casteloriso. It had been a fortuitous intervention in what could have been a decisive German assault.[7]

Two days later all this proved to have been in vain. The same three boats, 315, 266 and 307 set off on the evening of 15 November loaded with troops to attempt to relieve the pressure on the garrison of Leros. But it was too late: a withdrawal was in progress, and on the afternoon of the 16th the island fell to the Germans. The boats of the flotilla were kept busy for several nights making covert visits to remote beaches on the island, evacuating small parties of men who had evaded capture.

The German forces kept up their offensive in the Aegean and occupied more of the smaller islands. By the end of November, the British garrison at Samos was withdrawn, and also the main forces on Casteloriso. But it was recognized that it must be retained as long as possible as an emergency forward operating port, and fifty Coastal Force base staff were left there to provide fuelling, maintenance and light repair facilities. There was one other possible benefit in their continued presence: their activities could make it seem that the island was still occupied by a garrison.

The 10th Flotilla had survived its first two months among the Aegean islands, in a period when total German domination in the

air had enabled the Germans to seize control of the region and to make daylight movement hazardous. For the next four months the tactics were, perforce, to be based on 'hit and run' operations, involving quick surprise raids by the MTBs, commando landings from MLs and caiques, raids by Allied aircraft and submarine patrols.

In order to avoid using Casteloriso except when absolutely necessary, the boats of the 10th continued to spend their days hiding among the tiny islands close to the Turkish coast using camouflage netting. This proved effective in preventing attack from the air: the netting had to be in place before dawn on return from night patrol to be sure of safe concealment.

The operational objective was to harass enemy shipping from these hideouts, and they followed their orders night after night with only very few opportunities presented by the presence of enemy vessels. Those occasions were the highlights of their cat-and-mouse existence.

On 13/14 December 266 (Broad) and 315 (Newall) found a tug with two caiques in Trianda Bay off Rhodes, and set all three on fire until they sank, in a gun attack. 260 and 309 maintained a nightly patrol off Rhodes from Christmas Day 1943 until 20 January 1944, and only saw the enemy on one night. On 12/13 January they intercepted and destroyed a caique off Piscopi Island, and after this period they were relieved by 307 and 315.

During December there had been a considerable change in the personnel of the boats, as many members of the crews had been out in the Mediterranean since April 1941: these were sent back to Britain. Most had shared the early difficult days of North Africa and Tobruk, and then the exacting patrols off Tunisia and off Sicily. There were changes, too, among the COs. Lt Ross Campbell RCNVR flew to Canada for leave,

7   MO14246; ROP at PRO in ADM 199/1040.

and then returned to serve with distinction in home waters, being awarded a DSC for his boat's part in the Normandy landings. Lt J.R. Muir, the CO of 307 since she commissioned, also left for leave in Britain, having recently been awarded the DSC for operations in the Aegean.

In the interests of chronology, this narrative now turns to the Adriatic, to which the 20th and 24th Flotillas had been despatched in September 1943.

THE 20TH AND 24TH MTB FLOTILLAS

These two flotillas, which CCF had allocated to operate in the Adriatic, moved first to Taranto. The two SOs, Lt H.A. Barbary RN and Lt D. Scott RN, did not have all their boats available immediately, but most were able to join over the next few weeks. The first group sailed from Malta on 18 September and consisted of four boats from each flotilla. Almost at once, patrols on the far side of the Adriatic began, with the objective of intercepting any enemy shipping passing through the 40-mile wide Strait of Otranto. Until Brindisi became available as a base, the patrols from Taranto to the Albanian coast were long and tiring: it was necessary to set off in the early afternoon to ensure the cover of darkness as they entered the Adriatic. They had first to round the 'heel' of Italy before sailing north-westward to the vicinity of Valona Bay, a total distance of about 140 miles.

It was very gratifying for the two flotillas that almost at once they were able to mount a daring and successful attack on shipping in the busy port of Valona. Barbary had managed to obtain from the Italian naval authorities a chart which gave detail of the boom and the defences across the neck of the Bay, which protected the extensive anchorage. A plan was devised which envisaged the torpedoing of the boom by one boat, to clear the way for the entry of the others into the anchorage.

Five boats were allocated to the attack which was to be led by Barbary: three from his 20th and two from the 24th, as a second division led by Scott. The unit left Taranto at 1500 on 21 September, but the serene progress towards the target area was interrupted an hour later. Scott, embarked in 89 (Sub Lt W.J. Archer), sighted dense red smoke on the horizon and altered course to investigate, leaving 85 (Sub Lt K.C. Banks in temporary command) to join the boats of the 20th Flotilla after arranging a rendezvous. He found two rafts from SS *Almenara* which had been torpedoed during the previous night. The rafts were crowded with about eighty men and within a short time Scott had fifty-two, cold, wet and shocked survivors aboard his 71-ft Vosper. There was no way in which he could have joined the Valona operation with them on board, but very fortunately he found a landing craft, LCI (L) 6, and transferred his passengers. Now he had to try to make the rendezvous by the set time.

To do so, he pushed Archer's 89 – a Vosper approaching middle-age – very hard in an effort to maintain maximum speed for seven hours, and it was a tribute to the engine room crew that it was safely accomplished. But he was a few minutes late, and Barbary, anxious not to lose his best opportunity to attack, had just reorganized his force and moved off when 89 appeared. There was a hasty shouted conversation, and the original plan was put back in place.

Scott with 89 and 85 set off to search the northern end of the bay, while Barbary in 295 (Frenzel) with 290 (Austin) and 287 (Lancaster) moved to investigate the southern end. Strangely, they could find no signs at all of the boom that had figured so prominently as a hazard when planning the operation.

It was Scott who first sighted a group of three merchant vessels at anchor; one ship was slightly separated from the other two, so he ordered 85 to fire both her torpedoes at

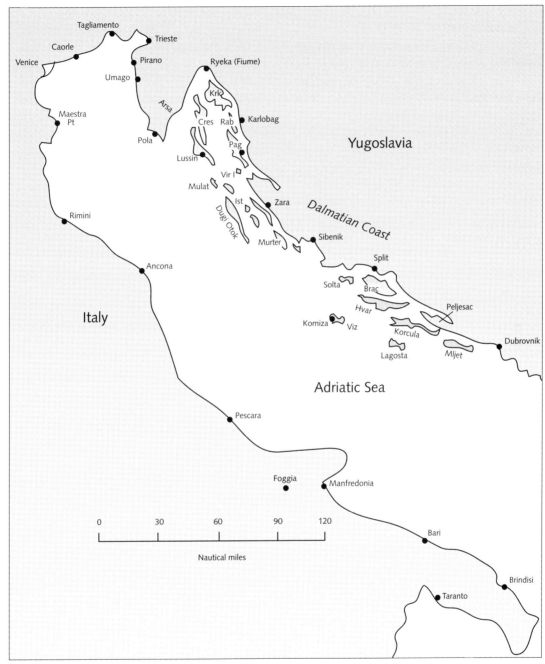

The Adriatic.

the single target, and 89 at the other two. One of the vessels – obviously carrying ammunition – blew up in a sheet of flame, another began to settle, and they could see that the third was holed for'd. Scott's two boats were so close that the explosion threw a sheet of water over them, drenching the crew of 89. They were then caught in the beam of a searchlight and came under heavy fire from the shore. Smoke floats were dropped over the stern to divert the enemy's aim as they withdrew at speed.

Meanwhile, Barbary to the south had found no targets, and he had moved northward. He too sighted the group of merchant ships and was about to fire torpedoes at the nearest when it blew up – the victim of Scott's attack. He saw the two boats of the 24th increase speed and disengage under fire, and moved in to renew his attack. As the smoke from the explosion cleared, it revealed a second target, apparently not damaged. 295 fired her torpedoes: one was thought to have hit, and the other ran off course. Later both were considered to have been fired at ranges less than the pistol safety range. But Barbary, seeing no conclusive evidence of a hit, decided to make a depth charge attack. He coolly took 295 along the side of the merchant vessel and dropped two charges abreast of the funnel. He disengaged across the bows of the ship and noticed a hole in the bow, confirming Scott's earlier observation.

Still not satisfied, he made another depth charge attack under the bow and again withdrew; although there was no immediate explosion one was felt and seen a little later. He made one more sweep southward, but the searchlights and shore batteries became active and he decided to withdraw. As he did so, 295, travelling at 25 knots towards the rendezvous point, suddenly checked and shook and had clearly hit a submerged obstruction. She vibrated violently, and Barbary stopped and sent a diver down to check the damage. He found that both the starboard and centre propellers were damaged. Inspection of the chart revealed that the incident had occurred in the position where the boom had previously been reported; but no boat had encountered it on entry to the bay, and only the last boat to leave had suffered.

295 was able to make 9 knots on her port engine, and reached the rendezvous at 0350.

She was taken in tow first by 85 and later by the destroyer HMS *Ilex*, and eventually arrived back at Taranto. None of the other boats had suffered damage or casualties.

In his final comments after considering the Report of Proceedings, the C-in-C wrote: 'This was a well-executed operation, carried through with dash and determination, and reflecting credit on the COs, officers and men of the flotillas involved.'

Their Lordships obviously agreed, as awards were announced much later: a DSO for Barbary, DSCs for Scott and the COs of 89 (Archer) and 295 (Frenzel), and DSMs for the key members of 89's crew – the Motor Mechanic, Sutcliffe, and the Leading Telegraphist, Langford. Several others were mentioned in despatches.[8]

Very shortly after this action, the opportunity was taken to reduce the distance for patrols by bringing into service Brindisi as a Coastal Forces Base. HMS *Vienna* arrived there on 28 September, enabling the boats of the 20th and 24th Flotillas to operate across to the far shore of the Adriatic more effectively. This move was totally in line with Mediterranean policy for Coastal Force operations, where the fluidity of land operations required constant movement of bases to provide support as close as possible to the front line.

In fact, in this case the Eighth Army's advance northward was so rapid that the port of Bari (60 miles north of Brindisi) had fallen by 23 September, and very significantly the major airfield complex at Foggia, inland from the small port of Manfredonia, was occupied by 1 October. This immediately pushed the operating area for the MTBs on the east coast of Italy much further north. For that reason, HMS *Vienna* was sailed to Bari and an Advanced Coastal Force Base set up there. The 20th and 24th moved up with her, and

8   MO12696; ROP at PRO in ADM 199/537; *Seedie's List of Coastal Forces Awards*, Ripley Press.

established their latest home (of many) in the older part of the harbour named Porto Vecchio. At the same time, CCF installed there a senior officer well known to virtually all Coastal Force officers: Cdr, A.E. Welman DSO DSC RN, previously the CO of HMS *St Christopher*, the training base at Fort William for all Coastal Forces personnel. He was now to be Commander Coastal Forces, Western Mediterranean (CFW), and was supremely well qualified to be responsible for operations in the Adriatic, having gained his decorations in the CMBs of the First World War.

Patrols northward first from Brindisi and then from Bari proved fruitless as the Germans were clearly not moving supplies by sea within range of the operations of the MTBs. This was largely the result of geography: the east side of Italy north of Bari for 180 miles to Ancona was in the main an inhospitable coast, with very few harbours of any size and with no protection for anchorages. One exception was the port of Manfredonia, to the south of the large promontory of the high land of Gorgano which forms such a feature on the map of Italy – the 'hock' above the heel. Manfredonia became important for the supply of fuel by pipeline to the huge Allied Air Force Base at Foggia, and was later brought into use as yet another Advanced Coastal Force Base.

It was obvious that, until the armies moved much further north, the next important area of operations would be on the Dalmatian coast, but for months it had been uncertain how such operations could be linked to military activity in Yugoslavia.

Churchill had been discussing as early as May ways of supporting the insurgents in Yugoslavia and Albania in their battle to combat the German troops which had occupied their lands. The difficulty had been to decide which of several very different groups to assist, and in the end it became a pragmatic decision based entirely on a calculation of the group most active in inflicting damage and casualties on the several German divisions. Churchill reasoned that the more effort the enemy had to put into the Balkan war, the fewer resources he would have to use against the Allies – and especially the Russians – on other fronts.

It was on this basis that he heeded the advice of his envoy Brig Fitzroy Maclean, a diplomat and MP on active service, that supplies and assistance should be given to the Communist Partisans headed by Tito. Once the political decision was made, the naval and military consequences followed quickly.[9]

Cdr Welman took an active part in this: he sent an advance party of officers to make contact with the Partisans, with the aim of setting up supply routes and of finding a suitable base for Coastal Forces. At this time the Germans had not occupied any of the southern islands off the Dalmatian coast. In mid-October, an RNVR Lieutenant Commander named Merlin Minshall had made contact with the Partisans, and had become the British Naval Liaison Officer, based in Hvar. At the same time, Lt Cdr Morgan-Giles RN – already well known in Coastal Forces having earlier been SOO at HMS *Gregale* – was busily setting up sources of supply of surplus material (officially Battlefield Clearance Stores) from Sicily and helping the Partisans to transport them across the Adriatic. The MLs were very active in these gun-running operations.

Cdr Welman himself set the example of active cooperation by taking three boats of the 24th Flotilla – 242 (Tonkin), 81 (Strong) and 97 (Bowyer), led by the SO David Scott – across to the island of Vis on 16 October. His aim was to arrange for the establishment of a base, and after inspecting the tiny harbour of Komiza at the western end of the island,

9   Maclean, *Eastern Approaches*; McConville, *A Small War in the Balkans*; Churchill, *The Second World War*, Vol. 5.

agreement was reached. Komiza was to become the setting-off place for all MTB operations for the next year. The island of Vis was the most distant of all the offshore islands from the Dalmatian coast (40 miles from the port of Split) and it alone of the major islands was never occupied by the German forces. It later became the base not only for the MTBs, but also for 9,000 Partisan troops, units of British Royal Marine Commandos, and an RAF fighter wing.

Even before Komiza was ready to receive boats, units of the 24th Flotilla began to operate among the islands. They would leave Bari (or a little later, Manfredonia) and take up patrol positions off the mainland north of Split. At dawn they would return to Vis Town harbour, collect 40-gallon drums of petrol, sail with them to a rocky islet named Ravenik

nearby, and hide in a huge cavern (the Green Grotto). Inside the grotto they were completely safe from observation from the air, and could fuel from the drums using hand-pumps. It was even possible to maintain wireless watch by means of an extended aerial through a hole in the roof of the cavern.

They met no enemy ships in the weeks before Komiza became an operational base, but established good relationships with the Partisans while gaining experience of these new waters. One thing they quickly discovered was the danger presented by the vicious north-westerly gales known as the 'Bora' which funnelled down the Adriatic with no warning: in mid-winter they could persist continuously for several days.

Gradually a pattern developed for the operations from Komiza. The MLs brought

Komiza, the Coastal Force Base on the Island of Vis. (Courtesy, G.M. Hudson)

The Bari Air Raid, December 1943. (Courtesy, G.M. Hudson)

in their supplies, the Partisan 'Tiger Boats' left for their raids on occupied territory, and the MTBs went further afield, often transporting small groups of commandos when they arrived. At first, there was only room for five or six MTBs at a time, and two of them were normally the much larger and more heavily armed Dog Boats. Occasionally there would be joint patrols, but most often the Vospers of the 20th and 24th Flotillas found themselves working together.

Patrols were out on almost every night when weather permitted. At first, little enemy contact was made, but it soon became clear that the enemy was well aware of their presence both at Vis and on patrol. This became even more obvious when German troops were despatched to take the major islands of Korcula, Brac, Hvar, Mljet and Solta in the belief that the Allies were about

to occupy them. This move had a twofold effect: it stretched the German forces on the mainland, and provided targets for the MTBs to attack. Their garrisons in the islands had to be supplied with food and ammunition and had to be reinforced or relieved regularly. This could only be achieved by the sea route at night, and the MTBs were constantly on watch to interfere with the process.

Just as the new pattern had begun to settle down, it was disturbed by two events in rapid succession. First, on 28 November, HMS *Hebe*, a Fleet minesweeper, was mined just outside Bari harbour. Several boats from the 20th and 24th raced to the scene of the explosion and rescued a number of survivors.

And then, on 2 December, came a sudden unexpected German air raid on Bari – the first the port had experienced – and it found the port's defences totally unprepared for air attack. The harbour was crammed with shipping: by ill fortune, there were two complete convoys massed at the quays. One was unloading and the ships of the one which had just arrived were anchored stern on, packed side by side, at the east wall. It was realized later that a reconnaissance plane which had flown over at high altitude earlier in the day must have taken film back to base showing how devastating a raid would be. There were ships of every description, carrying all the food and materiel (including fuel and ammunition) necessary to keep the Eighth Army, the RAF and Naval forces supplied. One of the freighters was specifically filled with Coastal Forces' requirements – spares for the 20th Flotilla, and sixteen Packard engines, a long-awaited cargo.

About six of the boats of the two flotillas were over at Komiza, and two were out of action under repair. That left 81, 242 and

Lt J. Woods RCNVR, CO MTB 297. (Courtesy, E. Young)

243 of the 24th, and 297, 289, 290 and 296 of the 20th in harbour. HMS *Vienna* had just welcomed CCF, with his staff. They had come to assess the needs of the boats and the organization before visiting Komiza to see conditions for themselves. Cdr Welman and Lt Cdr Morgan-Giles were there, too, reporting to CCF. They could not have chosen a more disastrous day.

Just before dusk a large group of bombers came in low over the sea, beneath the radar screen, catching the AA defences by surprise. A decode of the German signal reporting the raid secured by the ultra system gave the figure of eighty-eight involved. Bombs rained down and could hardly fail to hit their targets. A total of seventeen merchant ships were sunk, and many others, together with HMS *Vienna* and several of the MTBs, had damage of varying degrees from bomb blast and debris. The raid was all over in a few minutes. The aircraft had gone, and left behind an inferno of fire, smoke, acrid fumes, and the cries of wounded sailors, soldiers and civilians. There were more than 1,000 casualties including Italian civilians, and later reports put this on a scale for an air attack on shipping, second only to that at Pearl Harbor.

Every one of the MTBs in harbour distinguished itself. Many had depleted crews as some men were ashore: there was a film show for service personnel in a Bari cinema. The boats went round picking up survivors from blazing ships and from the water despite the hazard of their wooden hulls and tanks of high octane petrol. Laurie Strong in 81, with NOIC Bari aboard, approached a 5,000-ton Italian freighter on fire astern to tow it away from a Liberty ship which NOIC said was full of bombs and ammunition. The MTB, on maximum revs on all three engines, managed to pull the monster a hundred yards to safely.

297 (Woods), the duty boat that night, was ordered to torpedo a blazing ship just outside the harbour which was drifting back in.

The Bari Air Raid. (Courtesy, A.T. Robinson)

The Bari Air Raid. (Courtesy, G.M. Hudson)

Upper deck damage to MTB 296 in the Bari Air Raid. (Courtesy, H.F. Cooper)

Worst of all was the fact that the USS *John Harvey* was carrying a consignment of mustard gas in carboys on the deck as part of its cargo, and when the ship blew up, the contents were strewn all over the harbour. The liquid mustard gas was carried upwards in the blast and came raining down on ships and boats alike. But this particularly affected those survivors who were already in the water – and those who were attempting to rescue them. Many of the crews of the MTBs suffered: none worse than Lt C. Holloway (CO of 242), Sub Lt J.H.E. Collins (First Lt of 243) and his radar operator A/B Peter Bickmore, who were all badly burned. Tim Collins wryly remarked afterwards that he and Claude Holloway made the mistake of taking off their best uniform trousers before diving in! Holloway was in hospital for two

months. Collins was awarded the MBE and Bickmore the BEM.

HMS *Vienna* was so badly damaged that she was assessed as being no longer able to fulfil her function as the Coastal Force depot ship. She was towed to Brindisi and used as a store ship.

Although many of the boats had minor damage and many officers and men needed hospital treatment, it was the 20th Flotilla which suffered most. 296 had been so badly damaged that she was considered beyond repair, and was paid off and taken out of commission. 289 was assessed as needing major repairs, and was in fact not ready to resume operations until June 1944. Having lost MTB 288 months before in Augusta, the flotilla was down to five boats – and with the sinking of SS *Puck* in the air raid, carrying the replacement Packard engines, those five had to carry on with their old engines.

The air raid had its effect on the advance of the Eighth Army, too. Lack of essential supplies which had been lost in the sunken freighters held up the forward momentum of the campaign. The winter of 1943/4 found the front line stabilized near Ortona, about 100 miles north of Bari. With the weather deteriorating and long spells of rain, the tanks and transports became bogged down, and the swollen rivers created another problem. (Note 9, Appendix 1)

The boats which had been in the islands during the horrors of the Bari raid had not been idle. Until Hvar fell in the new German occupation strategy, some patrols had sailed from Hvar Town, but until Komiza was ready they used the grotto on Ravenik.

Soon after the Bari air raid, Lt Cdr Morgan-Giles established himself at Komiza as SNOVIS (Senior Naval Officer, Vis). He was charged with responsibility for operating the boats, liaising with the Partisans and with the other service units who were arriving, and gradually improving the rather primitive base facilities.

The enemy cruiser *Niobe*, previously the Yugoslav *Dalmacija*, sunk by torpedoes from 298 and 226 on 22 December 1943. (Courtesy, G.M. Hudson)

It was not long before patrols began to find enemy targets in this new phase of operations. The first Dog Boats arrived in Komiza: MTBs 637, 649 and 651 were the earliest to arrive, and they worked well with the 'short' boats, adding very considerably to the fire-power available. In fact, the first real success came on 18/19 December when Lt J.D. Lancaster, who had recently taken over from H.A. Barbary as SO of the 20th Flotilla, led a mixed unit of 297 (Lt J.R. Woods) and 637 (Lt R.C. Davidson) in support of a raid by a large force of Partisans on the garrison at Omis on the mainland north of the island of Brac.

The two boats became separated, and each working independently made successful attacks on enemy shipping. 637 met a Siebel ferry transporting troops, with three other small craft. After a fierce gun battle (the Siebel SF 193 was well armed) and sustaining some damage, she sank it with one torpedo and destroyed the others. Lancaster sighted a shape under a cliff which on closer inspection proved to be a well camouflaged ship about 200 ft long. Woods fired both his torpedoes at her, both hit, and she sank. At this stage no replacement torpedoes were kept at Komiza, and the boats had to return to Manfredonia to rearm.[10]

Lancaster was again involved three days later in a far more significant success. For

10   MO1442/43 and MO750/44; ROP at PRO in ADM 199/258.

Lt Peter Hyslop CO of MTB 85 of the 24th Flotilla, who was in command of 226 when *Niobe* was sunk. (Courtesy, H.F. Cooper)

months the Partisans had been troubled by intervention in their landings and patrols by what CCF later described as a 'hoary but agile old cruiser' with heavy armament and which naturally constituted a considerable threat to the Allied light forces as well as to the Partisans. The MTBs had sought her for weeks but had so far not found her. She had been built before the First World War as a German light cruiser, the *Niobe*. When she was passed to the Yugoslav Navy after the surrender in 1919, they renamed her *Dalmacija*. In 1941 she was taken over by the Italians, but since 8 November 1943 the Germans had returned to her original name and she was the *Niobe* again, working out of Pola to the north.

In Komiza news was received on 21 December from Intelligence sources that *Niobe* was aground on the south-west tip of Silba Island (not far from Zara), and that tugs were trying to salvage her. It is now known that one of the reports of her position came from Lt Owen Woodhouse RNZNVR, an officer of the 20th Flotilla who had temporarily been seconded from his boat to act as a Coastal Forces Liaison Officer with the Partisans. By chance, he had been on a clandestine mission in the area – in a 20-ft fishing boat with two Partisan sailors as crew – when he discovered the cruiser aground.

Lancaster set off immediately with two boats: 298 (Lt Shore) of the 20th, and 226 of the 24th, temporarily commanded by Lt P. Hyslop. They made a fast passage northward outside all the main islands at 25 knots (they had about 90 miles to cover from Vis) and approached Silba through the narrow channel between Skarda and Ist,

MTB 298 of the 20th Flotilla after the sinking of the *Niobe*. (Courtesy, G.M. Hudson)

99

Lt Cdr M.C. Morgan-Giles RN, Senior Naval Officer, Vis (SNOVIS). (Courtesy, IWM – HU 48871)

arriving at about 0100. Lancaster slowed to 4 knots to take stock of the situation, and sighted the cruiser surrounded by tugs and E-boats. Using silenced engines they crept in to 400 yds, and fired their four torpedoes. There was some inaccurate small-arms fire from the attending boats, but the cruiser was hit by two torpedoes, and the tug *Parenzo* alongside her was also destroyed. The *Niobe* was a total loss and played no further part in the war.

The two MTBs slipped away, quietly retraced a course past Ist and back to Komiza as dawn was breaking. The Partisan leaders were elated, as they had found this old cruiser a thorn in their flesh. In many ways this early major success by the MTBs was a very significant boost to the trust which built up between the Partisans and the Royal Navy. SNOVIS too was very grateful as this made his liaison role far easier from the start.[11]

On this note of success and the con-solidation of relationships with the Partisans, Chapter 7 follows to pursue the story of these four flotillas into 1944, all now established in their very different areas of the Mediter-ranean.

11 MO1442; ROP at PRO in ADM 199/258; notes from Sir Owen Woodhouse PC KBE DSC.

THE 7TH, 10TH, 20TH AND 24TH MTB FLOTILLAS

JANUARY TO SEPTEMBER 1944

THE 7TH MTB FLOTILLA

Apart from a small number of enemy contacts in the autumn of 1943, the 7th had seen very little action since the heady days of constant patrolling and frequent actions in the Strait of Messina many months earlier.

However, a new era was about to begin. By January 1944, the nine new boats had arrived, the transferred crews had taken them over, and they had been sailed to Malta from Algiers. Four of the replacement boats were of Vosper design, built at the Annapolis Yacht Yard in Maryland USA, off Chesapeake Bay. They were four of the eight boats originally intended to form a new flotilla for the Mediterranean, the 19th MTBs. A decision had been taken to change this, and to use them instead as replacements in the 7th and 20th Flotillas.

The four allocated to the 7th were numbered from 375 to 378, and they were fine new boats incorporating many new features in an improved Vosper design which benefited from years of wartime experience – an advantage denied to those who had produced the earliest boats. They were powered by three Packard 1250 b.h.p. engines and they had British 291 radar. The armament in addition to the two 21-in torpedo tubes, was a hand-operated 20-mm Oerlikon for'd, and a twin 0.5-in power-operated turret amidships. This was later replaced by a twin hand-operated 20-mm Oerlikon – far more lethal in its effect.

Making the 7th Flotilla up to nine boats were five Higgins boats built in the New Orleans Yard in the USA. They were originally built as PT boats for the US Navy, and twelve of these boats had been due to be shipped to Russia under Lease-Lend. It was by a perverse stroke of good fortune for the 7th Flotilla that the Britain to Russia convoys had been halted temporarily in March 1943 due to the sinking of seventeen ships in two days in the North Atlantic and the need to withdraw the Home Fleet destroyer screen in order to supplement the Support Groups in the Western Approaches. Five of the twelve Higgins boats had been on board ships in the last convoy, which sailed from Loch Ewe on 15 February for Murmansk, and the other seven had been unloaded in Britain and transferred to the Royal Navy in April 1944. It was five of these that had been shipped to the Mediterranean in November and December and allocated to the 7th.

By comparison with the Vospers, the Higgins boats were more roomy, and had more luxurious accommodation below. They were actually 78 ft in length, but the greater beam (20 ft) and high freeboard gave them the appearance of being far larger than the Vospers, disproportionately so for only 7 ft difference in length.

In addition to greater space, such items as a powerful generator, electric cooking, a refrigerator and sufficient bunks for the crew's sleeping quarters made them very popular with their ships' companies. They were also very heavily armed for 'short' boats: two 21-in torpedo tubes, a single hand-operated 20-mm Oerlikon for'd, twin 0.5-in turrets on each side of the bridge, a twin 20-mm Oerlikon amidships, and a 40-mm Bofors gun aft. The five boats were numbered MTB 419 to 423.

The boats were allocated to their new COs as follows:

375	Lt R.A. Johnson	419	Lt C.T. Finch
376	Lt A.H. Moore	420	Lt A.C. Blomfield RN
377	Lt R. Aitchison	421	Lt R. Varvill
378	Lt N.L. Ilett	422	Lt C.J. Cochran RANVR
		423	Lt E.S. Good

Tony Blomfield, the SO, was determined to use this opportunity to ensure that a well-drilled, confident flotilla with reliable boats and excellent equipment would return to operations. He put the boats through an extensive programme of night and day exercises off Malta, and by the end of April he was sure they could acquit themselves well. They also had the first delivery of the

MTB 421, a US-built Higgins MTB of the 7th Flotilla commanded by Lt R. Varvill. (Courtesy, L.C. Reynolds)

A Higgins PT boat with SO Radar, of the USN's 15th MTB Squadron (Ron 15). (Courtesy, A.T. Robinson)

latest mark of torpedo with the CCR pistols that had proved successful elsewhere but had only now become available to the MTBs in the Mediterranean. These pistols enabled the torpedo to explode within the magnetic field of the target, without needing to make actual contact with the hull before the warhead was detonated. They proved to be ideal for sinking shallow-draught vessels such as F-lighters – the principal targets in this area of operations – and the strike rate for the MTBs improved markedly from this time on.

Although it is not strictly within the scope of this history to describe the operations of the PT boats of the United States Navy, during the months that the 7th Flotilla were away Ron 15 (the 15th PT Squadron) led by Lt Cdr S. Barnes USN represented the sole

'short' boat presence on the west coast of Italy, and deserve a mention. The eighteen boats of the squadron (PT 201 to 218) were all of Higgins construction, quite similar to those arriving for the 7th, and had the advantage of the advanced SO radar set which had been fitted in them when they arrived in Bone in the spring of 1943. The problems they had with their torpedoes have already been mentioned, but they detected the enemy so often at long range that when they were able to get into perfect position they could be successful. Probably the most significant feature of their operational presence was the fact that they were welcomed warmly by SOIS and by Cdr Allan, under whose aegis they operated. They quickly built up a very close rapport with their allies in

British Coastal Forces. The Dog Boat flotillas, and particularly the 56th whose boats were all commanded by Canadians, found this particularly valuable, and the operational practice grew up of patrolling with one PT boat as radar control. Time after time this led to successful interceptions.

Bobby Allan realized the value of this system, and used it in an extended way to overcome the problems which were being experienced by PTs and Dog Boats alike in getting close enough to engage F-lighter convoys when they were provided with heavily armed escorts. He initiated, led and carried through tremendously successful 'battle group' attacks on F-lighter convoys off the Italian coast, two of which were Operations Gun and Newt. He used PTs for radar control and LCGs (Landing Craft, Gun), which had 4.7-in guns and were manned by expert Royal Marine gunners, to engage the enemy at long range. The Dog Boats took part each time in support and, after the LCGs had sunk or damaged whole groups of F-lighters at long range, were used to finish off damaged targets.

Sadly the 7th missed these operations, but they too were to enjoy a very fruitful association with the PTs on their return to the area.

When they sailed to Maddalena in the last days of April, the boats of the 7th found a very different operational situation from the one they had left in the previous December. Maddalena was now very much a 'back base', and the focus of activity had shifted to Bastia in north-east Corsica, only 30 miles from Elba. Both SOIS (Capt N.V. Dickinson) and Cdr Allan had established themselves at Bastia.

The landing at Anzio had taken place in January, and although it took months for the Army to break out and isolate Cassino, this movement coincided with the arrival of the 7th, and this meant that the coastal shipping routes available to the Germans would be shortened and more within range from Bastia.

The 7th found themselves sharing the Old Port at Bastia with the two squadrons of USN PT boats; the Dog Boats and the MLs used the New Harbour. They immediately built on the first-class rapport nurtured by Cdr Allan, and at once began to establish close ties with the officers and crews of the PT boats. This was greatly assisted by the fact that their boats were so similar. Ron 15 had been joined by Ron 22, also 78-ft Higgins boats, and numbered respectively from PT 302 to 313.

Blomfield, after discussions with Cdr Allan and with Lt Cdr Barnes USN, cemented the relationship by arranging that the normal pattern for the patrols of the 7th Flotilla would be to use three of his boats with one PT as radar ship. It was immediately fruitful, as on the first occasion it led to enemy contact and a successful interception and attack. On 9/10 May, with Lt Robert Varvill as SO, three of the 7th's Vospers, 378 (Ilett), 377 (Aitchison) and 376 (Masters), together with PT 203, were patrolling off the Tuscany coast between Elba and San Stefano when PT 203's radar identified two enemy targets. Despite a careful, silent approach they were detected and came under fire from two F-lighters. Mark VIII torpedoes with CCR pistols were used for the first time by Mediterranean MTBs. The spread of four torpedoes was fired at a range of 600 yds, and the leading F-lighter was hit, blew up and sank. An explosion was felt which indicated that the second, too, had been hit, but it was not seen to sink. This success by the new boats and their new torpedoes, with the help of the PT's radar, was a great boost to confidence.

Another unit patrolled on the next night, led by Blomfield in 420, with 421 (Varvill) and 375 (Johnson) accompanied by PT 214. This time they were off Vada Rocks to the north of Elba. Again the PT found the

Bastia, Corsica, in early 1944. (Courtesy, L.C. Reynolds)

contact at long range, enabling a planned approach to a good attack position, and six torpedoes were fired at a merchantman. She was escorted by five R-boats. One hit was seen on the main target, with another possible hit further aft, and some evidence of an escort also being struck. Shore batteries opened fire but the boats received no damage.[1]

Tony Blomfield, anxious to experiment to expand the flotilla's methods of attack, tried out a week or two later an ambitious plan involving multiple attacks from several units. He took the whole flotilla on patrol further north with two PTs, and when a convoy was detected, attempted to manoeuvre his boats into position by R/T (radio telephone). Unfortunately, the F-lighters were escorted by a destroyer and a corvette. The unit was sighted and came under heavy fire, and this rendered the experiment far more difficult, and led to a great deal of confusion. Only Bob Varvill in 421 fired torpedoes, acting independently, but no claims were made and the flotilla returned to Bastia without any

1   MO7215; ROP at PRO in ADM 199/268 (both 9 and 10 May).

damage but having learned little from the experiment.

This did not dampen enthusiasm, however, and a day or two later on 27/28 May, a patrol off Spezia produced even more startling results from the new torpedoes. Varvill led the unit in 421, with 419 (Moore), 420 (Good) and PT 218. Just after midnight, a convoy of five F-lighters escorted by one lone E-boat was sighted about half a mile offshore. The F-lighters were in close formation (presumably to enable concentrated defensive fire), which actually assisted the attacks as they presented an almost continuous target. Varvill ordered individual attacks by each boat in turn, having closed the convoy quietly at low speed using the underwater exhausts. One by one, each boat got into a favourable firing position and

made its attack. Varvill's came first, and brought a remarkable result. His two torpedoes hit two overlapping F-lighters. Moore fired one and missed astern. Good used his port torpedo for an F-lighter which had stopped, baulked by the two sinking vessels ahead. His target blew up in a sheet of orange flame and sank.

The escorting E-boat suddenly seemed to realize that three of his charges had been sunk and began firing at the MTBs, who withdrew and resumed patrol, hoping for larger targets. They were not disappointed, as an hour later PT 218 reported radar contacts nearly 2 miles ahead, close inshore. When sighted, they proved to be a KT ship (a War Transport) of about 1,500 tons, escorted by a warship – possibly a small destroyer, torpedo boat or sloop. The two vessels were steering south-

A German F-lighter. (Courtesy, A.T. Robinson)

east at about 15 knots, and Varvill decided to take his boat (with both torpedoes expended) close inshore to create a diversion while 419 and 420 attacked, each having one remaining torpedo. Moore in 419 fired first and hit the KT ship, which broke in two and sank. As Good prepared to fire at the escort, it opened heavy fire and at once 420 suffered hits on the bridge and in the charthouse, and two engines cut out. Good disengaged on his one engine, and tried to bluff the enemy by firing a red four-star cartridge from his Very pistol. It seemed to work, as fire from the escort ceased temporarily and the redoubtable motor mechanic (PO Joseph) had time to repair electrical faults, start up, and enable Good to withdraw to join up with the other boats.

They sped back towards Bastia, conscious of the remarkable tally of success. Three F-lighters and one KT ship had been sunk, and only five torpedoes used. This rate of success was such a marked contrast to the past experience of MTBs in the Mediterranean that they realized the significance of the new weapon for future operations. The American COs of the PTs bemoaned their different experience: in all these attacks in May their torpedoes had not hit once.

CCF commended the flotilla in his report, and months later POMM Joseph was awarded a DSM, and Bob Varvill a DSC for his part in all three attacks in May.[2]

One section of CCF's remarks was particularly appreciated when, commenting first on the success of the Mark VIII torpedo and CCR pistol, he added: '. . . But no matter how good the weapon, attacks will fail if they are not well executed . . . these successes were the fruits of well-conducted attacks resolutely and accurately pressed home.'

The system of analysing reports and learning from them was demonstrated in one comment at a higher level when this one reached Admiralty. Referring to the first attack, when 419 and 420 each fired a single torpedo, Operations Division wrote: 'According to the rules, both boats should have fired both torpedoes at their first target, in which case they would have had nothing left for the merchant ship later. Thus do the wicked prosper!'

With this string of successful attacks adding to those achieved by Dog Boats and PTs in the past few months, it was not surprising that the German Naval Command became worried by the continual sinking of their coastal waterway traffic. Access to German War Diaries after the war reveals that some attempts were made to affect the situation.

An extract dated early June 1944 reads:

Reconnaissance by the German Air Force and our own investigations reveal that the enemy MTB repair base is still at Maddalena, but also that the jumping off point is almost without exception Bastia. The elimination of Bastia harbour as an MTB base by naval bombardment is impossible because suitable heavy artillery carriers are lacking and because of enemy air superiority by day. Up to now, night bombardments have not achieved lasting results, especially as MTBs were not encountered during night operations.

Naval Staff is of the opinion that a single blow against enemy MTBs and their base at Bastia would for some time bring considerable relief for the traffic off the west coast of Italy, and thereby result in favouring the fighting on land by a temporary, and perhaps decisive, improvement in the supply situation.

The plea apparently fell on deaf – or powerless – ears. By mid-June, the Diary noted that: 'Due to developments on land [Rome fell to the Allies on 6 June] the necessity for increased supplies over the sea has decreased.'

---

2   MO8244; ROP at PRO in ADM 199/268; awards in *Seedie's List of Coastal Forces Awards*.

In fact, this proved to be a mistaken analysis, as the 7th Flotilla continued to find shipping targets along the coast of the Gulf of Genoa until April 1945. Nevertheless, Bastia was spared the blow which earlier could have affected the operations of the base considerably.

Between 8 and 15 June, the flotilla mounted patrols off Elba every night, as it was felt that the enemy might attempt an evacuation to the mainland in case the island was cut off by events on land. But there was no evidence of any such movement; instead, there was an Allied assault on Elba (Operation Brassard) on 16 June. It was carried out largely by Free French troops and launched mainly from Bastia, and thirty-nine Coastal Force craft were involved. Strangely, the boats which took the brunt of the direct assault were the HDMLs, as they led in the landing craft and encountered the first fierce opposition. The 7th Flotilla boats and a number of Dog Boats were used in support but were hardly called upon to do anything aggressive.

It took two days to clear the island of all German troops, but with Elba no longer in enemy hands the front moved northward and patrols were no longer required south of Elba. By the end of June the 56th Flotilla of Dog Boats had left to reinforce the operations in the Adriatic, leaving the 7th as the only MTB unit of the Royal Navy at Bastia, together with the PT boats.

Patrols were mounted constantly, and the next contact with the enemy was on 23/24 June off Spezia. Tony Blomfield, the SO, led in 420, and had 419 (Finch), 423 (Good) and PT 304 in company. The first purpose of this patrol was to recover Allied agents from the shore, but as soon as that was completed they met a powerful enemy force – a destroyer, a corvette and several E-boats. Blomfield prepared to make a torpedo attack but was greeted by fierce fire,

and his unit was beaten off before it was able to get into a good firing position. Blomfield got two torpedoes away, but in doing so 420 was badly damaged and no hits were claimed. He decided to withdraw rather than risk a mauling. In his report, it is suggested that the enemy seemed so well prepared that there was a possibility that this was a carefully laid trap – in line with the concerns of the German Naval Command.[3]

The regular search for targets continued into July, and came to a head in the middle of the month when contact was made with the enemy on three consecutive nights, all in the vicinity of Spezia. The first of these was on 12/13 July, when Bob Varvill was SO in 421, leading 375 (Johnson), 378 (Ilett) and PT 308. The radar plot led them to a convoy of four F-lighters escorted by two R-boats. Visibility was poor, which helped the unit to make a quiet approach. Varvill succeeded in torpedoing the leading F-lighter, which blew up and sank leading to heavy defensive fire which forced him to withdraw.

He returned on the next night with the same boats to the same area. Once again, one F-lighter was sunk, although six torpedoes were fired. On the third night – 14/15 July – the unit was made up of 419 (Finch, SO for the night), 376 (Moore) and 377 (Aitchison), with PT 306. Yet again they came across the F-lighter 'train' – a further three of them, unescorted. They were able to fire unobserved from a good position, but although they heard two explosions, only one target was seen to be hit and the 7th could just claim one more F-lighter as sunk.[4]

Soon after this purple patch, preparations began for the involvement of the 7th Flotilla in the South of France landings (Operation

3   MO10085; ROP at PRO in ADM 199/268.
4   Three actions 12/13, 13/14, 14/15 July 1944; MO9398, MO9503, MO9379; all three ROPs at PRO in ADM 199/268.

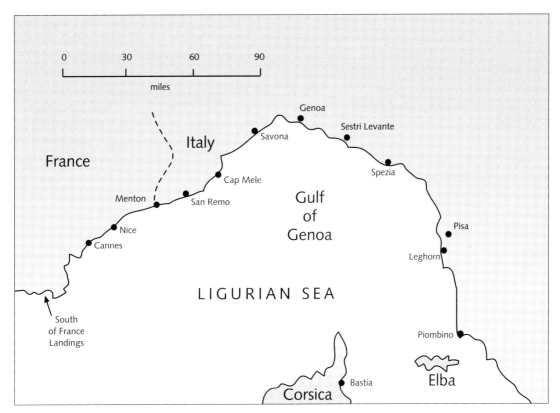

The Gulf of Genoa.

Dragoon). They, together with the PTs, were given the role of protecting the right flank of the assault force from any attack by enemy naval units based in Genoa or Spezia. The landings took place on 15 August, and opposition proved to be comparatively light. Fine weather and no interference from the Luftwaffe made this a very different operation from those at Sicily or Salerno which were well remembered; even the assault on tiny Elba a few weeks earlier had been contested far more fiercely. The only Coastal Force casualties were one ML sunk, and two damaged.

Almost immediately, the 7th Flotilla and the PTs returned to their normal role of patrolling the coast of the Gulf of Genoa, now from the French border round to Spezia. Leghorn (Livorgno) had fallen to the Army

on 19 July: the patrol distances had now increased – from Bastia it was 60 miles to Leghorn, a further 40 to Spezia, 40 on to Genoa, and 60 more to the border.

During Operation Dragoon, a third flotilla of eight PT boats – 'Ron 29' – had arrived. This group, unlike all the other Mediterranean PTs, was of 80-ft Elco design, which incorporated several important improvements. From the 7th Flotilla's point of view, the most significant was that its radar set was even more effective than the highly regarded early American sets. The PTs themselves regarded the greatest bonus to be their Mark XIII aircraft-type torpedoes launched from racks, which experience elsewhere had shown to be a great improvement. The new PTs were numbered between 552 and 563.

The first time one of them accompanied a unit of the 7th was on the night of 24/25 August when Blomfield in 420 with 423 (Good) and PT 559 patrolled off Genoa. Under heavy fire, they attacked a 200-ft torpedo boat (750 ton) and 423 sank it with one of two torpedoes fired. 423 also claimed to have sunk an E-boat in the exchange of fire.

This time it was the PT which first took shell damage from the torpedo boat, having two of her engines put out of action. 423 went alongside to render assistance, in particular to take off three badly wounded crew members, and to get them speedily back to base for medical attention. But while she was doing this, she was herself hit in the wheelhouse and (as it later transpired) on the port rudder, so that when she pulled away her steering was jammed solid, and she went round in circles. She made smoke and as soon as enemy fire ceased, stopped to investigate.

423's motor mechanic – Chief POMM Joseph Lee – then demonstrated the resourcefulness and expertise which typified so many of the Coastal Force motor mechanics in action. He discovered that it was the port rudder which was jammed hard over, and managed – with the help of the First Lieutenant – to drop it about nine inches to free it. It was then possible to rig steering by tiller down aft, connected only to that rudder, and to turn the starboard rudder by the bridge wheel. In that way it was possible to steer and maintain a course. CPOMM Lee was later awarded the DSM.[5]

The patrol on the next night (25/26 August) provided very clear evidence of the far-seeing eye of the PTs' new radar. PT 557, operating with 421 (Varvill) and 422 (Cochran) off Genoa, picked up the image of a destroyer or corvette at 37 miles. When the range closed to 1,000 yards, four torpedoes were fired, and although Varvill believed that one hit the target there was no confirmation later.

In the light of the remarkable performance of the radar in PT 557, a decision was made to adopt a new tactic. On the night of 27/28 August, Tony Blomfield, instead of taking out his own boat, was aboard PT 559, directing the unit from what was now regarded as the best control point, with a continuous view of the plot. It was the first time a British flotilla SO had led a combined patrol from a PT boat. The idea had clearly sprung from Bobby Allan's successes earlier in the summer in the LCG operations from Bastia.

The operation itself did lead to an enemy contact. 423 (Good) and 375 (Johnson) were put into an attack position when three F-lighters were sighted off Savona – halfway between Genoa and the French border – and fired their four torpedoes unobserved at 1,000 yds. The official report states that one was sunk and another damaged.[6]

Patrols were continued every night, with the nine boats of the flotilla maintaining an impressive record of reliability and availability. This enabled two boats to operate with a PT in rotation.

There were no sightings for two weeks, but on 10/11 September there began a remarkable series of actions as yet unmatched by any other flotilla. To record them in full becomes repetitious, as on each occasion the PT's radar made the interception and plot possible, the targets were F-lighters, and the torpedoes with their CCR pistols ensured hits. But a summary is justified to record the achievements of the flotilla in this period – the results of excellent equipment, skilful and experienced officers and crews, inspiring leadership and an insatiable appetite for taking the battle to the enemy.

5   MO11050; Summary of actions at NHB.

6   MO12454; Summary of actions at NHB.

10/11 September	Blomfield in PT 559 with 422 (Cochran) and 376 (Masters), off Cape Mele. Two F-lighters sunk with four torpedoes at 800 yds.
11/12 September:	Finch in PT 557 with 423 (Good), and 419 (Johnson), off Sestri Levante. Two F-lighters sunk with four torpedoes at 1,000 yds.
12/13 September	Moore in PT 557 with 378 (Ilett) and 421 (Aitchison), off Savona. Four F-lighters attacked; the MTBs hit with two torpedoes out of four, and the PT with one of four; three sunk, one damaged at 350 yds.
13/14 September	Blomfield in PT 559 with 422 (Cochran) and 376 (Masters), off Porto Fino. 422 sank a corvette, and the PT an F-lighter, at 1,000 yds.
17/18 September	Finch in PT 558 with 423 (Good), off Sestri Levante. Attack on five F-lighters, one sunk by 423 and one by PT 558.
18/19 September	Moore in PT 557 with 378 (Ilett) and 377 (Aitchison), west of Spezia. Two F-lighters attacked, one sunk with two torpedoes, the other missed with one.[7]

Not surprisingly, there were no contacts for the next week – perhaps the supply of available F-lighters was running short. The last patrol from Bastia took place on 26/27 September. Steve Moore was SO in PT 559, and the two MTBs were 377 (Aitchison) and 376 (Masters). It was a very dark night, but the PT's radar detected targets and Moore planned his attack, which took place off Sestri Levante. The visibility was so poor that the targets were very indistinct, and the first attack by the PT and 376 secured no hits. Aitchison had not had a good sight of the enemy, so held back his attack until he saw one larger target when he was in to 400 yds. This time there was no doubt about the result: there was a huge explosion and a brilliant flash which lit up the whole area and revealed a whole collection of F-lighters, a tug, R-boats and a corvette. The sinking provoked a fierce reaction, but fortunately the gunfire was not accurate, and 377 which had finished her attack very close to the convoy, withdrew at high speed.

Moore in his report considered that Aitchison had sunk a merchant vessel – possibly a tanker – of about 2-3,000 tons.[8]

It was a fitting end to the operations from Bastia. Two days later, the base was shut down (as was the base at Maddalena), and moved across the Ligurian Sea to Leghorn on the mainland of Italy. The new situation provides an appropriate point to move to the story of the 10th Flotilla in a very different operational zone.

THE 10TH FLOTILLA IN THE AEGEAN

In January 1944 the changes in the flotilla, resulting from the return home of Lt Campbell and Lt Muir, had required the appointment of two new COs. Command of 309 went to Lt M.S. Hannington, a South African and long-serving First Lieutenant in the 10th. Muir's replacement in 307 was Lt L.H. Blaxell DSC. This was his first command, but he had had long and varied experience in the 'long' boats. His DSC had been awarded after an action in the Dover Strait in July 1942 in a C class Fairmile MGB, and he had since been First Lieutenant of a Dog Boat in the Mediterranean for nearly a year.

Lionel Blaxell has provided a valuable insight into the conditions under which the boats operated during this time, in his privately printed memoirs, *Through the*

---

7 Six actions between 10 and 19 July 1944, all in MO12454 and ADM 199/268.

8 MO12454; ROP at PRO in ADM 199/268.

Hawse Pipe 1939–46. Some of his observations and descriptions add a great deal to an understanding of the problems and the tensions of the hide-away existence, the lack of supplies, and the comparative isolation of a small unit in a hostile area.

He describes how, with Newall 'showing him the ropes', he made his first ten-hour run up to Casteloriso from Alexandria, using 2,000 gallons of fuel, and immediately refuelled from a caique. The fuel came in 20-litre jerrycans, and had to be filtered through chamois leather to ensure no water or sand entered the system. They moved to a tiny inlet named Sertchi on the Turkish coast before dawn, set up their camouflage and settled down for the day in hiding. By climbing up the rocks to higher ground above, they could see Rhodes just 12 miles away, and study any local activity.

When darkness fell, they were off on patrol. Newall frequently chose a position close inshore off Rhodes; often they would cut engines and drift silently, watching transports running along the coast road. Occasionally a searchlight would switch on suddenly and if the boats were picked up, very quickly they would be 'boxed' by several searchlights. That would lead to a crash start and the beginning of a barrage from the shore batteries as the exhaust smoke, wash and spray were detected. There was even some beauty in the exercise according to Blaxell: 'When one or two of the batteries were firing fairly heavy shells, they would whine overhead and burst in large fountains of water which were illuminated by the searchlights. They made a beautiful firework display – but we didn't stop to admire the effect'.

When this happened, the Germans in Rhodes always assumed they had been laying mines off Rhodes harbour. The crews of the MTBs would watch next day from the peace of Sertchi as aircraft with a large magnetized ring would sweep for the mines they assumed to be there: they would reflect that in the absence of the targets they could not find, at least they were causing the shore batteries to waste ammunition and occupying the enemy's aircraft in useless activity.

Only once in this first period in January was there a real expectation of action. While patrolling between Symi and Rhodes, Newall in 315 flashed Blaxell in 307 to alert him to a torpedo target to starboard. He moved into position to attack and sighted the dark shape of a sizeable ship about 2,000 yds away on an ideal course and apparently unescorted. Newall challenged and there was no reply. Pins were removed from the firing levers. Newall challenged again, this time without the Aldis night shade. Its blinding white beam brought an immediate response: within seconds the whole ship became ablaze with all colours. She was a Swedish hospital ship with a broken down generator. She had a lucky escape, as the authorities had apparently not been notified of her possible presence.

Despite continuous patrols, targets did not appear, and frustration began to creep in, especially when the crews heard of the successes the other flotillas were having in the Mediterranean areas further west. Fortunately there were just enough boats for a rotation system to operate, with the periodic return to Alexandria bringing regular opportunities for relaxation and for maintenance

MTB 315 of the 10th Flotilla. (Courtesy, G.M. Hudson)

requirements. The Elco boats stood up well to their operational demands, and their officers and men took great pride in them.

On 2/3 March came the opportunity – at last – to engage the enemy. 315 (Newall) and 307 (Blaxell) were once more the unit on patrol on an idyllic night with a full moon, a smooth sea, and the surrounding islands sharply silhouetted against the bright sky. The 2 MTBs were in an ideal position against the darkness of the shore when at 2215 they sighted what appeared to be three destroyers steaming fast towards them, aiming to enter Rhodes harbour. They were up-moon, 70 degrees off the bow, and still about 2 miles away, giving the MTBs time to manoeuvre into the best firing positions when the range closed.

At 1,000 yds and the correct firing angle, both 315 and 307 released their torpedoes. Unfortunately, 315's port tube flared on firing, and 307's port tube misfired – infuriating and unusual mishaps – leaving a spread of only three torpedoes in the attack. They saw the destroyers alter course, combing the line of the torpedoes, and knew that only luck could now bring a hit. Full of disappointment they realized that they had missed, and with only one torpedo and now seen and under fierce attack, they made smoke and withdrew at high speed.

Blaxell later obtained information from the log books of the German ships, which were TA15, TA16 and TA19 (Torpedo Boats of similar size to British Hunt class destroyers). The three ships had been ordered to deliver troops and had been delayed by their embarkation, and were therefore running at 20 knots. The flotilla commander aboard TA15 recorded that at 2230 they sighted shadows abeam to port, recognized them as enemy MTBs, and fire was opened with all weapons. Almost at once they then saw the flash of a torpedo discharge and sighted the wake of torpedoes especially one which ran

on the surface. The ship keeled over violently as it 'combed the tracks' and this locked the main armament turrets, allowing the MTBs to escape without further attack by the three Torpedo Boats.

315 and 307 headed first for the entrance of Rhodes harbour at full speed, hoping to intercept and use the one remaining torpedo, but they were just too late: the three ships were inside the harbour making a great deal of smoke.[9]

A few days later, on the night of 9/10 March 1944, Lt J.N. Broad RNZNVR in 266 with 260 (R.W. Beaumont) intercepted a convoy which consisted of three schooners, a caique, an F-lighter and an R-boat. The MTBs were, apparently, up moon when they sighted the convoy and were drawn into action before they could achieve a better position. They attacked at speed, but found themselves heavily outgunned. In the exchange, 266 was hit by an 88-mm shell on the bridge, and both Norman Broad and his coxswain at the wheel were killed. 266 was left circling under fire until the First Lieutenant rigged an after hand-steering position and extricated the boat from her dangerous situation, allowing withdrawal to Casteloriso.[10]

The constant patrols off Rhodes, Leros and Samos continued without any enemy sightings, but on 16 April, 315 (Newall) and 309 in company with MLs caught a caique and a small merchant vessel off Kos. A brief gun battle ensued: the caique was set on fire and both enemy vessels escaped into Kos harbour. 315 suffered shell damage below the waterline, and as she was making water too fast to control, she made for the nearest Turkish port of Bodrum. As they approached, they were fired upon from shore, but with 315 clearly down by the head they were

9 Blaxell, *Through the Hawse Pipe 1939–1946*.
10 ROP at PRO in ADM 199/268.

MTB 315 alongside at Casteloriso. (Courtesy, IWM – A23353)

allowed to enter the harbour and Newall beached her, and entered negotiations for time to effect repairs.

In neutral Turkey, the reception of warships from either of the warring nations very often depended upon the attitude of an individual local Turkish diplomat or senior officer. Many were very willing to give assistance within limits of time, but some were hostile. At Bodrum, after serious discussions and what Newall described as 'energetic bartering', generous hospitality and the time to effect temporary repairs were accorded. By 2000, within the time set, the boats were able to leave and return to Casteloriso by the following morning.

In this history of the Mediterranean MTBs, there is, for obvious reasons, little mention of other units of Coastal Forces which were operating in the region – usually separately from the MTBs – taking an equal share in the pattern of activity. Four Dog Boats had played their part in the period up to Christmas 1943, and the MLs and HDMLs were the longest serving of all the boats among the islands. In view of the general lack of torpedo targets and of fast enemy craft, the slower boats could be very effective, and certainly the MLs were excellent in bad weather and had a considerable range. They were greatly respected by the men of the MTBs.

The loss in March of the New Zealander Norman Broad, a highly regarded long-serving officer in the 10th, was in April compounded by the departure to New Zealand of his great friend Lt Len Newall. After well-deserved leave, he became one of the few experienced Coastal Force officers to serve in the Pacific, as CO of an ML for the rest of the war. Fortunately, there was a battle-hardened replacement for Newall, as Lt L.V. (Laurie) Strong DSC, arriving from the 24th Flotilla, took over as half-leader of the flotilla and as CO of 315.

The remainder of April and May 1944 was a quiet period for operations. Although night patrols were regularly mounted, the boats of the 10th found no enemy ships plying between the German-held islands. The reason was clear. With complete mastery of the sky, movements of enemy troops and supplies could be made by day under the protection of the Luftwaffe. Vulnerability to air attack kept the MTBs hidden under camouflage until dusk approached.

They did, however, play their part in the many successful raids by detachments of the LRDG (Long Range Desert Group), SBS (Special Boat Squadron) and commandos upon the islands garrisoned by the German military. The policy, as in the Dalmatian islands, was not to capture land but to attack the garrisons, take prisoners, and thus compel the enemy to weaken their mainland forces if they wished to reoccupy or reinforce each island. The grand strategy was to help the Allies on the Russian Front and the imminent Second Front in France by tying up divisions in the Balkans and the Aegean.

In these raids, the MTBs joined the MLs and the Levant Schooner Force in transporting and escorting these special troops to and from their missions.

Along with the dearth of night patrol targets – so frustrating for the boats – came an increasing concern over problems of their maintenance. Only 260, 266, 307, 309 and 315 were now operational, and to sustain a constant presence in the Aegean was no easy task, as there was a shortage of the specialist supplies which that required. CCF was warned that the boats were now needing exceptional care and supervision if they were to be kept running, and of course when they were isolated at Casteloriso or in their hideouts, they were unable to receive it. There were instances of boats having to be sailed to Alexandria for a major refit and engine maintenance and, having received that care, still breaking down on their return to the forward area.

Although it only involved MTB 309 (Lt M.S. Hannington), the raid on Symi on 13/14 July is worth describing as an example of the sort of operation which for the MTBs broke the frustration of the absence of targets.

The raid was codenamed Operation Tenement. It could not be despatched from Casteloriso because the distance to Symi was too great to meet the necessary time factors in safety at night. The force therefore gathered in the Gulf of Dorio on the Turkish coast, where the Coastal Force boats laid up under camouflage netting to avoid detection by enemy reconnaissance planes by day.

There were 224 men involved in the raiding force, to be carried and escorted by eight MLs, four HDMLs, two schooners and MTB 309. Intelligence had reported that the German garrison numbered 200, and that they were in a high state of tension, expecting a raid by night, and therefore relaxing their guard by day. In addition, the main German naval threat in the area was currently not available to them, as the four destroyers which normally patrolled there were all reported to be under repair in Piraeus. For these reasons, the raid was timed for 0700 on 14 July. An advance party of raiders had been landed on the north-western side of the island during the preceding night.

Many of the troops landed were Greeks, supported by commandos. They were put ashore at three points, and the MLs which carried them were then held ready to move into Symi harbour to bombard the castle in which the German garrison was established.

MTB 309 and three other MLs, covering the landings, were called into action at 0640 when two MAS boats in the harbour came out with three barges. As they appeared they were engaged at close range, the barges were sunk, and the MAS boats turned back into the harbour, one on fire. They were later captured by the Greek troops. Eventually, the garrison surrendered and 135 prisoners-of-war were taken. The commandos destroyed the enemy installations and captured a large haul of arms.[11]

The Luftwaffe became active, and MTB 309 and the MLs were withdrawn to hide up through the remaining daylight hours, returning at dusk to evacuate the troops, the prisoners, the captured arms and the two MAS boats. The operation had been successfully concluded in 24 hours and the objectives all met.

The following day the Germans showed the importance they placed on the island by mounting first a heavy air raid, and then a landing in force to reoccupy it. An even larger garrison was established, thereby achieving for the Allies their second objective, which was to deplete the enemy reserves on the mainland and continue to tie up troops in this region.

Evidence began to appear of other effects that this operation – and other similar raids – had on German strategy. During August the enemy began to strengthen their forces on all the islands they had occupied. But other pressures soon began to change the Aegean situation yet again. The war had at last turned in favour of the Allies, who were now advancing on all fronts – in Normandy, in Italy and in Russia. At the same time, the Russian advance and political pressures on Romania and Bulgaria caused these two Balkan states to defect to the Allies on 25 August and 5 September respectively. Together these factors completely undermined the German presence in the Aegean, and throughout the autumn they began to evacuate first the islands they had held, and then mainland Greece itself, to avoid being cut off and captured.

---

11 Report by Military Commander, Brig Turnbull.

Units of the 10th Flotilla were involved in operations connected with the Allies' movement into southern Greece – first taking the island of Kithera on 16 September, and then moving into the Pireaus and Athens, while the Germans carried out a 'skilful retreat and evacuation' of the Greek islands and mainland.[12]

The 10th, briefly reinforced by the return of 265 (now repaired after losing her bow in the Strait of Messina in August 1943), was reduced again almost at once by an accident to 263 in Kos harbour. Thereafter she could only be used as a training boat. Effectively, the three 77-ft Elcos 307, 309 and 315, which had remained operational despite all the difficulties, were the only sound and fully reliable boats left.

They now also lost their long-serving SO, Lt Cdr Peter Evensen DSC and Bar RNVR. He had been ill for some months, and was invalided home to Britain. He had been with the flotilla since January 1942, and even before that had held commands in home waters in 1940 and 1941. Throughout the whole of the Aegean campaign he had been required to solve many problems of supply and maintenance for the flotilla, and plan a new style of cat-and-mouse operations in an area under constant threat from the air and isolated from the base at Alexandria. His awards had been well deserved.

By the end of September 1944, a new flotilla of replacement boats had arrived at Alexandria and a new – and final – phase of operations for the 10th Flotilla was about to begin.

THE 20TH AND 24TH MTB FLOTILLAS

When 1944 opened, these two flotillas had been operating around the Dalmatian islands whenever the weather and sea conditions allowed, for about six weeks. After an initial period of hiding-up under camouflage, they were now able to use the rather primitive base at Komiza. The two SOs, Lt J.D. (Butch) Lancaster DSC of the 20th, and Lt David Scott DSC RN of the 24th, had rather different boats to lead: Lancaster had five Vospers built early in 1943 in the USA, while Scott's eight Vospers were of an earlier design and build, and had operated in home waters for six months before entering the Mediterranean in time for Operation Husky. They were beginning to feel their age.

A pattern was developing during January when no more than four or five Vospers and two or three Dog Boats could operate from Komiza at a time. This was a period when patrol units were mixed up with little reference to flotillas. At this early stage, it was common for Vospers to join a Dog Boat on patrol, and this was the case on 13/14 January when David Scott was SO of a patrol off the island of Brac. He sailed in 226 (which had Peter Hyslop temporarily in command) with 651 (Lt Ken Horlock).

It was known that German troops were being landed on Brac, and the plan was to intercept shipping either reinforcing or supplying the assault. The first enemy sighting was of a small merchant ship entering Sumartin harbour on the coast of Brac. Hyslop waited until she had tied up alongside, and fired two torpedoes through the harbour entrance. Both hit, and she sank at her berth.

As they continued their search, a Siebel ferry was sighted, and 651 fired her torpedoes at her from a good position. They ran true, but although they were set at minimum depth there was no explosion, so they must have passed below the shallow-draught troop carrier. Both boats then attacked with all guns, and the ferry was very badly damaged.[13]

---

12 Churchill, *The Second World War*, Vol. 6.

13 MO2016; ROP at PRO in ADM 199/268.

This was the only action the 20th or 24th saw until the very end of January, but not for want of trying. Captain Stevens (CCF) who visited Vis to see the problems for himself and stayed sixteen days, reported to C-in-C that in the period of his visit there were patrols on thirteen nights. He also illustrated the arduous conditions existing at the time, referring to the fuelling from drums by hand, the constant calls to action stations during the day for air raids, and the atrocious weather throughout his stay.

Another mixed unit met with success on 29/30 January, when Lt Cdr Tim Bligh, the new SO of the 57th Flotilla of Dog Boats in his own MGB 662, with 97 (Bowyer), sank the 330-ton tanker SS *Folgore* and the schooner *Roma* carrying a large cargo of cement. This gun action in the Drevnik Channel was Bligh's first 'in the Islands', as his flotilla had been operating off the west coast of Italy for several months. Bowyer put a boarding party on to the tanker and found that it had a crew of eight Italians, with two Germans manning the guns. They had not had a chance to fire, being killed in the first attack. The Italians were taken prisoner.

Two nights later, on 31 January/1 February, Scott once again led a successful mixed patrol – this time of 85 (Hyslop) with 297 (Woods) and 298 (Shore) of the 20th Flotilla. They sank two schooners with depth charges off Silba Island, well north of Vis, after taking off two German and six Italian prisoners.[14]

Butch Lancaster had his turn on 2/3 February, when with 242 (Tonkin) and 298 (Shore) he found two unescorted schooners, took off eighty-five prisoners including twenty Germans, and then sank the vessels.

February was only notable for a series of raids on the German garrisons, particularly

Lt Cdr J. ('Butch') Lancaster (right), SO of the 20th Flotilla, with Lt J. Woods (CO 297) at Komiza. (Courtesy, E. Young)

on Brac, involving commandos, US Rangers, or Partisans. During this month, when the enemy was smarting under the loss of so many small supply vessels and their crews, there were indications (later confirmed) that an assault on Vis was being considered, and anti-invasion patrols were regularly mounted. In reality the German plan was delayed for two months and then rejected. The air raids on Vis subsided as the Allies built up supremacy in the air.

Major raids on garrisons continued to be mounted, and the boats of both flotillas were always involved. In much the same strategy as that used in the Aegean Islands, the object of the raids was not to attempt the capture of each island, but to defeat and take the

14 Actions on 29/30 January and 31 January/ 1 February 1944 in MO2874 and MO3986, and in ADM 199/268 and 269.

119

garrison troops prisoner and thus stretch the German reserves and tie down their hard-pressed occupying force.

This was demonstrated to be effective when, on 10/11 March, the Dog Boat 674 (Davidson, SO for the night) with 85 (Hyslop) first attacked a 120-ton schooner and disabled it, then boarded and took off twenty-seven prisoners. The boats stood off to sink it, and were met by a hail of fire from a group which had been left behind. 674 then totally destroyed and sank the vessel. Interrogation of the prisoners on Vis later discovered that the schooner was carrying seventy-five German troops in addition to the Italian crew: they were being taken to Hvar to reinforce the garrison there.[15]

Peter Hyslop was a busy man at this time. He followed up on the next night by leading a patrol from the 24th Flotilla – 85 (his own boat), 243 (du Boulay) and 84 (Gilpin) – off Murter. They found a target on a very dark night and shadowed it until it disappeared into a cove. Hyslop's torpedoes failed to register a hit, and 85 was damaged as he withdrew when she came under heavy fire.

Soon after this, David Scott, the SO of the 24th since August 1943, left the flotilla to return to General Service, and was replaced by Lt J.B. (Brian) Sturgeon DSC, who had made his name in MTB 77 of the 7th Flotilla.

Sadly he was killed in action on his very first patrol as SO. On the night of 2/3 April, he led a patrol of two boats, 242 (Holloway) and 81 (Strong) which met an I-boat – not large, but heavily armed – and attacked it vigorously. The return fire was spasmodic only, but Sturgeon, who was standing beside Holloway on the bridge of 242, was struck by a single bullet and died instantly. In many ways his death in such a way was a replica of that of Robert Hichens, the most renowned

of all Coastal Force officers, a year earlier. Brian Sturgeon had come through countless actions unscathed and was greatly respected by his colleagues in the Mediterranean MTBs.

He was buried next day with full Naval honours in the cemetery on Vis, where his grave stood not only among those of other British personnel who died in 1943 and 1944, but also some from 1811. In that year, three frigates of the Royal Navy fought a battle with Napoleon's ships off Vis (then known as Lissa) and routed them.

The main activity of supporting the raids on the garrisons continued and got larger in scale through March. Other than those operations, the boats of the 20th and 24th began to find themselves at a considerable disadvantage in regard to attacks on targets. As always, their primary value was in torpedoing larger vessels; here, almost all the targets were of shallow draught, and many were well armed. The Dog Boats with their heavy fire-power were generally far more effective in those circumstances. The weather turned bad throughout April and May, and that too affected the 'short' boats seriously. Many patrols were cancelled before they even set out, and on others they had to return during the night due to deteriorating conditions.

The month of April belonged emphatically to the Dog Boats, at this time mainly led by Tom Fuller, late of the 10th Flotilla. Early in the month he initiated a technique of boarding schooners and taking them back to Vis as prizes. Their cargoes were very welcome to the Partisans. This method was rapidly developed by carrying specially trained boarding parties of commandos. Later, the boats competed to record the shortest overall time from putting the party aboard to taking the vessel in tow.

Other changes during April included the arrival of a new Coastal Force depot ship at

15 MO5312; ADM 199/268 and 269.

Brindisi. She was the 5,000-ton Italian Navy seaplane tender *Almirante Miraglia*, which had taken the place of HMS *Vienna*. She could provide good facilities, and in particular was greatly appreciated by crews whose boats were out of the water and not habitable. They had the luxury of spacious quarters, with showers and good messing facilities in considerable contrast to their normally very cramped lives in the boats.

Another event which had a significant if indirect effect on operations was the arrival on Vis of a contingent of American Pioneer Corps troops who built an air strip in the centre of the island. Its completion in nine days enabled a fighter wing to be kept on the island, and also proved invaluable to damaged aircraft returning from bombing raids who could not reach their bases.

Early in May the 24th Flotilla tried a new strategy, taking patrols much further north in an attempt to find torpedo targets. In par-

ticular, there were reports of enemy destroyers (possibly Torpedo Boats) in that area.

On 2 May three boats escorted a commando landing on the island of Plocica. The troops found no opposition so were re-embarked. Then on 11 May, 242 (Holloway), 85 (Hyslop) and 81 (Gilpin) set off for a prolonged patrol 100 miles to the north, refuelling from drums as they expended petrol en route. They arrived at the island of Ist at about 0400, and anchored in a sheltered spot between two wrecked schooners. The next day they sailed before dusk to move as far north as any boats had yet been, off Pesaro. They made no enemy contact, and returned at dawn to spend another night at Ist. The following night, they left to patrol around the islands of Silba and Olib. Having been alerted once again to the possible presence of destroyers, they were hopeful of contacts, but they did not come, and having used their reserves of fuel, they returned wearily to Vis.

The ex-Italian seaplane tender *Miraglia*, Coastal Force Base, Brindisi. (Courtesy, A.T. Robinson)

The harbour at Ist, Dalmatia. (Courtesy, L.C. Reynolds)

They tried again a few days later on 16 May, this time to lie up in a cove on Skarda. It was much less peaceful than the previous week – they had several aircraft scares during the day, although they were not attacked. This position enabled another night's patrol off Pesaro but, just as before, their efforts were fruitless and they were faced with the long flog home.

These descriptions illustrate the fact that Coastal Force patrols here (as in every sphere of operations) were more frequently unrewarded than culminating in action. And even the nights that brought no sightings of enemy ships had their hazards: on the long passage back to base at first light – especially from the northern islands – there were occasional attacks by German fighter aircraft. On 30 May, 84 (Gilpin), 243 (du Boulay) and 674 (Bowyer – until recently CO of 97) were caught and despite an impressive anti-aircraft

barrage, 84 was hit and damaged, and Lt F.A. Gilpin was badly wounded.

On 6 June, two simultaneously released items of momentous significance were broadcast and were received by the men of all Mediterranean flotillas. From that 'different war' in Northern Europe came the news that at last the invasion of Normandy had been launched. It had long been expected and awaited, and once it was confirmed that the beachhead had been successfully established, there was great elation. This was surely the sign that the final phase of the war had been entered. Despite a rather natural attitude among the crews that they had, after all, experienced a whole succession of 'D-Days' – Sicily, Salerno, Anzio, to name a few – there was undoubtedly a huge boost to morale. It was enhanced by the fact that in the Italian campaign the fall of Rome was reported on the same day, following the long delay after Anzio. That too added to a fresh sense of purpose, coming as it did at a time when new boats were arriving, and flotillas were being reorganized.

June was indeed a decisive month for the future of both the flotillas. The 20th, which had been reduced by losses to five boats after the Bari air raid, had just been reinforced by four new Vospers built in the USA. They were a group of boats which had been intended to form a 19th Flotilla, but were instead used to build up the 7th and the 20th. Their officers and crews had first taken over the boats in Algiers in January, and after fitting out moved to Malta in March. There they completed a working-up programme before arriving in the Adriatic, ready for operations, late in May. 289, now with Frenzel in command, also rejoined the flotilla after her damage at Bari. The boats were:

MTB 371 Lt B.G. Syrett
MTB 372 Lt K. Golding
MTB 373 Lt L. Cruise RANVR
MTB 374 Lt R. Keyes RN

Vice Admiral, Malta, inspects the men of the 20th MTB Flotilla. (Courtesy, H.F. Cooper)

At much the same time, an important decision was made about the role of the 24th Flotilla. It had been clear for some time that all nine boats were showing the ravages of two years of operations first in home waters and then in the Mediterranean. They were needing more and more time out of the water or on engine maintenance, and so spent less time on operations. The hulls had taken a pounding, and continual constructional problems of leaks and rotting timber arose so that their reliability was in serious doubt. 226 had already been laid up at Brindisi because of her deteriorating condition, and her crew was being used to man 289 of the 20th Flotilla.

For these reasons the role of the 24th Flotilla was changed. It became a Special Service Flotilla, used to escort commando raids, or to land other small units of LRDG and SBS personnel on occupied coasts. Five of the remaining boats (85, 86, 89, 97 and 243) had to have their torpedo tubes removed and were each fitted with an additional 20-mm Breda gun to increase their fire-power. The other three boats (81, 84 and 242) retained their torpedoes in order to be able to operate as MTBs when required to do so. They were, of course, available to carry out the Special Service missions which were planned while the five boats being stripped of their torpedo tubes were all out of action in Brindisi, Bari and Manfredonia.

All five boats returned for operational use during the last two weeks of July 1944 but, shortly after, there was another change of plan. 81, 86, 89 and 243 were sent to pay off so that their crews could stand by to man the first four new USA-built Vospers of the 28th Flotilla. This left 84, 85, 97 and 242, all now dedicated to the Special Service role, led by Lt Roger Keyes RN. Keyes had served in command of boats of the 7th and 20th Flotillas since 1942.

Four Vospers in dock at Brindisi. (Courtesy, A.T. Robinson)

MTB 81 (Lt E.H.G. Lassen RNZNVR) returning to Komiza with a damaged bow. (Courtesy, L.C. Reynolds)

Meanwhile, the newly reinforced 20th Flotilla was playing its part in the largest of all the raids to be staged from Vis by a combined force of commandos and Partisans. A total of 3,600 troops was landed on Brac on 3 June – 2,500 Partisans, 1,000 British, and 100 Americans. The Germans mounted a spirited response and used the mountainous terrain very effectively. As a result there was bitter fighting, and after three days the assault force had to withdraw, the commandos in particular having suffered grievous losses. The CO of 40 Royal Marine Commando, Lt Col P. Manners DSO was killed, and Lt Col Jack Churchill, the CO of Number 2 Commando, was taken prisoner. A total of 120 were killed and 274 wounded.

The dearth of targets continued, and most of June and July, although certainly not uneventful, produced no results for the 'short' boats. On 23/24 July, however, a mixed group, 297 (Woods) and 372 (Golding) of the 20th, and 81 (Lassen) from the 24th, was patrolling off Korcula when a convoy of five E-boats escorting several supply vessels, including at least one F-lighter, was sighted. As the enemy were up-moon, they closed as quietly as possible but were obviously seen, and as soon as they opened fire they were greeted by a hail of return fire. The first salvo hit 372 in the engine room, and she stopped in her tracks. 81 in close station astern could not avoid her, and collided with her port quarter. 81 went alongside, and took off 372's crew with fire spreading rapidly through the boat. Stoker McLennon was killed in that initial burst of fire, and one crew member swam to a nearby island and was eventually returned to Vis by the Partisans. 372 did not sink, but was finished off the following morning by a Spitfire sent out from Vis to make sure she did not fall into enemy hands.[16]

Claude Holloway in 242 played a protracted solo role in a series of Special Service missions from Vis between 27 July and 3 August. They involved escorting a landing force on the first night, then taking troops to the southerly island of Lagosta, staying overnight and returning early to Vis. The next night she was involved in Operation Decomposed 2, a combined operation on Korcula over two days – an exhausting schedule.

The first major operation in which Roger Keyes led the reconstituted 24th Flotilla was a large commando raid on the mainland of Albania on 28/29 July. 85 (Keyes) and 97 (Tonkin) were involved, and led the Landing Craft, Infantry (LCIs) in which 712 commandos were embarked, towards the beach close to the objective, the garrison of Himare. Two destroyers bombarded before the assault, and at one point the MTBs were called upon to attack a suspected enemy gun position on a nearby promontory. Once the troops were ashore and moving towards Himare, it became obvious that they had met strong opposition, and when they withdrew to the landing beach they brought with them sixty-two casualties. These were loaded aboard the two MTBs – the seriously wounded on the upper decks, and the walking wounded below, tended by doctors and medical orderlies. In good sea conditions, the boats were able to maintain high speed back to Brindisi, and delivered their charges to the ambulances. The decks had to be hosed down, so much blood had been lost by the casualties.

Ashore in Italy, the Army had progressed painstakingly northward since the summer offensive began and by the end of July had taken the major port of Ancona, and cleared it ready for operations.

Ancona, only 60 miles from the northern Dalmatian islands, was earmarked as the next Coastal Force Base, and the mobile base lorries had set off from Manfredonia, following the Army's advance, in mid-June. Eventually, after an epic journey over bad roads, worse diversions and deep fords, it reached Ancona. By 8 August, the base was established and boats began to arrive there to take advantage of its promixity to the patrol areas.

The first to do so, on the day the base opened, moved north from Manfredonia on 7 August. The urgency was caused by the planning of a commando raid in the northern Dalmatians on the following night. The six boats which sailed to Ancona, led by Keyes, were 85, 97 (Tonkin), 242 (Holloway) with 295 (Cassidy) of the 20th, together with two Dog Boats. The early stages of the operation were dogged by breakdowns and bad weather, leading to a postponement and the need for replacements, all provided by the 20th Flotilla. Once again the unreliability of the old boats of the 24th had surfaced.

But once under way, Operation Gradient was completely successful. The objective was to destroy strong points at Ossero on Cherso, the enemy HQ at Neserine on Lussin Piccolo Island, and the swing bridge connecting the two islands. The MTBs carried 85 commandos, 5 collapsible boats, and 25 bicycles, distributed over 5 boats. The three Vospers were now 297 (Woods), 295 (Cassidy) and 371 (Syrett), and they had no problems at all. The Force Commander remained aboard 297 with Keyes, and received continuous reports from each unit ashore. By 0320, all the troops were back aboard with no casualties, the bridge had been blown up, and the telephone exchange at Ossero destroyed. It had been a copybook combined operation.

16   MO10063; Summary of actions at NHB.

The 24th Special Service Flotilla having missed the success of Operation Gradient was conscious that time was running out in the operational life of its boats. The base staff continued to make every effort to get them ready for a series of clandestine operations during August, and Keyes led several from Ancona, Manfredonia and Bari. Each time they carried small parties of LRDG men and successfully put them ashore at a variety of pinpoints, mostly in the more northerly Dalmatian islands. One of the first was particularly important for future operations by Coastal Force craft. On 10 August, 85 and 295 made straight for Ist Island where it had long been known that two sunken schooners provided cover for boats under camouflage alongside. Keyes and four LRDG officers went off in a dinghy to nearby Mulat, where Morgan-Giles hoped to set up a fuelling point for future operations in the north. They established a good relationship with the local Partisans, and in the evening 85 and 295 joined them there to re-embark the recce group, well satisfied with the progress made. This type of mission continued regularly, with 84, 85, 97 and 242 all playing their part.

In the meantime, the 20th, now reinforced by their new boats, were operating from Ancona. They had lost one of their most experienced COs when Lt The Hon Freddie Shore DSC was summoned home on the death of his father, Lord Teignmouth, and instead of returning, was appointed to a flotilla in home waters, joining Owen-Pawson, Ross Campbell and Jeff Aimers, all previously distinguished COs in the Mediterranean. His place was taken by Sub Lt F.E. Dowrick, a long-serving First Lieutenant in the flotilla.

On the night of 17/18 August, Lancaster led three of his boats – 295 (Cassidy) 371 (Syrett) and 297 (Woods) – northward to patrol for the first time in the Gulf of Venice.

It was a calm, moonless, dark night and after an uneventful passage, by midnight the unit was lying stopped off Parenzo inside the convoy route. It was two hours before a cluster of five red stars was seen inshore, and the boats, on silenced engines, closed the range. Suddenly, the lookouts reported a large ship moving south at about 10 knots, distance three quarters of a mile. Lancaster ordered a silent approach, and 295 and 371 moved in to firing position. The target was seen to have a high funnel and raised forecastle and stern, with a balloon flying from the deck. She was estimated at 400-ft length and possibly of 4,000 tons.

At 0154, Cassidy fired 295's two torpedoes at 600 yds, and Syrett in 371 followed with two more at 450 yds. There was a considerable explosion abaft the funnel – possibly a hit in the engine room – and two more under the bridge and for'd well deck. The ship sank immediately. Lancaster, in his report, expressed 'the satisfaction of all that the flotilla's incursion into these waters should be rewarded so soon by such a handsome prize'. He also commended the unhurried deliberation with which the attack was carried out by the COs. It was later learned that the ship was the 5,339-ton *Numidia*.[17]

The flotilla soon had two more sightings of the enemy, on both 21 and 24/25 August. On the first night they fired at two F-lighters but could record no hits. But on the second, a coaster of about 1,000 tons was sunk between Venice and Trieste by one torpedo hit from the two fired by 373 (Lt L. Cruise RANVR). The end was, however, in sight for the 24th Special Service Flotilla, the news having arrived that four boats were being paid off. On 30 August, Lt Keyes handed over as SO to Lt Claude Holloway, the CO of 242, who had just the last four boats 84, 85,

---

17 MO11249; ROP in authors' collection.

Lt L. Cruise RANVR, the CO of MTB 373. (Courtesy, H.F. Cooper)

97 and his own to meet the continuing demands on the Special Service Flotilla until the end of October. Lt Woodhouse took over as CO of 85.

The 20th, with its newer boats, had longer to serve both in the northern Adriatic and in the new situation developing in the Dalmatians as the Germans withdrew northward. However, on the west coast of Italy the 7th Flotilla was entering a new phase of operations, which now demands attention.

CHAPTER 8

THE 7TH, 10TH AND 27TH, 20TH AND 24TH MTB FLOTILLAS

SEPTEMBER 1944 TO MAY 1945

THE 7TH MTB FLOTILLA – WEST COAST OF ITALY

The 7th Flotilla had moved to Leghorn from Bastia on 29 September 1944 with a summer of continuously successful operations in the Gulf of Genoa behind them. Led by Lt A.C.B. Blomfield DSC RN, and with total confidence in the American-built Vospers and Higgins boats they had worked up so carefully in the spring, the officers and crews were experienced and battle-hardened. The PTs of Ron 15 and Ron 22 moved with them, enabling their close cooperation to continue uninterrupted, and Cdr R.A. Allan was still there as CO of the base with Capt N.V. Dickinson RN as SOIS just as he had been in Bastia.

In other respects, though, a combination of circumstances led to a considerable reduction in the number of contacts with the enemy, despite the fact that patrols were still mounted whenever the weather permitted.

Perhaps the most obvious reason was that the length of coastline along which German convoys were required to sail had been greatly reduced, together with the volume of traffic. After the invasion of the South of France, and with the northward advance of the 5th Army, it was only the stretch of the coast of the Gulf of Genoa between Savona and La Spezia (about 70 miles) which had to

be patrolled. Further to this, the numerous losses the enemy had recently suffered at the hands of the 7th and the PTs had led not only to a local shortage of F-lighters but also to an increase in the strength of suitable replacement escorts. In addition, the number of coastal batteries had been increased.

Virtually all this coast had deep water close inshore, so that enemy convoys invariably sailed as tight to the cliffs as they could, to take advantage of the dark background this provided. Once this was realized, plans were devised to counteract it by the use of flares dropped by aircraft between the convoy and the shore as an attack was about to be made.

To try out this idea, an exercise was arranged using a trawler from Leghorn as a target. The trawler had Silas Good (the CO of 423) aboard to observe the effect from an enemy point of view. The trawler left in the afternoon, and the boats and aircraft after dark. Despite their excellent radar, the boats could not find the trawler, and good radio contact with the aircraft revealed that they too could find no trace. Somewhat puzzled, the boats returned to base.

It was not until the following afternoon, when Silas Good had not returned to the base and the trawler had not appeared, that the shore radar plot revealed that the echo from the trawler had been lost from their screen on

An MTB among the bomb damage rubble of Leghorn. (Courtesy, IWM – A 27461)

the previous evening. Boats were immediately despatched and found a Carley float with only a few survivors on board. One of them was Silas Good, and he was able to confirm that the trawler had hit a mine and sunk.

It is not always recognized that although weather and sea conditions in the Mediterranean are generally by no means as severe as those in more northerly waters, local conditions can provide some sudden and very unpleasant experiences for small craft. At this time the flotilla was occasionally being assigned to air-sea rescue duties, searching for airmen who had ditched. The Chief Motor Mechanic of MTB 423, J.L. Lee DSM, recalls one such rescue attempt which nearly ended in tragedy for his boat. The weather was really atrocious, but Silas Good, the CO,

decided the risks were worth taking and set out. By the time they reached the search area, a full gale was blowing with very steep seas. 423 was running with a stern sea, and suddenly she ran along the crest of a giant wave before plunging down into a deep trough and diving into the next wall of water. No one on board had experienced anything like this before. Chief MM Lee was in the engine room, and felt the impact. Water poured down through an open hatch, and at once there were several inches of water above the bilge boards. On deck, the wheelhouse structure had been badly damaged, the door ripped off, and the wave had sucked out the radio. Every compartment below was flooded. The boat was in grave danger of foundering if the engine stopped.

Static electricity sparked between the engines and the deck head, but frantic operation of the bilge pumps, aided by hand bailing, gradually reduced the water level, and the engines were kept going. 423 made her way to a small island and found shelter in a cove with high cliffs around each side. It took two days for the boat to dry out. The electrics all had to be checked, and a tarpaulin lashed over the battered wheelhouse. When the sea abated, she was able to return to base, sadly without ever having found the ditched airmen.

It was not until the end of October that enemy sightings were next made. On 22nd/23rd, a two-boat patrol off Spezia (Johnson in 423 was out as SO, and he was accompanied by PT 563) picked up an echo which turned out to be three F-lighters. The unit tracked the convoy and got into a good torpedo firing position without being detected, and one F-lighter was seen to be hit, and then to blow up and sink. 423 was credited with the hit.

On the following night, Tony Blomfield led a unit in PT 559 with 378 (Ilett) and 420 (Aitchison in temporary command) and two other PTs. In much the same position as the previous night – off Mesco Point near Spezia – they found a barge convoy escorted by one of the German Torpedo Boats (small destroyers) which could heavily outgun the attackers if they were sighted. As a result, Blomfield decided to attack at longer range than usual, using a radar plot. All the torpedoes fired by 378 and one of the PTs failed to secure a hit, and a subsequent closer attack also proved inconclusive.[1]

In the last few days of October, patrols off Sestri Levante were troubled by a coastal battery of two heavy guns. On the first occasion they were encountered, they engendered great respect for their accuracy. Blomfield was leading a large unit of six boats in line ahead, about 2 miles off shore, moving northwest. Suddenly the battery opened fire, and in three salvoes established the range: the first shells were over, the second short, and the third straddled the unit, one shell over and the other short. The SO immediately ordered all boats to turn to seaward, increase speed, and withdraw independently.

Far from shaking off the attention of the battery, it continued to fire with remarkable accuracy, with shells constantly falling close by until the boats were at fully 10 miles range. Binoculars trained on the battery site revealed very clearly vertical streaks when it fired, allowing evasive action to be taken before the shells arrived. Even so, some shells fell close enough to 377 for Aitchison to be able to see them spiralling down into the sea, once throwing up an immense column of water which showered down over 377.

The following morning a small fragment of shell was found on deck, and was sent to Army ballistic experts who later expressed the view that it was from a shell of 230-mm calibre (about 9 in). The Intelligence experts refused to believe that there were guns of this size in the area, but a destroyer was sent to deal with the threat it presented – whatever calibre. To the destroyer captain's surprise, the first salvo from the battery was very close indeed, and he beat a hasty retreat, later finding a large fragment of shell on the foredeck, reinforcing the Army's verdict. Aircraft were sent to locate the battery in daylight without any success, leading to the presumption that it was set within the cliff face.

The weather deteriorated markedly in November, reducing the number of patrols which could be mounted, but on 18/19 November a long action was fought off Sestri Levante. Steve Moore was acting as

1   MO354, MO307; two actions 22/23 and 23/24 October 1944, both ROPs at PRO in ADM 199/268.

MTB 378, a US-built Vosper of the 7th Flotilla, at speed in the Gulf of Genoa. (Courtesy IWM – A 27449)

SO, and was aboard a PT boat, in company with 421 (Raper) and 377 (Aitchison).

An enemy convoy was detected, very close to the shore as usual, and travelling north-west towards Sestri Levante. Thinking that they might be bound for the harbour, Moore increased speed to gain bearing in order to make an attack. But as the approach began, another group of ships was detected steering south-east, so he stood off to await developments. The two convoys met in the bay off Sestri, and both stopped. The run-in was started at once – such a gathering of targets promised a rich reward – but before they were even sighted visually, the whole area was lit by starshell, and heavy gunfire began both from shore and from the ships in the bay. Tracer was flying in all directions and starshell continued to burst overhead.

In fact, there was utter confusion, as the enemy ashore seemed not to be able to distinguish their ships from the MTBs, and were firing at both, while the ships of the convoy were firing at the MTBs and each other. Moore rapidly decided this was a melee to be avoided, and quietly withdrew, leaving the battle to rage by itself – which it did for some time while the MTBs watched from a safe distance.

Eventually the gunfire ceased, the starshell faded and peace was restored. The convoys left the bay and Moore began to track the group which set off south-eastward along the coast, still hugging the shore. Twice more, as bearing was gained, an approach was tried; but each time it was greeted by the barrage of starshell and preventative fire. Indeed, after the last withdrawal, the escorts sent up starshell as the convoy proceeded, and Moore began to feel that the enemy's vigilance was going to succeed. He tried once more, and was greeted by an even heavier hail of fire.

Moore, in the PT, was watching the plot in the charthouse below the bridge conducting operations, and did not realize immediately that the PT had turned away to port and

begun to retire at high speed. But he did know that 377 and 421 had pressed home the attack in the face of the barrage, and fired their four torpedoes. He opened the chart-house door and stepped up on to the bridge, and as soon as he looked towards the convoy he saw an immense explosion and identified the victim as a KT ship (a gun-coaster or 'flak ship') which he estimated at 1,500 tons. He also thought he saw a Vosper at the foot of a great column of white water.

421 and 377 had in fact been so close that they had both experienced a violent concussion when the torpedo hit, and later it was discovered that a shell had passed right through 377's bow.[2]

It was at this stage in the 7th Flotilla's history that a series of major changes took place which resulted in several new appointments. The most significant was the departure of Lt Blomfield, who left to command a Hunt class destroyer. He had led the flotilla with flair and aggression for eighteen months, seen it through the Sicily operations, and then masterminded its transition from the vulnerable, unreliable boats of its early days to the highly tuned new craft which had had so much success throughout 1944. Bob Varvill, too, left to become the SO of the new 27th Flotilla which had joined the 10th in the Aegean. Lt A.H. (Steve) Moore, already prominent as a successful unit leader over many months, became the new SO, and took over command of 419. 'Nick' Ilett moved to command 420, and there were new commands for highly regarded First Lieutenants in the flotilla, Sub Lt G.R. Masters, Sub Lt G.P. James and Sub Lt J.S. Raper.

The next major excitement for the flotilla came on the night of 16/17 December, when Cdr Allan, now appointed as SOIS in place

2 CCF's Report at PRO in ADM 199/268; Rohwer and Hummelchen, *Chronology of the War at Sea*, Vol. 2.

MTB 378 viewed from one of the Higgins boats of the 7th Flotilla, showing her Bofors gun aft. (Courtesy, IWM – A 27448)

of Capt Dickinson, decided to mount another operation in the same mould as his highly successful LCG forays of the spring. He could see that enemy convoys were being more and more heavily escorted, and wanted to increase the range at which attacks on them could be effective. No LCGs were available, so he used five armed trawlers based in Leghorn, with the 7th Flotilla and a strong group of PTs to scout and then make torpedo attacks. Operation Nimrod did find an enemy convoy of F-lighters and R-boats, and the trawlers had a fierce battle with them, sinking one R-boat; but the MTBs and PTs were unsuccessful in finding targets in their area.[3]

January continued the period of bad weather, and patrols were only possible on

five nights out of thirty-one. The first of these, on 10/11th brought success. The unit employed was a single MTB – 422 (Bullwinkle) – with a PT, and after tracking an enemy convoy, torpedoes were fired at 1,500 yds by radar without visual sighting, and Bullwinkle obtained hits on F-lighters with each of his torpedoes in a classic undetected attack.

A few nights later, on 15/16 January, this success was repeated, this time by one of the new COs, Sub Lt G.P. James, in 378. His accompanying PT fired another long-range attack by radar, but missed. James went in to 700 yds under fire from five F-lighters, and secured one hit. It was an advantage that the shore batteries fired starshell which lit the targets rather than the attackers. [4]

---

3 MO2937; CCF's Report; Summary in list of actions.

4 For both 10/11 and 15/16 January: MO3629; Summaries in list of recorded actions.

Sub Lt G.P.H. James, CO of MTB 378. (Courtesy, IWM – A 27452)

The weather improved considerably in February, so that patrols were possible on 50 per cent of the nights: but the number of convoys had decreased so markedly that there were few enemy sightings. On 7/8th, however, Bullwinkle in 422 was again able to achieve success when, with two PTs, a convoy of two merchant ships was detected about to enter the port of Savona. One of the PTs fired at 1,600 yds by radar and secured a hit on a merchant vessel. Bullwinkle closed – still unobserved – to 700 yds and fired both torpedoes at the second vessel as it slowed at the harbour entrance. Both hit. For his successful attacks in January and February, Bullwinkle was awarded the DSC.[5]

March was only really significant for the 7th Flotilla when they were involved as a scouting force in connection with another of Cdr Allan's LCG operations. Steve Moore took 377 and 378 to the north-west of the main force, and, finding a target which could clearly not be reached by the LCGs, received permission to attack independently. The standard tracking procedure was followed, and the attack launched a few miles south-east of Sestri Levante. One F-lighter was hit by 377, which came under heavy and accurate fire and began to take in water after near-misses from heavy shells.[6]

The pace of the war was quite definitely slowing down during April 1945, with the Germans despatching far fewer convoys. The

5   MO4120; summary in list; *Seedie's List of Coastal Forces Awards*.

6   MO5070; summary in list of actions.

7th Flotilla maintained its patrols throughout the month and fired its last torpedoes on 11/12 April when a convoy close inshore was found, with – unusually – an escort force well out to seaward. Moore in 422, with 423 and 377, mounted a skilful attack after manoeuvring between the two groups. Just when it seemed that surprise had been achieved, starshell lit the whole area and the boats came under fire from both sides. All six torpedoes were fired, and three explosions seen.

As soon as hostilities ceased, the boats sailed to Malta, and it was not long before those officers and men who had served throughout the flotilla's commission were sent back to Britain. Those that remained manned the boats until the US Navy was ready to receive them back, and they were handed over at Palermo. The nine boats had carried out 122 patrols since the flotilla was re-formed and returned to operations in April 1944, in 40 of which they had engaged the enemy. The official record credited them with 31 enemy ships definitely sunk, and 19 others hit and damaged. Even more astonishing was the fact that the crews had suffered no casualties, and none of the boats had received damage which could not be repaired.

It was a proud record, highlighting the progression from 1942, with the problems of boat unreliability when the flotilla was based in Alexandria, and its renaissance during 1943 in the waters off Tunisia and then during the Sicilian campaign, to culminate in the extraordinary successes off the west coast of Italy and particularly in the Gulf of Genoa. It demonstrated clearly that the officers and

An MTB at speed. (Courtesy, IWM – A 27462)

Cdr R.A. Allan says goodbye to officers of the 7th and 27th Flotillas. (Courtesy, IWM – A 29010)

men under the leadership of Robert Hennessy, Tony Blomfield and Steve Moore, once given boats and equipment of quality had by their skill and aggression been able to achieve results rarely matched over such a long period. (Note 10, Appendix 1)

THE 10TH/27TH MTB FLOTILLAS – THE AEGEAN

By September 1944, the 10th Flotilla had effectively been reduced to only three boats in fully operational state, and had for many months been awaiting reinforcement. When it came, it was in fact too late to be able to make a major contribution to the war in the Aegean, as the Germans had already begun to reduce their garrisons and withdraw from the southern islands. The period when a higher intensity of patrols might have brought more opportunities of enemy contacts had passed.

Nevertheless, the arrival of the 27th Flotilla of brand-new Vosper boats built in the USA, fitted with the latest SO radar with PPI (Plan Position Indicator) which had been so effective in the PT boats and enabled both the 7th Flotilla and the Dog Boats on the west coast of Italy to detect targets, was warmly welcomed by the long-serving veterans of the 10th.

The first four boats, completed two months before the second group left the Robert Jacob Yard on City Island, New York, had arrived in Alexandria at the end of July. Their completion and handing over had been carefully supervised by the flotilla's Engineer Officer Lt (E) W. Aldridge RN, who had previously gained considerable experience at Lowestoft, and proved to be a great asset.

These first four boats were numbered 396 to 399, and were quickly crewed up, commissioned, and put through a rigorous and valuable working-up period before sailing north in September. There they joined the three remaining boats of the 10th (307, 309 and 315) at the newly established Coastal

Force Base on the island of Khios, north-west of Samos.

To lead this group of seven boats, a new Senior Officer had been appointed, whose name has already become familiar in this narrative. Lt Robert Varvill DSC RNVR had been active in MTBs since May 1940, when as a midshipman he had briefly joined MTB 04 of the 1st Flotilla soon after it had returned from the Mediterranean through France. For nearly two years he served with the legendary Lt H.L. (Harpy) Lloyd RN in both 04 and 34 in operations from Felixstowe and Dover. His first command was of MTB 78, which joined the 7th Flotilla in Alexandria. Together they worked their way along the North African coast and took a major part in the operations throughout the Tunisian and Sicily campaigns before moving to Maddalena and Bastia late in 1943. His exploits with the 7th in the Gulf of Genoa both in 78 and then in 421 had earned him a DSC and the respect of all, and it was no surprise when he became Senior Officer of the combined 10th/27th Flotilla.

He decided to take over command of 309, one of the three Elco boats of the 10th, which had a very experienced crew, and long service among the Aegean islands. His available boats at Khios in September were MTBs 307 (Lt L.H. Blaxell DSC), 309 (his own), 315 (Lt L.V. Strong DSC), 396 (Lt J.D. Whipp SANF,V), 397 (Sub Lt R.J. Lubbock), 398 (Sub Lt B.F. Farmer) and 399 (Sub Lt D.W. Lea).

It was not long before the new flotilla was plunged into action. At 0915 on 9 October, the base at Khios received a signal from HM Submarine *Vivid*, which was patrolling in the vicinity. It reported the position of an enemy convoy with details of its course and speed. The three boats in harbour were 307, 397 and 399, and they were brought to immediate notice and were ordered to intercept and engage the enemy – a daylight attack which emphasized the perceived significance of this convoy.

Blaxell, as the most senior and by far the most experienced of the COs, was SO for the operation, and when they slipped at 1035 their first task was to gain an advantageous intercepting position. Working on the information provided by *Vivid*, it was calculated that the convoy would pass close to the westward of Psara Island, several miles off the north-west corner of Khios. Signals were exchanged with *Vivid*, and they set off at 25 knots.

The masts of the convoy were first sighted to port at 1346, and as they closed they could see that it consisted of one tanker, two armed F-lighters, and two trawlers. There was no doubt that the much heavier armament of the F-lighters would make a daylight attack very hazardous, so a fast approach and accurate torpedo firing would be essential.

Blaxell took his unit inshore of the convoy and gained bearing on it, but in so doing, with the weather worsening, the MTBs began pounding into a steep head sea. They were obviously sighted by the ships of the convoy, which altered course 30 degrees to port to increase the range. But by 1410 the unit had drawn ahead of the enemy, which was now in line ahead with the tanker in the van. At 1430 the boats had reached a favourable position to begin an attack, and ran in towards the enemy, now with a beam sea and the sun in an advantageous position. At 1436 they were ready to turn in for the firing bearing, and as they did so the convoy turned towards them. Blaxell at once ordered an independent attack and designated a target for each boat. They dispersed, and as they did so the escorts opened heavy fire with 75-mm and multiple 20-mm cannons, some bow-mounted. At first, the aim was high and wide, but as the boats closed it improved. As the range decreased, the tanker turned away, and Roger Lubbock in 397 was presented with an ideal opportunity to fire her torpedoes. At 900 yds, with the gunfire heavy, he fired and

immediately turned away and made smoke. At 1449 the other boats saw the tanker blow up and disappear very quickly below the surface, leaving a huge pall of black smoke which rose to 1,000 ft. It seemed probable she had been carrying ammunition as well as fuel.

307 and 399 continued to attack the escorts, and miraculously suffered no hits. One of the trawlers was seen to founder off Psara Island and one of the F-lighters was clearly hit by a torpedo.

All three boats returned to Khios without major damage or casualties, having carried out a highly successful daylight attack on a heavily defended convoy. Their feat was recognized later with a batch of awards which included a DSC for Roger Lubbock and a DSM for his coxswain L/Sea Taylor.[7]

Almost immediately after this action two of the 27th were sent across to the western side of the Aegean into the Northern Sporades islands, to bottle up enemy shipping in the Gulf of Volus, about 70 miles due north of Athens. Intelligence was reporting the presence of about fifty enemy ships trapped there which might attempt a break-out.

A few days later a signal was received at Khios that these two boats were running short of fuel, and 307 (Blaxell) with one of the 27th was despatched to the island of Skopelos, each with 800 gallons of 100 octane petrol in 40-gallon drums on the upper deck. Before leaving Khios, Blaxell was briefed that Force H, consisting of the escort carrier *Emperor*, the cruiser *Black Prince*, and a destroyer escort group, were patrolling in the area.

The two boats made the run to Skopelos without incident, except that soon after

7   MO13409 and MO1027; ROPs at PRO in ADM 199/268 and 269; Blaxell, *Through the Hawse Pipe*; *Seedie's List of Coastal Forces Awards*.

midnight they sighted *Emperor* and then the other ships on the horizon, and were astonished that they were not challenged despite the fact that had they been E-boats they were in an ideal position to make a torpedo attack.

They found 398 and 399 at the head of a bay, and they secured outside each to transfer their cargo of drums. Almost at once there was a roar of approaching aircraft, and four single-engined fighters appeared over the hilltops astern from the direction of the entrance to the bay. They were Hellcats with British markings and obviously came from the escort carrier *Emperor*.

Blaxell didn't like the look of their approach formation which looked suspiciously like an attack, and first ordered his telegraphist to fire the recognition signal – a two star cartridge from the Very pistol – and then a crash start on the engines. The lines of the two outboard boats were cast off and they roared astern. The inboard pair had no chance to move, and in swept the four fighters with their eight 0.5-in machine guns already firing. They both had to put helm on as they went astern, and presented a broad-side target. At once, the first burst punctured the drums on the upper deck of 307 and petrol spurted out all over the deck.

The fighters then turned their attention to the two boats alongside, and they were badly hit. It was a nightmare. Blaxell did all he could – he ran his boat towards the beach, put out a kedge anchor to hold her steady, and speedily ditched the leaking drums and washed down the deck. Any further hits with everything saturated in petrol would have been fatal. Mercifully, the fighters seemed to have realized their error, and disappeared from view. But the damage had been done. Two men had been killed and seven wounded.

Blaxell sent signals requesting medical attention, and shortly after, a Walrus seaplane appeared with a Surgeon Lieutenant to tend the wounded, followed later by the arrival of *Black Prince*. Blaxell went aboard, was received with great courtesy and sympathy, and supplied with shells to act as sinkers for the burial of the dead. The service was held aboard 398, and with great solemnity the two canvas-wrapped bodies were committed to the deep in age-old Naval tradition.

307 (on two engines) and 397 made their way to Khios and 307 was sent on to Alexandria for repairs.[8]

This was effectively the last operation of note by the 10th/27th Flotilla in the Aegean, as the Germans evacuated the Greek mainland and the Aegean islands completely during November. The flotilla therefore returned to Alexandria to effect any necessary repairs, and stood by for a call elsewhere.

It did not come until January, when Varvill received orders to sail the flotilla via Malta, Messina and Ischia to Leghorn, where he had operated so successfully the previous autumn. Blaxell, after fifteen months in the flotilla, handed over 307 to Lt J.D. Whipp, a South African, and took passage in his old boat to Ischia to join a destroyer in Naples.

In Leghorn they teamed up with the 7th Flotilla. The volume of German shipping in the Gulf of Genoa had reduced to a trickle, and although they patrolled, their main hazard came from the vigilant shore batteries. Just as the 7th had only one significant action in this period, the 10th/27th, too, despite their SO radar sets, were able to find nothing. But on 15/16 April a unit (396, 307 and 397) received an aircraft report of a convoy in their area. They soon found it on radar and tracked it. Aircraft dropped flares to silhouette the enemy, but only succeeded in blinding the MTBs and revealing their presence. They attacked under fire, and two boats despatched three torpedoes at under 1,000 yds,

8   Blaxell, *Through the Hawse Pipe*; Summary in list.

VE Day in Leghorn from the CF Base. (Courtesy, Peter Shorer)

and saw two big explosions, sinking a fast armed merchant ship and one other of the convoy.[9]

There was great relief in the flotilla that the short period of operations in this area had yielded at least one success, albeit in the last Coastal Force action in the Gulf of Genoa.

In June 1945, with the war in Europe over, the nine boats were sent to Malta and paid off. The crews were dispersed and the officers and men who had been with the 10th in the Mediterranean for two years or more were sent back to Britain. The boats were placed in reserve, but in September and October were sailed to Palermo and returned to the US Navy.

So ended the 10th Flotilla's distinguished record in the Mediterranean. It had operated longer and in a greater variety of battle zones and conditions than any other in Coastal

Forces as a continuing unit. The scars of Crete and Tobruk, of Tunisia, Sicily and the Aegean, had not deflected the flotilla with its succeeding generations of new craft and personnel, and they had maintained a great spirit to the very end.

THE SPECIAL SERVICE 24TH MTB FLOTILLA IN THE ADRIATIC

The 24th Flotilla was conscious that when September began, only two months would elapse before the boats would be paid off and the officers and men transferred to the boats of the 28th Flotilla which were about to leave the American yard where they had just been completed.

Claude Holloway, the newly appointed SO, had only four boats left in commission, and was determined to keep them running and to carry out any Special Service mission to which they were assigned. MTBs 84, 85, 97

9   MO5516; Summary in list.

and 242 were all prone to breakdown, but had high quality and experienced crews and determined COs.

They carried out seven operations in September, and one remarkable aspect was the variety of objectives and pinpoints they covered. Almost every one was in a different area, ranging from the northern Yugoslavian mainland and the Istrian peninsula to points much further south such as Dubrovnik and Albania. This entailed lengthy passages between missions, as some were from Brindisi, although most were from the rapidly developing base at Ancona, where they were now joined by the 20th Flotilla and a number of Dog Boats.

The first two operations, simultaneously mounted on 5 September to different locations, both involved landing and picking up either individuals or groups of SBS and LRDG personnel. On each occasion, too, they were denied the luxury of an unobserved approach, which in these operations was always the intention, because they were identified and engaged by shore batteries either through vigilance or possibly through radar. Owen Woodhouse, newly in command of 85, whose pinpoint was in a southerly position, showed great coolness in zig-zagging out of range of the batteries and using calcium flares as decoys before creeping in to carry out the pick-up successfully after seeing the recognition signal from shore.

Claude Holloway in 242 had made the passage to Brindisi and then across to Dubrovnik. He too met heavy shelling, but still got in to the assigned position and picked up a group of infiltrated troops to return them to Bari as required.

On 11 September, 242 and 97 took an LRDG officer across from Ancona to land him on the Yugoslav coast. On their passage over they met and sank two fishing vessels and took seventeen Italian prisoners before carrying out their main task.

The same two boats successfully landed other agents three nights later on the Istrian coast. The last weeks of September were more disappointing, when 242 was frustrated first by engine trouble and then by appalling weather and had to return to base. Holloway made a final effort, this time to pick up RAF personnel from the Yugoslav mainland coast, but patrolled off the pinpoint for three hours without receiving any contact from shore before returning to Bari.

Both 85 and 242 were experiencing more and more defects, but when 85 returned from an engine overhaul at the end of September, she set off on the 26th with 373 of the 20th Flotilla across the northern Adriatic to land personnel. They were at first diverted by the appearance of three E-boats which obstructed their approach. They tried again the following night, and although there was again enemy shipping near the pinpoint, they were able to land the LRDG and their supplies in Vignole Bay by a well-rehearsed method: 85 went in first to unload while 373 guarded the entrance to the bay, and then roles were reversed and the operation completed.

The Special Service role of the 24th Flotilla finally came to an end in mid-October in two missions made additionally hazardous by bad weather. Both were to the Albanian coast from Brindisi. The first, on 12/13th, involved 242 and 97 taking off a number of Kurdistanis, Albanians, Italians and Germans from the Gulf of Drin. During the pick-up the conditions were entirely unsuitable, with heavy waves rolling in to a shelving beach. 242 was caught by one enormous wave, touched bottom, and only just managed to regain the safety of deeper water. In the attempt, three of the would-be passengers drowned in the heavy surf.

The last mission of all almost ended in tragedy. 85 and 97 set off from Bari in worsening weather to carry two Albanian politicians and a seven-man LRDG group to Albania. As they had tried two days before and been forced by bad weather to return, they were determined to carry out what was obviously regarded as an important assignment. They had almost reached the Albanian coast when at 2258, MTB 85's engines cut out and could not be restarted. In the rough seas a leak in the engine room had opened up, causing a 'short' in the main electrical circuits, with the engines stuck in ahead gear. Water in the bilges was rising.

Lt R.P. Tonkin in 97 tried to take 85 in tow astern, but when this proved impossible, he attempted a tow alongside to no avail, both boats being in danger of seriously damaging each other. The next try was to tow 85 astern, but stern first. With a full gale blowing from the south-east, and 85 unable to assist, this too proved hazardous, but Tonkin and his men got a wire hawser across, and for two hours made 4 knots to westward before the tow parted. Over the next four hours it parted six times, and everyone was exhausted. When daylight came, the scene aboard 85 was indescribable. All the passengers and many of the crew were violently seasick as the boat pitched and rolled, and with the gale gaining strength, towing was no longer possible. They had tried pumping oil on the water with no success. All the towing gear was now unusable.

Woodhouse, determined to save his boat, hoisted a rudimentary sail made from a bale of pusser's canvas from the very short mast. With this puny assistance and hard work on the wheel, it was just possible to control the drift, keeping it between West and N70W, making 1–2 knots and very very slowly increasing the distance from the Albanian coast. 85 drifted all that day and all the next night, with 97 standing loyally by. A signal was received saying that ML 577 had been despatched to tow 85 back, so a burst of tracer was fired every fifteen minutes to assist her search, with no success.

With daybreak, the weather abated a little, and at 0540 the Flower class corvette K O4 (HMS *Saxifrage*) was sighted and offered to tow 85 back to Brindisi – an offer which was very gratefully accepted. She also took off the passengers who had been through an ordeal they would never forget.[10]

Within two weeks, the battered flotilla – or rather the three boats still in commission – was ordered to pay off, to grant leave to the crews, and then to report to the base at Ischia to await their new boats to form the second division of the 28th MTB Flotilla.

THE 20TH MTB FLOTILLA IN THE ADRIATIC

By the beginning of September 1944, 'Butch' Lancaster had seven boats in his flotilla – three of the new Vospers and four of the older design. They established their main base in Ancona, and were available to carry out normal offensive operations either in the northern Adriatic if targets were available, or in the Dalmatians if called upon by SNOVIS (Lt Cdr Morgan-Giles).

The enemy were now busy laying surface mines in the northern Adriatic, and this new strategy was to inflict grievous blows to the Dog Boats in the area over the months ahead. Patrols were organized to catch the E-boats which were so engaged. On 7 September, 289 (Frenzel) and 298 (Dowrick) were patrolling off Rimini and encountered two E-boats thought to be mine-laying. They immediately attacked with guns. They were driven off, and damage and casualties were inflicted on both sides.

Shortly after, on 10 September, Peter Hyslop in 374 with 295 (Cassidy) were seeking targets off the Istrian peninsula when they found and captured a 300-ton barge, took the crew prisoner and scuttled the barge.

10 Eyewitness accounts by C.R. Holloway DSC and H.F. Cooper.

MTBs 371 and 287 of the 20th Flotilla aground on Levrera Island. MGB 658 attempts to pull them off. (Courtesy, L.C. Reynolds)

In the Dalmatian islands, a major change was taking place. The Germans had evacuated most of the southern islands, and, immediately, Allied and Partisan forces landed on Hvar and Brac in early September. This left Vis too far south of the significant operational area, and Morgan-Giles had decided to move northward in his headquarters ship, LCH 282. The LCH was an adapted LCI(L) with sophisticated radar and communications equipment. After reconnaissance by the Special Service Flotilla and Partisan intelligence sources, it was decided to base the LCH at Ist, and she moved up on 20 October. Almost at once the 20th Flotilla moved from Ancona to Ist, and the next day 371 (Syrett) was sent northward to the island of Rab to bring off a group of LRDG officers and local officials.

The immediate problem for Morgan-Giles was the knowledge that larger enemy units (possibly destroyers but more likely to be corvettes or Torpedo Boats) were roaming the area, having come down from Pola and Rijeka. Morgan-Giles decided to help track them down by taking LCH 282 to operate north of Olib Island where they had previously been sighted. The Vospers sighted them and fired torpedoes at them, but missed.

SNOVIS's next move was to request the presence of destroyers to seek out and destroy these ships. The two Hunts HMS *Wheatland* and *Avon Vale* arrived on 1 November, and Operation Exterminate was mounted on the same night. The two Hunts were joined by MTBs 295, 287, 374 and by three Dog Boats, 633, 638 and 642. The Coastal Force boats were deployed to the north of Rab, covering probable passage routes the enemy ships might take. At 1950 the MTBs reported that they had sighted two destroyers on a southerly course. Twenty minutes later the Hunts opened fire and set the enemy ships on fire before sinking them. They closed to pick up survivors, but broke off when their radar detected another target. It was promptly engaged and both their first salvoes struck the enemy's bridge, killing all the officers and

The SO, Lt Cdr J.D. Lancaster (holding papers), with officers of the 20th Flotilla on the quayside at Ancona. (Courtesy, W. Holden)

wrecking the fire control system. She was doomed, and sank soon after. It was established that the enemy ships were the German Torpedo Boat TA 20, formerly the Italian *Audace* and the two submarine chasers UJ202 and UJ208, which were the former Italian corvettes *Melpomene* and *Springarda*.[11]

The 20th suffered an unfortunate loss on 24 November when, returning from patrol in the extreme north, 287 (Reed), 371 (Syrett) and 298 (Dowrick) were making their way back to Ist through thick fog when the first two boats went aground on the very low island of Levrera. Dowrick, who had avoided the same fate, rushed off to get help, leaving the two helpless craft stranded in full view of enemy personnel on the mainland and with the very real danger of air attack. Three Dog Boats arrived to try to get them off, but could not budge them, so they were abandoned, all secret gear removed or destroyed, and the boats destroyed by close range gunfire from the Dogs.[12]

January was a busy month in the northern Adriatic. All enemy seaworthy craft were bottled up in the Gulf of Venice, but there was little movement, and although patrols were mounted on 29 of the 31 days in the month, only one contact was made. On 4/5 January, 374 (Hyslop) with 298 attacked a small convoy in bad visibility as it was entering Parenzo harbour, but no hits were claimed.

Although patrols continued, there were no more actions for the 20th Flotilla, and in due course they were sailed to Malta to pay off.

Their place as the main strike force of 'short' boats in the region was taken by the 28th MTB Flotilla, whose first division arrived in Ancona at the end of January. (Note 11, Appendix 1)

11 ROP at PRO in ADM 199/268.

12 Eyewitness accounts by B. Syrett (371) and L.C. Reynolds (658).

CHAPTER 9

THE 28TH MTB FLOTILLA: THE NORTHERN ADRIATIC

JANUARY TO MAY 1945

The officers and men of the old Vospers of the 24th Flotilla had waited for some weeks to hear their fate, having been told as early as July 1944 that they were to take over the boats due to arrive from the USA to form the 28th MTB Flotilla.

The first four boats arrived in Naples in October, were towed across to Ischia and almost at once were taken over by their new crews and commissioned into the Royal Navy. The background to their arrival is a saga which demonstrates the long-drawn-out process of acquisition, production and completion, despite the urgency of war and the efficiency of the American production line. It had begun with a directive dated 20 January 1943 which ensured the inclusion of sixteen Vospers of British design in the US Navy's Building Programme for 1943. They were initially given hull numbers PT 384 to 399, and on 15 March 1943 the order was placed with Robert Jacob Inc, City Island, New York, and they were designated MTBs 396 to 411. Of these, the first eight – 396 to 403 – formed the 27th MTB Flotilla, already referred to in Chapter 8. The last eight – 404 to 411 – formed the 28th MTB Flotilla. (Note 12, Appendix 1)

They were laid down between 18 October 1943 and 26 January 1944, and eventually completed between 22 July and 30 October 1944.

During their construction, the motor mechanics who were to be responsible for their engines were sent to Detroit to take a course in the latest Packard engine design. Each boat would be fitted with three 1250-b.h.p. petrol engines, and their maximum speed was calculated to reach around 50 knots before the armament was installed.

The motor mechanics accompanied the boats when they were despatched across the Atlantic on cradles on the upper decks of American freighters. There was great excitement in Ischia as the new COs and crews inspected their long-awaited boats, and they were thrilled with the quality and the technically advanced equipment they carried. Engine trials over the measured mile in the Gulf of Gaeta revealed speeds between 48 and 51 knots before the armament was fitted. It was the radar which excited most attention and anticipation. Each boat had the latest PPI (Plan Position Indicator) set with its continuous scan screen and high definition giving long-range echoes. The two 21-in torpedo tubes would carry the Mark VIII torpedoes with CCR pistols enabling detonation within the magnetic field of the target, rather than only on contact. As the explosion normally took place beneath the target's keel, the damage it caused was far greater than that which resulted from impact.

All had a single Oerlikon for'd, and twin

Three boats of the 28th Flotilla on passage. (Courtesy, H.F. Cooper)

0.5-in amidships in a power-operated turret, which was later replaced by a hand-operated twin Oerlikon.

The COs of the first four boats (which formed the first division) were:

404   Lt E. Lassen DSC RNZNVR, from MTB 81
405   Lt F. Scoble RNR from MTB 226
406   Sub Lt J.E.H. Collins MBE from MTB 84
407   Lt H. du Boulay from MTB 243

The Senior Officer of the new flotilla was not appointed until 22 November 1944, and to the surprise of the COs was not chosen from any of the 'short' boat flotillas. Lt Charles Jerram DSC RNVR was a very experienced Coastal Forces officer. He had

been at Dunkirk, and spent the years between 1940 and 1942 in MLs in the Channel, where he won the first of his DSCs. He had then been appointed to the Dog Boat MTB 667, arriving in the Mediterranean in May 1943 and serving with distinction in the 33rd and 60th Flotillas in Sicily, on the west coast of Italy and in the Dalmatian islands from Vis. He had just returned from the Aegean, where 667 had been active in operations during the reoccupation of Greece.

He reported to CCF at Malta, and when all four boats had completed their fitting out they joined him, to carry out a working-up period at HMS *Gregale*. He and his crews made very good use of this period, and concentrated particularly on maximizing the value of the radar and the first-class torpedo armament. They found the PPI radar to be every bit as effective as they had hoped, and embarked on intensive training in plotting and attacking target ships made available to them by both night and day. They soon found that their exercise torpedoes (with dummy heads) were passing beneath targets, proving the accuracy of the plotting methods. The navigators and radar operators learned to work in close harmony, and were able to pass accurate information to the COs both for the approach and the attack. By the end of January 1945 they were ready to put their skills into practice, and moved up to Ancona, arriving in the first week of February.

Meanwhile, the second division, in a programme some eight weeks behind the first division, had completed their fitting out in Ischia and began working up in Malta just as operations started from Ancona. Jerram appointed Claude Holloway – fresh from his period as SO of the Special Service Flotilla of the 24th – as leader of the second division, with the responsibility of overseeing their training period in Malta.

The boats were allocated as follows:

408 Lt R.P. Tonkin from MTB 97
409 Lt C.R. Holloway (Divisional Leader) from MTB 242
410 Lt A.O. Woodhouse RNZNVR from MTB 85
411 Lt B.G. Syrett from MTB 371 of the 20th Flotilla

The 28th Flotilla berthed at HMS *Gregale*, Malta. (Courtesy, A.T. Robinson)

Left to right: Lt C.J. Jerram (SO 28th), Lt Franklin, Lt C.R. Holloway (Division Leader), Sub Lt N. Evans. (Courtesy, H.F. Cooper)

Woodhouse's First Lieutenant was Sub Lt H.F. Cooper, the co-author of this history who had served in the 24th Flotilla from June 1944.

On 5 February 1945, Jerram led the flotilla's first patrol northward from Ancona. It was the start of a momentous three months in the history of Coastal Forces. The strategic situation was propitious, so long as the enemy were able to send ships along the coast at the head of the Adriatic. The end of the war was clearly in sight. The German Army was in retreat on every front, and the Allies were converging on Berlin from every direction. In the Mediterranean they were retreating up both the east and the west coasts of Italy and through northern Yugoslavia towards Trieste. Enemy shipping only ran between Venice and Trieste, and along the Istrian peninsula. The Allied Air Force ruled

the skies during the day, and the Italian resistance movement increased its activities, taking over the hinterland area between Venice and Trieste. The only method of moving supplies available to the enemy was by the sea route during the hours of darkness.

That first patrol on 5/6 February was carried out by 406 (Collins, with the SO aboard), 405 (Scoble) and 407 (du Boulay). Their orders were to patrol between Parenzo and Umago, on the coast of the Istrian peninsula south of Trieste. They left Ancona at 1430, and by 2119, having reached the patrol line and slowly moved southward, they picked up their first radar echo. The plot soon established that a target was moving northward at 6 knots towards the small port of Daila. They closed, but there was thick fog and no visual sighting was made. Jerram ordered Collins to fire torpedoes by radar at

Lt H. ('Duke') du Boulay, CO of MTB 407. (Courtesy, H.F. Cooper)

1,000 yds, but no hit was observed, and the target was plotted entering Daila.[1]

Although this proved to be an unsuccessful patrol, there were two beneficial outcomes. When Jerram's report was received, the RAF sent Beaufighters over Daila and sank a 100-ton schooner by rockets. And secondly, the plotting routine was improved. Jerram reasoned that the plotting craft should be stopped while taking bearings, and this became standard procedure, resulting in more precise ranges and bearings and establishing the enemy course and speed more accurately.

The lesson was well learned. Two days later, on 7/8 February, they repeated this patrol, to the same area and with only one change – 404, Lassen's boat, replacing 405. This time they stopped one mile off shore, and after first tracking two small echoes, a

much larger blip was picked up moving southward towards the unit at about 2 miles range. Almost at once, the target was sighted on the radar bearing, and appeared to be a corvette moving at about 12 knots. The unit had begun to deploy into firing position when the target opened fire with a heavy-calibre gun and turned abruptly towards the coast. Jerram ordered all three boats to fire independently when their sights were on, and at 2014 they did so. Shortly after, two hits were observed on the target, and there was a loud explosion and a red glow, followed by the sight of the corvette sinking. The flotilla was to learn that the screen provided excellent confirmation of a sinking when a hitherto bright and positive echo simultaneously disappeared.

Jerram considered that Lassen in 404 had obtained the two hits, as 406 had one misfire, and du Boulay in 407 seemed to have fired a little after the others. But the battle was not over, as the three boats were under fire from several directions, the shells appearing to be from an 88-mm gun and quadruple Oerlikons. They withdrew speedily to the west, when radar revealed a large new echo closing from the north. 406's torpedoman reported his misfired torpedo ready to use, and Jerram told Collins to stand by to attack the new target. But 407 had been hit below the water line for'd and was making water rapidly. She was ordered to withdraw to a rendezvous point to the west, and 406 moved in to attack. This time, at greater range, it was possible to plot accurately and to fire at 1,700 yds on a radar bearing. All the training paid off: the single torpedo hit and a double explosion was heard.

Rendezvous was made with the other boats, and du Boulay reported that the flooding in 407 had been reduced by fixing a tingle over the hole and working the pumps hard. He thought that at a higher speed on return, the bow would lift high enough out of

1   MO4248.

the water to prevent further flooding, so passage back to Ancona was achieved very rapidly, with 407 setting the pace.

As the boats left the scene of the action, radar held the echo of the ship that had been hit. It was still there, stopped, at 25 miles, clearly a very large vessel. When Jerram made his verbal report, it was decided to send two Dog Boats to Parenzo later that day to see whether the damaged ship could be finished off. Jerram accompanied them, and they arrived off Parenzo in daylight, passing floating debris at the site of the action. They sighted the ship in Parenzo harbour, and once again the RAF was sent to finish her off. It was later learned that she was the 6,300-ton *Pluto*, formerly the British merchantman SS *Dalesman*.[2]

The 28th were fortunate to find that weather conditions were remarkably calm for February – not always the case in the Adriatic at this time of the year. Night after night there were smooth seas and excellent visibility.

This was the case on 12/13 February, when for the third time Jerram led a patrol, this time off Caorle, a point midway between Venice and Trieste. He was aboard 404 (Lassen) with 405 (Scoble) and 407 (du Boulay), whose damaged hull had been speedily repaired by the base shipwrights. They reached a point about 5 miles south of Caorle Tower at 1750, and cut engines. The tower provided an accurate fix from which any plot could begin with certainty. All three boats kept radar watch, but it was only 405's set which picked up a stationary echo at 6 miles, just to the east of their patrol area. By 2330 nothing else had appeared on the screens, so Jerram decided to investigate 405's echo.

A slow approach on one engine brought the unit to a position where the echo was dead ahead at 5 miles, and all three boats

now had it on screen. As they got closer, it grew appreciably larger, and when it was sighted at 2,500 yds it could be seen to be a large merchant vessel of about 4,000 tons with two masts and a funnel amidships. Jerram took 404 in very quietly and slowly, followed at extreme visibility range by the other two boats. At a range of 2,000 yds, he ordered Lassen to fire his torpedoes on a radar bearing with the ship's head directly pointing at the centre point of the target's hull. Both torpedoes hit, and explosions were seen both for'd and aft. The funnel was seen to fly into the air. After a quiet, unobserved withdrawal, radar showed the echo was still held on the screen, so Jerram returned to investigate, and at 0110 was able to see the remains of the target, with its stern protruding vertically. As they watched, it slid below the surface.

Intelligence later revealed that this was the SS *Mediceo*, a 5,000-ton ship which had been operating between Venice and Trieste. She had been built in Glasgow in 1915 and was owned by an Italian shipping company based in Genoa.[3]

The weather deteriorated for a short period at this stage and provided an opportunity for further refinement of the tactical lessons learned in the flotilla's first three attacks. Without doubt the advantages provided by early detection of targets by the excellent radar were the basis for success, but had to be used to the full by sophisticated plotting.

The decision was made, in the light of experience, to incorporate several steps into the approach to the patrol area. First, to stop at a point about 5 miles to seaward of the known shipping route along which any attack was expected to be made. This was particularly appropriate for the low coastline and shallow sea bordering the patrol areas off

2   MO4123.

3   MO5381.

MTB 405 (Lt F. Scoble RNR). (Courtesy, G.M. Hudson)

Caorle. The distance allowed more time for plotting once an echo was picked up, to establish an accurate target course and speed, and thus to plan the angle of approach to the firing position. Now there was confidence in the true running of torpedoes, firing on radar bearings even without visual sighting became viable, and had the great advantage that if the attacking MTB was not sighted by the enemy, there was no probability of a change of course.

All these tactics were to lead to some astonishing results in the weeks ahead. The navigators became proficient at plotting, and the radar operators increasingly efficient at their interpretation of the information on their screens.

The flotilla's next contact with the enemy came on 9 March, when Jerram in 406 (Collins) with 405 (Scoble) and 407 (du Boulay) patrolled once again off the Istrian coast. By 1900 they were 10 miles off Parenzo, and course was set on silenced engines to the agreed plotting point 5 miles off Port Daila. With engines cut, and all three boats on radar watch, it was not long before the first echo was detected, at 5 miles to the north-east, clearly a large ship moving southward. After only a short period of observation, the course and speed were accurately resolved, and Jerram was able to move his unit silently into an attacking position at about 2 miles range. By then the screen revealed one large and three small echoes. By 2145 all boats could see the target, and they had closed to 2,000 yds. Jerram ordered 406 to fire first and turn away to port, followed by 405 and 407 – a zonal attack in view of the size of the target. All six torpedoes got safely away, but soon after 407 had fired there were two explosions on the track to the target, followed by another major explosion, after which the large echo disappeared from the radar screen. Clearly the target had been sunk; but the only explanation of the two earlier explosions seemed to be that 407's two torpedoes had run together, collided, and 'countermined' each other some 400 yds after leaving the tubes.

Jerram estimated the destroyed merchant ship to have been of about 4,000 tons, and concluded that both 406's torpedoes had hit. He was well satisfied that the zonal attack had been successful, and that the plotting had led to the precision of approach he was seeking. In his report he made one further tactical recommendation: in future, he suggested, only one of the unit's radar sets should operate while the boats lay cut; communication was easy by megaphone if they were within hailing distance. This would eliminate a tendency for two or more sets to give a distinct 'grass' effect upon the others and thus make the echoes less clear. He also believed that the sets gave better results if they were not run continuously: a rest every hour or so seemed to improve performance.[4]

The flotilla was out again on the night of 15/16 March, with Jerram once more aboard 406 (Collins), and 404 (Lassen) and 407 (du Boulay) in company. This time the patrol area was midway along the northern coast of the Adriatic, between Caorle and Tagliamento. They were at their agreed plotting position 5 miles offshore just east of Caorle, by 2020. Several complications arose: first an echo which proved to be false, and then, when a true echo was found of a target moving westward at 8 knots towards Venice, the need

for care as the patrol briefing had referred to the fact that MGB 191 would be carrying out a clandestine operation west of Caorle that night. She was a 78-ft Higgins boat of the 45th MGB Flotilla, manned by former African Coast Flotilla crews.

Jerram followed the target westward on a parallel course to seaward, and was soon certain it was not MGB 191. By 2240 it was necessary to increase speed to gain bearing on the target, and at the same time 407 reported that her screen showed a second echo astern of the first. Even though he was anxious not to reveal the unit's presence by displaying too obvious a bow wave or wake, Jerram found it necessary to increase speed to 14 knots to gain bearing.

Sub Lt J.E.H. ('Tim') Collins, CO of MTB 406. (Courtesy, H.F. Cooper)

4   MO6308.

MTB 406 (Sub Lt J.E.H. Collins) off Malta. (Courtesy, H.F. Cooper)

Throughout this long stalking manoeuvre, the navigator of 406, Sub Lt Norman Evans RNVR, had been keeping a meticulous plot with minute by minute adjustments of the bearing and range and ship's head. The targets, now at 4,000 yds, could still not be seen even through binoculars. Jerram reasoned that they could not be large, and might not merit torpedo attack, so ordered all boats to be ready for a gun attack. By 2326 the convoy was nearing the entrance to the swept channel into Venice, and radar picked up a stationary echo there, probably a harbour defence craft. Jerram decided he could not delay his attack any longer. The unit was in a good position, so he turned in towards the enemy and reduced speed to 12 knots, closing to 2,000 yds, then slightly altering course for the attack and reducing to 6 knots. Suddenly at 2345 the first target was sighted and revealed as an F-lighter. When Collins reported that he had it in his bridge sight, he ordered him to fire a

single torpedo, and away it went at a range of 1,300 yds. At the same time, the radar operator reported more echoes, and Jerram saw several more F-lighters astern of the first, in close formation.

He took the unit to starboard to give each boat a clear sight of the group of targets, and ordered all the boats to fire when their sights were on. Lassen fired at the first, du Boulay fired singly at the next two, and Collins with his remaining torpedo at the last. As soon as their torpedoes had gone, each boat disengaged to starboard at 12 knots to the south. Almost simultaneously, there were six explosions in succession commencing with the leading F-lighter, and columns of water rose 200 ft into the air. All this happened with no return fire from the targets, although at 2359 a shell burst overhead, causing no damage to the nearest boat, 407. It presumably came from the harbour defence craft, although no one was looking in that direction.

Jerram stopped the unit, and watched the last of five echoes disappear from the radar screen. As it did so, a final violent explosion occurred, and seemed to be the last F-lighter blowing up. Considering that the targets had not been fully revealed until the last few minutes, it was a remarkable performance. They were back at Ancona by 0455, and had time to discuss the detail of the attack. After hearing from his COs, Jerram considered that Collins in 406 had sunk two F-lighters, du Boulay in 407 also two, and Lassen in 404 had sunk the remaining target, both his torpedoes hitting the vessel.

Capt Stevens, CCF (Mediterranean), in passing on the action report to C-in-C, commented:

The results of this action are proof enough of the quality of the performance. Indeed this attack may well be described as a classic of 'short' MTB tactics. This is due entirely to the unit being well equipped and well trained, and to the skill, patience and determination of the Senior Officer, Lt C.J. Jerram DSC RNVR, to whom the highest credit is due.[5]

Two days later, the boats were out again on the night of 17/18 March, to the same patrol area off Caorle. This time, Jerram gave 406 (Collins and his crew) a night in harbour, and took passage in 405 (Scoble) with 404 (Lassen) and 407 (du Boulay). They were reminded of the danger of mines, which had already claimed many Dog Boats in this area, when on the passage north they sighted a mine and when they closed, could see snag lines attached to it. 405 sank it with gunfire. By 1957, they had reached their plotting position 4½ miles south of Caorle light.

They only had to wait an hour before 407 – on radar watch – reported an echo 5,800 yds to the west, moving eastward. Jerram decided

to increase the distance offshore by steering south for ten minutes until he felt he had a better range for plotting accurately. He turned east on a parallel course, and followed the tactic which had been so successful on previous patrols. Once precise course and speed had been established, he increased speed to gain bearing, and eventually turned towards the target and reduced speed to 8 knots until the enemy was sighted and identified as a convoy escorted by at least one F-lighter of the heavily armed variety.

At 2139, Scoble was ordered to fire 405's torpedoes. In doing so, the starboard tube emitted a brilliant cordite flash, disclosing the presence of the unit to the enemy. Almost immediately, starshell burst overhead followed by 20-mm, 40-mm and 88-mm shells from the convoy. 404 fired her torpedoes, but as they were launched, explosions were heard and seen as 405's target – the escorting F-lighter – was hit. Jerram decided that the situation merited a speedy withdrawal and disengaged southward at high speed, the boats laying smoke as they went. The enemy's fire continued, but was too high and thus ineffective.

After a while, Jerram turned north again to give 407 a chance to fire her torpedoes. However, a persistent heavy rain squall reduced visibility to barely 50 yds, and Jerram decided to return to Ancona. As they left, at 2226, a large explosion was heard by all three boats' crews, and a dull red glow was observed in the direction of the convoy. There seemed no doubt that Scoble's two torpedoes had hit and sunk the F-lighter.[6]

It was now nearing the end of March, and the first four boats of the 28th Flotilla had been actively engaged on offensive patrols since early in February. In those few weeks, they had fought 6 actions, fired 26 torpedoes, hit with 15 of them, sinking or heavily

5   MO6308.

6   MO6305; ROP at PRO in ADM 199/181.

damaging 10 vessels including 3 merchant vessels, 1 corvette, and 6 F-lighters. The SO and 407 (du Boulay) had been involved in all six actions. There had been not one casualty from the crews, and only 407 had suffered damage, which had been quickly repaired.

It was now the turn of the second division, which had arrived in Ancona. Jerram sent the first division down to Manfredonia for engine maintenance, and the crews were given a few days' leave, one watch at a time, in a local rest camp.

He himself remained in Ancona to settle in the second division, to acquaint them with the patrol conditions and pass on the lessons learned. He had evolved his own method of conserving his energy: he would rest in the wardroom of the leading boat until the patrol area was reached, and would then be summoned to the bridge to take control of the operation.

The division had its first contact with the enemy on 9 April, when Jerram in 410 (Lt A.O. Woodhouse RNZNVR) with 411 (Lt B.G. Syrett) and 408 (Lt R.P. Tonkin) carried out a patrol off Caorle Point. It was a fine night with slight haze, calm sea and, without moon, a visibility of nearly 2 miles. On the way north they came across a small sailing craft. There were six Italian deserters aboard, enthusiastically waving a white flag. Their vessel was sunk and two of the prisoners taken aboard each boat.

At 2147, the unit reached its plotting point 5 miles south of Caorle Point, and stopped with engines cut. It was only twelve minutes later that 410's radar operator reported an echo at 13.5 miles to the westward. Over the next forty minutes, the navigator (Sub Lt H.F. Cooper, co-author of this history) plotted the constant flow of information from the radar and established the target's course as 053 degrees at 8 knots.

During the early part of the plotting operation, the echo was lost on all three

screens for about fifteen minutes. When they picked up the blip again the enemy was on the same course and at the same speed as previously recorded and worked out. It was later established that during the time of the disappearance of the echo, enemy aircraft had dropped a large quantity of strips of silver foil ('chaff') over the area. This had been responsible for the loss of the blip on the radar screens, and was an indication that the enemy now realized that the MTBs were equipped with the latest radar detection equipment.

At 2241, Jerram ordered the boats to start up and begin to close at 8 knots on silenced engines, until at 2259 the unit could see the target and identify it as the first of three F-lighters. The boats took up attack position in echelon to starboard and stood by to fire torpedoes. As they closed further, they could see three more F-lighters in a second line. At 2307, still unobserved, the three boats fired in turn, and astonishingly all three suffered a misfire in one torpedo, leaving each boat with a torpedo still to fire. But at 2309 came a loud explosion, clearly a hit on one of the F-lighters. The boats turned away to port and withdrew slowly and quietly to the south before stopping to regroup a few minutes later.

Jerram decided to attack a second time, his unit having three torpedoes left, and five F-lighters still in the convoy. The MTBs were still apparently unobserved. Once again careful plotting enabled a precise approach, involving an increase of speed to gain bearing: by 2355 the slower approach on the attack bearing could begin, and once again the three boats moved in undetected until at 2,000 yds 410 fired her remaining torpedo. It seemed there was a jinx on this attack: 410's tube misfired again causing a ten-second delay before the discharge: she missed astern. 411 also misfired with no discharge. 408 redeemed the position as her torpedo

Lt R.P. Tonkin (right) CO MTB 408, with his First Lieutenant, Sub Lt E.M. Newsome. (Courtesy, H.F. Cooper)

Lt C.R. Holloway, the Divisional Leader in the 28th and later the SO. MTB 409, which he commanded, is in the background. (Courtesy, H.F. Cooper)

fired perfectly and secured a hit on the leading F-lighter.

As the unit withdrew, the remaining enemy ships at last seemed to realize an attack had taken place, but their fire was so spasmodic and wildly directed that they clearly had no true idea of the direction from which it had come. Efforts were made to enable 411 to fire her second torpedo, but without avail, so the unit returned to Ancona. Despite some embarrassment at the torpedo failures, the second division had opened their account with two hits out of five, and no damage or casualties.

The conclusion was reached afterwards that if all six torpedoes had left their tubes at the initial attack the toll of enemy vessels sunk could well have been three or four. The approach and firing courses were ideal, and

all three boats were in the optimum position to ensure successful strikes.[7]

Two days later, on 11 April, they had another chance when for the first time the divisional leader, Lt C.R. Holloway, led a unit to the same patrol area. He was in his own boat, 409, with 408 and 411. However this operation was dogged by ill fortune. First, 411 had to return with engine trouble, so 409 and 408 proceeded alone and reached the plotting position at 2202. And then, when an echo was detected and plotted, and the approach begun, the whole process suddenly became complicated by the appearance of two more echoes. One showed ships steering straight for the unit from dead ahead, and the other a group approaching from the opposite direction. It seemed that three groups were converging simultaneously on the two boats. Holloway decided to mount an immediate attack on the first targets, which had been revealed as three F-lighters. He had less time than he had wished to position the unit for this attack, but at 0050 both boats fired their two torpedoes. Once again each suffered a misfire, and sadly neither of the running torpedoes hit. Holloway turned away and watched the enemy ships open fire on each other. By 0108, the radar showed ships steering westward towards Venice, and Holloway moved in to attack again praying that the remaining torpedoes would not misfire. By this time it was far more difficult to get into a good firing position, and although both fired, neither secured a hit. There was great disappointment, but undoubtedly circumstances had not been favourable.[8]

But they were to have their morale restored on the very next night (12/13 April), when the same two boats were out again, but with Jerram leading in 410 (Woodhouse). The

7   MO6362.
8   MO6360.

beaten track to Caorle Light was followed again, but cruising speed had to be reduced from 30 knots to 18 when 410 had an oil leak from one engine. They reached patrol plotting position at 2201.

In the way to which Jerram had become accustomed, an echo was detected to the west at 3.7 miles. As it seemed to be steering too close to the unit, he manoeuvred to gain more distance and time, and after twenty minutes was in a better position for Sub Lt Cooper to provide an accurate course and speed, enabling Jerram to move into a more advantageous attack position. It was this patience and professionalism that was Jerram's hallmark. Once again it led to success. As they closed, by 2354 six long dark shapes could be discerned – two main bunches, with a single ship some way astern. Carrying out their well rehearsed approach, the boats moved into echelon to starboard. Just before midnight, with the convoy now south of Tagliamento, 410 fired, swinging round to aim at the second group (two F-lighters close together) before disengaging to port, while 409 and 408 fired at the leading group. Shortly after, two explosions in the second group signified two hits by 410, and both blips disappeared from the screen. A few seconds later, three more 'crumps' and a great cloud of smoke came from the leading group. All three F-lighters in that group had been sunk, and the only echo on the screen was the ship astern, which now came to life. She pumped starshell over the unit, which had been creeping southward at 6 knots to avoid detection. When the boats were starkly illuminated, the enemy opened up with the full array of 20-mm, 40-mm and 88-mm guns.

A feature of this particular action was that although the CO of 410 had fired his torpedoes with the aid of his bridge sighting equipment, the bearing of the echo on the radar screen registered the correct director

angle for the target's course and speed and the torpedo speed. The torpedoes could have been successfully fired by either method.

Jerram did not hang around. The three boats surged ahead at high speed and in open order to provide less of a target, and were soon out of range. By 0520 they were alongside at Ancona, with the second division's morale boosted dramatically as they matched the performance of the first division on 15 March by sinking five ships with six torpedoes.[9]

The war in the Mediterranean was now grinding to a halt, with the enemy forces retreating on all fronts. In the Adriatic, they had lost so many ships, and the need for movement of supplies had been so reduced, that most of the shipping left was holed up in the few remaining ports available to them. Recently only F-lighters had been venturing out to sea at night.

There were, however, two last operations by the 28th Flotilla, both on 16/17 April when for the first time units from both divisions were despatched on patrol simultaneously, to two different areas. The first of these concerned 409 (Claude Holloway leading the unit) with two PT gunboats of the Royal Yugoslav Navy, 217 and 207. Their destination was Umago, on the Istrian coast south of Trieste.

They reached their patrol position at 2200 and the two Yugoslav boats came alongside 409, which had set radar watch. An hour later radar contact was established at over 7,000 yds to the north. Holloway moved his unit ahead of the convoy to a position close inshore, invisible against the dark coastline. As the range closed, the convoy was revealed as three or more F-lighters and five barges each clearly illuminated in silhouette by bright moonlight. Holloway told the Yugoslav boats to wait in

9 MO6220.

position while he carried out a torpedo attack on the last F-lighter in line. He fired at 2,200 yds, and had the satisfaction of seeing both torpedoes hit, for'd and aft on the same target. There were two large explosions followed by exploding ammunition.

By 2345 he was back with the Yugoslav boats, and decided to allow them to make a gun attack on the convoy from astern. For eight minutes the two boats engaged the enemy closely and hits were seen on four enemy craft, including an E/R boat which failed to reply. The enemy's other return fire was heavy and accurate, and 207 suffered damage and casualties. As they disengaged to

the north-west, no signals were received, and Holloway lost contact with them. They had in fact returned to Ancona at best speed to secure medical aid for their casualties. 409 followed them and reached Ancona at 0640. The convoy had been seen to turn northward and retrace its steps towards Umago or Trieste.[10]

Meanwhile, shortly after Holloway had set out, Jerram led 406 (Collins), 404 (Lassen), 405 (Scoble) and 408 (Tonkin) for a final patrol off the favoured position of Caorle Point. It was still daylight when they were

10 MO6622.

An F-lighter off Ancona, May 1945. (Courtesy, H.F. Cooper)

20 miles to the south, so Jerram reduced speed and stopped for a time before moving in to the plotting position. The first echo was received at 14 miles range, so Jerram moved his unit northward to close, and starshell was fired by the enemy, lighting up the area to the east. There had been evidence that the F-lighters had been taking up positions in line abreast rather than in line ahead, to counteract the beam attacks which had been so successful against them. The COs had discussed this and Jerram had planned that if they met this formation, he would be prepared to use a different kind of tactic. He had deliberately taken the fourth boat on patrol to enable two attacks, each with two boats.

This was precisely what they met on this occasion. After the moon had set, the convoy, now approaching Tagliamento, was sighted and seen to consist of two lines of F-lighters in line abreast.

The first attack – by 406 and 405 – was from a poor beam position at the head of the convoy. But they deliberately attracted attention, rather like gunboat diversionary tactics earlier in Coastal Forces operations, which allowed 404 and 408 to fire their torpedoes undetected at the rear end of the convoy, at the much closer range of 1,200 yds. Although the beam torpedoes missed, both 404 and 408 scored hits on an F-lighter. Both pairs disengaged to the south and rejoined 7 miles from the coast, while the radar watched the remaining enemy units increase speed and round Tagliamento Point. Jerram returned to the scene of the action to search for wreckage and survivors, but nothing was found.[11]

Although there were no more offensive patrols by the 28th, some of the boats assisted in cloak-and-dagger landings and pick-ups. Early in May seven boats of the

The 'Jolly Roger' of the 28th Flotilla, with twenty-three torpedo hits recorded. (Courtesy, H.F. Cooper)

flotilla set out with a group of Dog Boats for Tagliamento Bay where the remains of the enemy naval forces in the Adriatic were gathering. There was no clear idea what their attitude would be – whether they might fight or scuttle or surrender – and Jerram wanted to be there, in the area of his flotilla's greatest triumphs. But the weather deteriorated so much that the Vospers were forced to return to Ancona; the Dog Boats had a very rough passage, but carried out their delicate diplomatic mission with distinction.

The last act of the drama was played out two days later off Ancona. Very early in the morning a flotilla of E-boats from Trieste suddenly appeared off the harbour, each flying a white flag. The signal station alerted the base and boats of the 28th together with the Dog Boat 658 rushed out to assess the situation. The E-boats were loaded to the gunwales with German Army personnel, and the distinguished E-boat commander who led them – Capt Wupperman – had come to plead for permission to be allowed to return to Trieste to bring out more troops. But he was not allowed to do so, and the E-boats were led into Ancona, the boats were surrendered, and the men led off to prisoner-

One of the 28th joins MGB 658 to investigate E-boats surrendering off Ancona. (Courtesy, L.C. Reynolds)

of-war camps. It was a proud symbolic end to operations for the Coastal Forces boats and their crews.[12]

The 28th Flotilla had not quite finished its duties. On VE day, 8 May, the eight boats sailed for Malta via Brindisi and Catania, arriving at HMS *Gregale* on 12 May. Almost at once Jerram and six of the COs were returned to Britain. They had all seen long service in the Mediterranean and were among the first due for home leave.

12 Pope, *Flag 4*; Reynolds, *Gunboat 658*; Reynolds, *Dog Boats at War*.

The flotilla was quickly reorganized. Claude Holloway was appointed SO, and commands went to five of the First Lieutenants who had played a major part in the success of the flotilla as navigators. They were kept busy during June and July 1945, engaged in exercises with all the major ships of the Royal Navy passing through Malta en route to the Far East where the Pacific war was still raging. When the atom bombs were dropped and Japan surrendered, the war was truly over. It was a time for celebrations, but when these were over there was a tedious period until, in November, the boats were sent on their final passage to Palermo where they were handed back to the US Navy.

It is doubtful whether in any operational period of only twelve weeks, any flotilla in Coastal Forces had ever made such an impact. They had made 11 attacks on the enemy and fired 51 torpedoes, 26 of which hit their targets – an astonishing proportion. And this was achieved without suffering a single casualty, and with damage to only one boat which was repaired within two days. Not only was their equipment of top quality, but they were brilliantly led by an outstanding Senior Officer, and had Commanding Officers and crews who were all experienced from years together in the 24th Flotilla.

Shortly after the end of the war, the London Gazette published lists of awards to men of the flotilla to mark their achievements in this remarkable series of actions.

Jerram received a DSO and a Bar to his DSC; Lassen a Bar to the DSC; Collins first a DSC then a Bar; and Scoble, du Boulay, Tonkin, Holloway and Woodhouse DSCs. There were also DSMs for six coxswains and torpedomen of the flotilla, and a number were mentioned in despatches.[13]

On this high note, the story of the Mediterranean MTBs ends. The 28th had completed the task begun by the 10th Flotilla in Alexandria in 1941, and continued by the 15th and 27th, the 7th and 8th, the 20th, and the 24th over four years in which they had harried the enemy and covered all the war regions of the Mediterranean.

13 *Seedie's List of Coastal Forces Awards.*

Four of the 28th Flotilla at HMS *Gregale*, Malta, dressed overall for VJ day. (Courtesy, A.T. Robinson)

CHAPTER 10

A SUPPLEMENTARY HISTORY OF THE 2ND MTB FLOTILLA IN HONG KONG

1938–41

To help the aim of producing a definitive history of all the British-operated MTBs of the Second World War, it is necessary to conclude this volume by adding a supplementary chapter to cover those 'short' boat flotillas which were sent to parts of the world other than the Mediterranean.

There were in fact four such flotillas. The 2nd Flotilla of British Power Boats shipped to Hong Kong in 1938 were of the same design as the pre-war 1st Flotilla in the Mediterranean, and their activities from the outbreak of war to the abrupt end to their operations in December 1941 make a fascinating story.

The 16th (SO: Lt Cdr K.A. Cradock-Hartopp RN) and the 17th (SO: Lt Cdr E.F. Hamilton-Meikle RN), both of US-built Vospers, were based in India and Ceylon from 1943 to 1944. The 19th (SO: Lt H.A. Barbary RN) of Canadian-built British Power Boats, served in the West Indies from 1942 to 1943.

The two flotillas in Indian waters were despatched to their distant area of operations for strategic reasons which proved in retrospect to have had no ultimate justification. Whether their mere presence was a factor leading to their lack of involvement is difficult to assess, but the many experienced officers and senior ratings removed from the opportunities of frequent enemy contacts in home or Mediterranean waters were certainly glad to return after long periods away.

The 19th, in the West Indies, was intended for anti-submarine and rescue duties, and had no torpedoes but additional depth charges – of little value as they had no submarine detection equipment. In their eight-month existence, however, they did rescue 600 survivors from torpedoed ships.

These three flotillas had no lack of activity during their commissions, but their battles were against the elements in these tropical waters, and against problems of supply in their remote and sometimes primitive bases. None had any direct contact with the enemy, and for this reason the remainder of this chapter is devoted entirely to the story of the 2nd Flotilla in Hong Kong.

The composition of the flotilla and the background to the construction of its boats are largely covered in Chapter 1. MTBs 07 to 12 had all the initial problems encountered by the 1st Flotilla in Malta, although it had been possible for some lessons to be learned in regard to operations in hot climates. Little detail is known of the personnel who manned

The 17th MTB Flotilla on exercises off Madras, India. (Courtesy, E. Robertson)

MTB 335 of the 19th MTB Flotilla in the West Indies. Canadian BPBs without tubes. (Courtesy, G.M. Hudson)

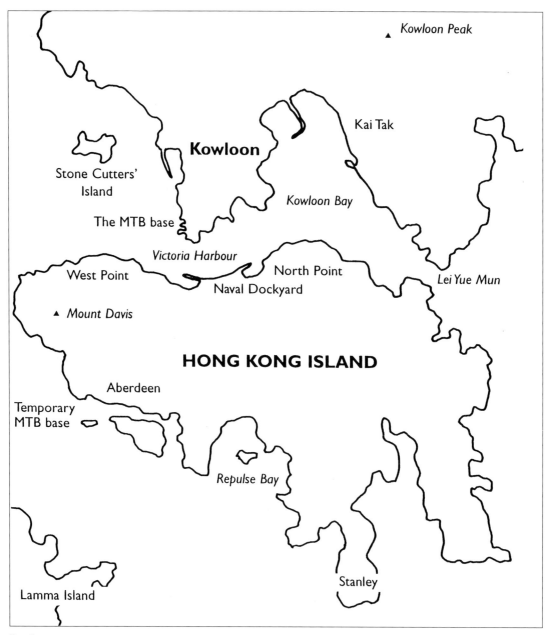

Hong Kong.

the boats in the pre-war period, although there is a direct link with the Mediterranean MTBs in that Lt R.A.M. Hennessy RN, who later became SO of the 7th Flotilla, was CO of MTB 07 from September 1938 to March 1940. (Note 13, Appendix 1)

In addition to the six British Power Boats, two Thornycroft 55-ft boats with stepped hulls – MTBs 26 and 27 – brought the flotilla up to eight in number in September 1939. They had been ordered by the Chinese Navy and completed in September 1938.

MTB 09 of the 2nd MTB Flotilla at Hong Kong. (Courtesy, A. Kennedy)

It is fortunate that there is one first-hand account of the flotilla's activities from October 1939 onward, written by Alexander Kennedy at the end of the war and privately published many years later. Kennedy, in common with many other reservists, was called up in August 1939 as a Sub Lieutenant RNVR, one of a small group from the Clyde RNVR, and immediately found himself bound for the Far East, appointed to the 2nd MTB Flotilla.

When he arrived at Hong Kong, he was allocated initially as First Lieutenant to Lt Cdr D.G. Clark RN, the SO who had led the flotilla since its formation in 1938. Kennedy was part of a complete reorganization programme which saw the first group of COs – all RN – replaced by the end of 1939 by officers from the Royal Hong Kong NVR and the RNVR.

From that time on, the boats were commanded as follows:

MTB 07	Lt R.R. Ashby RHKNVR (from MTB 26, April 1940)
MTB 08	Lt L.D. Kilbee RHKNVR (from MTB 27, April 1940)
MTB 09	Lt A. Kennedy RNVR
MTB 10	Lt Cdr D.G. Clark RN (SO)
MTB 11	Lt C.J. Collingwood RN (from MTB 27)
MTB 12	1. Sub Lt W.E. Richards RNVR
	2. Lt J.B. Colls RHKNVR
MTB 26	1. Lt R.R.W. Ashby RHKNVR (to 07, April 1940)
	2. Lt D.W. Wagstaff RHKNVR
MTB 27	1. Lt C.J. Collingwood RN (to MTB 11)
	2. Lt L.D. Kilbee RHKNVR (to MTB 08)
	3. Lt T.M. Parsons RHKNVR

The majority of these officers, and their crews, were to remain with their boats in

Hong Kong right through to the end of 1941.[1] Almost from the first month of the war, the normally strong naval presence in the Colony began to disperse. The cruisers, destroyers and submarines of the China squadron moved westward to the Mediterranean or back to their home ports, and soon three small destroyers, some Canton River gunboats and the MTBs of the 2nd Flotilla represented the only offensive forces in the area.

In the autumn of 1939 the political situation in the Colony showed little evidence of the 'war back home', or indeed of the Sino-Japanese war near at hand, in which Japan had established many troops in southern China, and was in nominal control of the country north of Hong Kong. But in the minds of the Naval authorities was the thought that that situation had arisen from a landing only 50 miles from Hong Kong, in Bias Bay.

A minefield had been laid in the approaches to the port, and one of the duties of the MTBs was to patrol its limits and the swept channel. Mines frequently broke loose from their moorings and caused alarm along the shore line.

Lt Cdr Clark (known inevitably to his officers as 'Nobby') was energetic and efficient, and had the respect and confidence of all. He put his inexperienced Reserve officers through a course of intensive training. The flotilla's duties were largely perceived as defensive, but they did also include the possibility of attacking large vessels with their only potent weapons – the torpedoes. In common with the boats of the 1st Flotilla and indeed those of the early Thornycrofts of the 10th Flotilla in the Mediterranean, their torpedoes were stern launched and required the acquisition of considerable skill in aiming,

and then evading, the weapon as it overtook the boat.

Early in April 1940 the lull in Europe was shattered by the Nazi attack on Norway, followed rapidly by the fall of the Low Countries and then of France. Tension in Hong Kong increased rapidly, with an all-pervading sense of isolation. Japan occupied Indo-China, and the evacuation of women and children from the Colony began.

In August, Japan signed a Tripartite Pact with Germany and Italy, and although the Japanese made no warlike gestures in the area at this stage, the apprehension and expectation of escalation was now clearly established. As Hong Kong was still an international port, Japan's merchant ships still visited, and plied their trade on the Canton River. There were also many Japanese businessmen and their families in the Colony, and these facts indicated that there should be some warning of an invasion, if or when it came.

This state of mounting unease continued into 1941. Lt Cdr Clark had been required for General Service, and his place as SO was taken by a much older officer, Lt Cdr G.H. Gandy RN, recalled from retirement, and with a seniority dating back to 1924 – indicative of his age. It was not until November, however, that things began to change rapidly. Two infantry battalions from Canada arrived to strengthen the garrison. By 6 December, most ships had left the harbour, and the Volunteer Defence Corps had been mobilized.

Suddenly, early in the morning of 8 December, a signal was received by the MTBs alongside their base (and indeed by all the naval vessels in harbour) ordering 'Raise steam' – interpreted by the boats as 'Prepare to sail as ordered'. This involved the recall of officers from lodgings ashore, loading of guns and a final check on engine readiness. At 0630 a second signal was received: 'Commence hostilities against Japan'. Those four

1 Kennedy, *Hong Kong Full Circle*.

long-expected words created a new tension, and yet at the same time resolved the uncertainties of two years, and strangely settled the atmosphere. But no further orders were received.

It was not for several hours that the news broke that a large Japanese convoy was approaching Malaya, and then – even more astonishing – that Pearl Harbor had been attacked and the United States Navy in the Pacific crippled in one fell swoop. Clearly there was a coordinated and wide-ranging programme of aggression. Within minutes it came even nearer home. Explosions were heard from the direction of the airport on Kowloon Bay, and the air-raid sirens woke the citizens of Hong Kong to the realization that the aggression included them.

The available boats of the flotilla were based at the Kowloon Naval Yard, where their torpedo store and engine workshop were nearby. The first step – planned in advance – was to disperse the boats so that they would not be caught alongside, close together, in a raid. Orders were soon received that stores were to be moved to Aberdeen, and that the boats were also to transfer there. This was accomplished during the day between 1000 and 1600, the last MTB escorting the stores lighter and base staff. MTB 12 was under repair and was left in Hong Kong Dockyard, but rejoined the flotilla a day or two later.

Bombing of all locations continued, and the boats were busily engaged in patrolling and ferrying troops and staff officers. These duties meant that there was no time for sleep, and after two days and nights there was urgent need for some respite – but none came.

The air of impending doom was not relieved by the news from elsewhere. They heard – and had difficulty believing the unbelievable – that both the *Prince of Wales* and *Repulse* had been sunk in an air attack off Malaya. All around were merchant ships

either bombed or scuttled and lying heeled over at grotesque angles.

The installations at Kowloon – including the fuel storage tanks – were being demolished, and that created more problems for the boats running low in petrol. A lighter moored near Aberdeen (albeit with a defective pump) became the only source, the petrol being transferred by bucket-loads – literally bailing her out. But hour after hour the ferrying of troops from Kowloon to the island continued until it was completed by 0300 on 12 December.

The air raids came in rapid succession throughout the day, mostly kept high by the Army's anti-aircraft guns. In the early evening, just as the boats were ready to sail to various patrol locations, a single Japanese plane flew in low from the west. At last there was a chance for the boats to use their light machine guns, and as the guns were manned ready, the boats did not hesitate and poured tracer into the fuselage as it passed over. It was reported as plunging into the sea to the east. A small incident, but it was immensely important to flotilla morale. It was necessary, because during the night the boats were sent to evacuate a regiment of Indian troops – the Rajputs – who having fought gallantly for a week had withdrawn to the east of Kowloon Bay. It was pitch-black at 0600 when four MTBs began to evacuate troops – as many as fifty to a boat packed tight and sitting or lying with amazing discipline and calmness on deck – to the destroyer *Thracian* lying as close inshore as she could venture. Dawn began to break and there was no time to lose, but incredibly there was no Japanese barrage from their position on the ridge above. By 0715 several hundred men had been delivered to the *Thracian* and by 1000 they were disembarked and the evacuation had been completed without loss.

Despite another night with no sleep, the next task, during a lull in the bombing, was

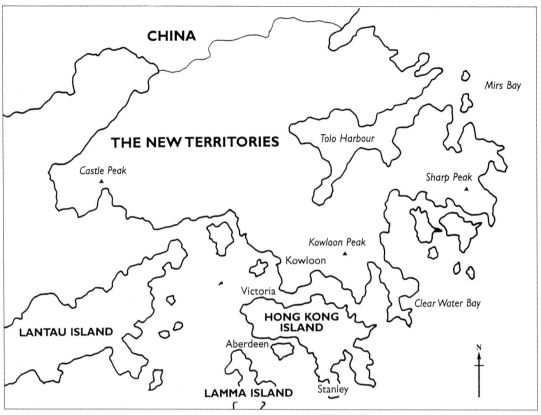

Hong Kong and the New Territories.

to give a quick coat of paint in a mixture of dark camouflage colours to cover the existing pale blue/grey hulls and decks. It was considered that this would reduce vulnerability from air attack rather than the lighter shade suitable at sea in the tropics. That night, patrols continued but with no incidents, but on the 15th, after a day of heavy bombing, four of the flotilla were sent in two pairs to the westward. MTBs 10 (Gandy) and 27 (Parsons), and then 11 (Collingwood) and 12 (Colls) were each in turn engaged by two large vessels so close inshore that they could not be identified, holding both units in their searchlights and firing 3-in and lighter calibre guns at the MTBs quite accurately. MTB 11, 12 and 27 all fired torpedoes but no results were seen: possibly the water had been too

shallow. However, a Tokyo newspaper report was later found which stated that Japanese naval forces had been engaged in Hong Kong waters and suffered losses.

On 16 December there was a day of heavy bombing during which boats' crews and base personnel were involved in fire fighting and assisting casualties, but still mounted patrols. Much the same pattern was repeated on 17th and 18th, with the situation getting more and more desperate as communications systems and ability to defend against air attack through lack of ammunition weakened.

It was on 19 December that the flotilla was involved in its fiercest confrontation with the enemy. At 0830 the SO received an urgent signal requiring immediate despatch of a unit to Hong Kong harbour to engage Japanese troops in landing craft crossing from Kowloon Bay towards Taikoo: the actual words were 'shoot anything inside the harbour'.

He sent 07 (Ashby) and 09 (Kennedy) which proceeded at 30 knots towards the western entrance of the harbour. Ashby and Kennedy's reports were not written until 12 January – several weeks later – because of the intervention of far more pressing action, but they reveal the detail of a very resolute daylight attack under fire, and a complete success in dispersing the landing forces.

Ashby led the way, with 09 a cable astern, and as he passed the Naval Dockyard and neared North Point, both boats came under heavy machine gun attack, the first indication that some Japanese troops had actually landed and established themselves on Hong Kong Island. As 07 entered Kowloon Bay, he sighted numbers of landing craft in lines of three crossing from the mainland towards Taikoo. They seemed very light and frail, with the first of each three equipped with an outboard motor towing the other two. Each boat contained 12–15 men.

Ashby signalled 09 to attack independently, and as he increased speed to about 37 knots, aircraft dived at him firing cannons. When the range was about 100 yds, he opened fire with all his Lewis guns and passed down the leading string at point-blank range. He dropped two depth charges but they failed to explode, although this mattered not at all as each barge in turn capsized in the boat's wash and there seemed to be no survivors. 07 had already been hit several times, but now the barrage came from shore and wrecks in the harbour – howitzers and

MTBs 07 and 09 under camouflage on 25 December 1941 during the Japanese attack. (Courtesy, A. Kennedy)

light artillery fire – and from the aircraft. A cannon shell exploded in the engine room, killing the Leading Stoker and putting the starboard engine out of action. Ashby was still able to turn and make a second attack at about 32 knots, again sinking the next string of three. He saw 09 also attacking and realized that any landing craft still afloat had turned 180 degrees and were beating a hasty retreat for Kowloon. Another cannon shell now put the port engine out, and sadly the Leading Telegraphist who had been sent down to render assistance was also killed. 07's speed was now down to 12 knots and she was making water in the engine room, so Ashby knew it was time to extricate himself and get back to the base. The attacks from aircraft continued, with shelling from shore, but 07's gunners scored hits on one fighter which made off and did not return.

MTB 09 rejoined and stood by, and when 07's centre engine also failed, she took her in tow. They got back to Aberdeen at 1000.

Kennedy's report adds further detail of the success of the raid. After sinking another three craft in his first attack, he roared round the bay looking for more targets, and firing at several. Ammunition was running out, so he rejoined the damaged 07 and stood by her until Ashby shouted over that his centre engine had now failed and he had no power at all. She was then taken in tow.[2]

There was more drama to come. MTBs 10 (Gandy) and 27 (Parsons) and then 11 (Collingwood) and 12 (Colls) had been sent to follow 07 and 09, the third unit to wait before entering the harbour. But 10 had engine trouble and Gandy sent Collingwood on into Kowloon Bay. His report also indicates surprise when fired on from North Point; but having passed it he explored the bay and found that no Japanese craft were

afloat anywhere in sight. He turned to withdraw, but found to his dismay that MTB 12 was no longer in company. One of the crew reported that the last time he had seen her she was stopped and clouds of white smoke were issuing from her. Nor had MTB 11 escaped unscathed – in one of the early attacks from shore, the coxswain had been wounded in the neck. In addition she had to run the gauntlet of air attacks, including one bomb which was a very near miss astern. As she left the area, 27 (Parsons) and 26 (Wagstaff) were awaiting orders to enter the bay. They arrived at 0940.[3]

The two boats set off, but almost at once the Signal Station on Mount Davis called up MTB 27 (leading the unit) and passed a signal which told them to wait off Green Island. Unfortunately, 26 had gone ahead without waiting, and entered the bay. She was never seen again and it had to be presumed that she had been sunk with all hands.[4]

The flotilla was shocked that on the one day they had been able to achieve something tangible in halting the ferrying of troops to the island, they had also lost two boats with all their men, as far as they knew. Morale plummeted, and was not helped by the bad news which constantly reached them. No orders were received and day followed day in the period up to Christmas with no respite from air raids and from the continuing tales of losses ashore and at sea. The old river gun boat *Cicala* with her two 6-in guns gallantly persisted in bombarding targets ashore, and seemingly bore a charmed life. She was finally crippled, but would not sink, after a concentrated attack by nine dive-bombers. Her crew were taken off by MTB 10, and 09

2 ROPs at IWM by Lt R.R.W. Ashby RHKNVR and Lt A. Kennedy RNVR dated 12 January 1942.

3 ROP at IWM by Lt C.J. Collingwood RN, dated 12 January 1942.

4 Report by Lt Cdr G.H. Gandy RN, dated 8 March 1942 held at IWM.

174

was given the task of attempting to sink her. It took six depth charges to do it, but eventually this gallant ship disappeared.

Now the five MTBs were the only naval craft afloat. Rather purposeless patrols were mounted around those parts of the coast the Japanese had taken: but the enemy were not mounting any more landings. Eventually, with the SO in MTB 10 remaining in Aberdeen to receive orders, the other four boats were dispersed under camouflage, waiting for news and the inevitable end. Fuel was running out and Hong Kong in any case too isolated for any breakout by sea to succeed.

Finally, at 1515 on Christmas Day 1941, white flags flying from Mount Davis proclaimed the truth – that Hong Kong had fallen.

There had been much discussion on the course of action to be taken when this happened. Preparations had tentatively been made to equip the crews for service, or even for escape overland through China. The fate of the boats was less explicit, but clearly they could not be allowed to fall into Japanese hands. Soon after dusk the signal to the flotilla to rendezvous south of Aberdeen was received. MTB 10 was crowded with a horde of British and Chinese dressed in a strange assortment of clothes, and they were shared out among the boats. The party consisted of a few survivors from the base, and a group from the Chinese Military Mission in Hong Kong led by their Senior Officer, Admiral Chen Chak.

They had left Aberdeen in a small launch which had been spotted and sunk. Of the twenty aboard, eleven survived by swimming ashore, several of them wounded. Admiral Chen Chak was one of them: this gallant officer, who had already lost a leg earlier in the war, and had just received a new wound to his wrist, managed to swim ashore having discarded his wooden leg. The cold bedraggled

group were found by MTB 10, and had just been taken aboard and kitted out when the other boats arrived.

The Admiral was irrepressible, remaining on deck now wearing one of Lt Cdr Gandy's uniforms. He was largely responsible for the plan hastily made. The boats sailed southward from the island, and then doubled back into Mirs Bay to a section of the coast known to be free of enemy occupation, near the village of Namoa where local guerrillas were expected to be camped.

In deep water, the confidential books were dumped overboard in their heavy iron boxes. They then moved towards the coast, and contact was successfully made with the guerrillas ashore. All the worthwhile gear aboard was handed over, and then – most poignant of all – the time had come to scuttle the boats. They were taken out a short distance, and in each boat the bottom was holed with hatchets and seawater intakes opened. Slowly, as the weight of the engines took them down, they each sank out of sight. With heavy hearts the crews paddled back to the beach.

The 2nd MTB Flotilla was no more. There could surely be no sadder fate than to end its life in this way.[5]

The postscript to this brief history of the flotilla is a story worth telling. It is unique in British Coastal Forces that the personnel of a flotilla, with some base staff, having been overcome by invasion and conquest of their isolated operating port, should set out as a group to find their way to freedom through enemy territory in order to be able to fight again.

When the crews reached the beach after scuttling their boats, they found that the party had grown in size and was now almost

5 Kennedy, *Hong Kong Full Circle*; Report by Lt Cdr Gandy.

seventy strong. It had been reinforced by the arrival of Cdr Montague, who had been in overall command at Aberdeen, with some of his staff who had made their escape by finding a small dockyard launch with some fuel in it. It was necessary to get inland as quickly as possible, and as dawn broke, the long straggling line of weary men wound its way inland like pack-mules on the trail.

The first leg, to get beyond the zone of occupied Japanese territory, was the 80 miles northward to Waichow. They were fortunate to have the expertise of three British members of the Hong Kong Volunteer Force who had been involved for months in guerrilla activities, and had not only a fluent command of Cantonese, but knowledge of the terrain. They also discovered that Admiral Chen Chak, who held high political office in South China, was a popular and highly respected figure whose presence brought many advantages as they passed through villages. Food, green tea, and shelter were always offered and gratefully accepted.

The going was desperately hard. They crossed two mountain passes, forded rivers and detoured to avoid known Japanese pockets. The majority were totally unaccustomed to such conditions, although the eight MTB officers and their thirty-six ratings were young and fit and made the best of it.

At the end of three days they had covered 60 miles, and were beyond the sphere of Japanese influence on land. A message arrived that for the last 14 miles to Waichow, bicycles would be sent out for the older men later in the day.

They found Waichow to be a much-bombed city of some size, with a British Liaison Officer and Red Cross centre and even an ex-German mission hospital where they were to be billeted. But before they could rest, there was a procession – a march past – with cheering crowds, and then a

banquet given by the Commanding General of the area.[6]

They stayed two nights in Waichow, while plans were made to enable the party to travel on westward across South China into Burma and thence to Rangoon: a journey which had in prospect been impossible to visualize, but seemed now to present a real hope of rejoining British forces and avoiding capture by a ruthless enemy.

It was the last day of the year when the party embarked on the next stage of its journey. This leg was to take them 150 miles up the East River in two flat-bottomed motor boats each towing a sampan. Engines broke down, the boats grounded on shallows, and in the end the sampans were abandoned and everyone packed into the motor boats. It took five days to reach their destination, Lung chun, where they transferred to six motor trucks, but not until they were again treated to another feast in their billet, the village school. They discovered later that the villagers had killed a bullock for them, a wonderfully generous gesture in a poor country area.

The next stage – at last westward rather than northward – was by truck for 200 miles over a mountainous road rising to 5,000 ft to Ku Kong, now the capital of the province. Once more the two days were punctuated by breakdowns, but on arrival they found the people at Ku Kong to be very hospitable. It was just as well, since they had a week to wait there before setting out by train along the Canton–Hankow railway which took them circuitously in a great sweep but eventually westward towards Kweiyang. In fact, after five days they reached the railhead still far short of their destination, as the railway was still being built. They pressed on by truck, but it took three more days to reach

6 Kennedy, *Hong Kong Full Circle*; Report by Lt Cdr Gandy.

The crew of MTB 09 (CO Lt A. Kennedy is kneeling front right) at Waichow in South China during the breakout from Hong Kong, December 1941. (Courtesy, A. Kennedy)

Kweiyang, on the third of which one of the trucks overturned, and five ratings were injured. It was now 24 January and they were still less than halfway to Rangoon. The next stage was by Red Cross trucks, mainly along an old section of the Burma Road, passing through Kunming, the capital of the province.

Lt Cdr Gandy, conscious of the news he had picked up that the Japanese were making progress towards Rangoon from Siam, tried to inject urgency into the travel plans, but found it impossible to shake the Chinese disregard of hurry! They could not leave Kunming until 1 February, and continued slowly westward until they crossed the border from China to Burma and finally reached the railhead at Lashio: six weeks had now passed.

They waited for a train to run, and after passing through Mandalay they entered Rangoon on 14 February, finding a city which seemed to be bleeding to death. The station area was packed with people trying to get away: the news had come through that Singapore had fallen, and when people realized that it would be Rangoon's turn next, panic had spread.

After two days of uncertainty during which the MTB crews were kitted out by the Burma RNVR and able at last to discard the rags they had hardly changed since December, the official notice of civil evacuation was issued. Then an armoured brigade arrived from the Middle East and the tanks rumbled out to assist the defence of the city during the seemingly inevitable military evacuation.

Gandy and the bulk of the MTB party left Rangoon in the Commodore's HQ ship, *Jessen*, on 8 March. She went on to Calcutta

Admiral Chen Chak (right) of the Chinese Navy, at Ku Kong. (Courtesy, A. Kennedy)

Officers of the 2nd Flotilla, with their hosts, at Kweiyang, 26 January 1942. (Courtesy, A. Kennedy)

where they disembarked for onward passage to Britain, followed not long after by those who had been temporarily detached, some to command and crew patrol vessels for the Burma RNVR.

The long 'breakout' from Hong Kong had finally been accomplished. It had been a remarkable experience for the men of an MTB flotilla, who throughout had displayed their typical bond of comradeship after two years together in their tiny boats.

Lt Cdr Gandy's handwritten log of the last stage of operations and then the experiences during the breakout, laboriously kept in very primitive conditions on the march, was

ultimately typed up and submitted to the C-in-C Ron Ashby (MTB 07), who was awarded a DSC for his boat's attack on the Japanese landing craft on 19 December 1941, went on to command briefly a Dog Boat flotilla which went to the Mediterranean, and then returned to command the MLs in Burma; John Collingwood (MTB 11) also stayed in Coastal Forces, as Training Officer at Dover and later as SOO at HMS *Gregale* in Malta. Alexander Kennedy (MTB 09), author of *Hong Kong Full Circle*, spent two years as an instructor at HMS *St Christopher*, the Coastal Force training base at Fort William. In 1945 he had the remarkable

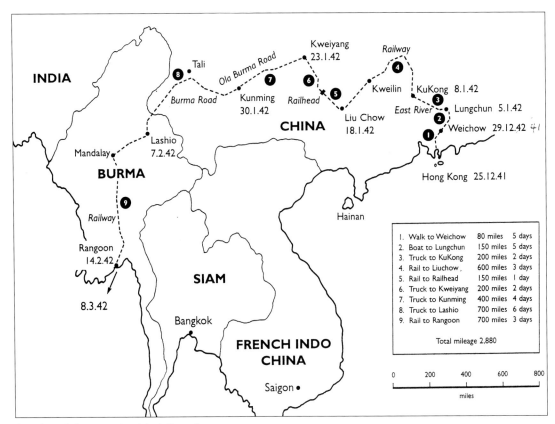

The 2nd MTB Flotilla's journey through South China to Rangoon.

experience of returning to Hong Kong soon after its recapture, when as a Staff Officer aboard the maintenance carrier HMS *Pioneer* he sailed into the harbour on 9 September.

Nothing is known with certainty of the fate of the ships' companies of MTBs 12 and 26, who were all listed as 'missing believed killed', nor indeed of the officers and men of MTB 08, which had been under repair in the dockyard at the time of the surrender, and had been destroyed. It is believed that the crew joined up with the Army in the final defence of the Colony, and that many were lost.[7]

7 Kennedy, *Hong Kong Full Circle*; correspondence with Lt Cdr A. Kennedy VRD RNVR and Lt Cdr C.J. Collingwood RN (Rtd).

EPILOGUE

This account of the operations of the Royal Navy's smallest surface fighting vessels in the Mediterranean is of particular interest because their war was so closely linked to constant military movement over a period of almost five years. It was a very different war from that fought by the MTBs in home waters.

From 1941 to 1945 the various MTB flotillas were called upon to carry out a wide variety of tasks, and the Army had cause to be grateful that these small craft provided much of the support for the protection of its seaward flank as the troops advanced (or, in the Desert years, retreated).

Many of the operations were in areas where larger warships – not as 'expendable' as the MTBs – could not be used. One excellent example was the blockade of the northern section of the Strait of Messina throughout the Sicilian campaign. Only low-silhouette craft could have patrolled nightly despite the concentration of coastal batteries and their attendant searchlights across the 3 to 4 miles of the narrowest section, successfully denying the enemy access to attack the shipping further south.

The experience of the Mediterranean MTBs in many other ways mirrored that of all the flotillas of Coastal Forces. It began with a legacy of neglect of any of the experience gained by the CMBs in the First World War – in boat design, weaponry, engines and tactics, and most of all in the employment and operations of the boats. The result was a long hard path to effectiveness.

The vacillation of Government and Admiralty, first over the need for *any* offensive small craft, then over which designs of both boats and power units to choose and support, meant that it was the second half of 1942 before Coastal Forces began to receive in quantity the craft their enthusiastic and aggressive crews deserved.

However boldly they were operated, the early boats lacked reliable power units or adequate armament to enable them to achieve significant results. Envious eyes were cast at the obvious superiority of the E-boats, which began to sink major targets very frequently from May 1940; their first success was against HMS *Kelly*, hit by a torpedo from S31 on 9 May. She did not sink, but was under repair for three months.

The early Thornycrofts were very similar to the CMBs of 1915 design; the Scott-Paine boats were a step forward in design, but with their stern-launched torpedoes and their Lewis gun armament they were inadequately equipped. The early 1939 Vospers, designed to be powered by Isotta-Fraschini engines, were fine – but when these Italian engines became unavailable, the Hall Scott and Packard engines which replaced them were not at first compatible with the hull and led to unreliability in some of the boats of the 1940 and 1941 programmes.

The 70-ft British Power Boats paved the way for their successors, and the Elcos began to show the advantages of construction of many boats in the USA. The later Vospers were a vast improvement on the early models, and armament increased in quantity and effectiveness with the introduction of Oerlikons and twin 0.5-in guns in power-operated turrets.

The early boats had no radar, and there is no doubt that its development changed the whole nature of patrols and attack techniques. The Mark VIII torpedo with the CCR pistol had been in use in submarines for some time before they were able to be made available to the MTBs, but when the pistols arrived the strike rate improved dramatically.

Added to these vast improvements in equipment, the whole concept of training and working-up developed, when the benefits of analysis of tactical success by early leaders like Hichens and Dickens were taught and put into practice at HMS *Bee* and HMS *St Christopher*.

All these stages have been clearly demonstrated in this history of the 'short' MTB flotillas in the Mediterranean. To compare the unreliable and poorly armed boats of 'The Wobbly 10th' which sailed to Crete in 1941 with the sophisticated and lethally effective Vospers of the 28th in 1945 is unfair: in these and indeed in all the flotillas between, the officers and crews could do no more than use the boats and the equipment they were given with all the skill and determination they could muster.

It was the massive recovery from the initial unpreparedness and the scientific and technical revolution accelerated by the impetus of war, that were the main ingredients which led to the totally different picture of Coastal Forces in 1944 and 1945. Nor must the human aspects be forgotten. The handful of RN officers and General Service ratings who manned the early boats had of necessity to be replaced by a large number of RNVR and Commonwealth officers, and hostilities-only men. Britain's seafaring heritage was rarely better exemplified than by the way in which men of all backgrounds, and many with no previous experience of the sea, rose to command the MTBs. The crews were even more likely to consist, on commissioning, of a small backbone of officers and men with some experience, but with many 18-year-old newcomers to the sea who within weeks found themselves in close combat with the enemy.

The enormous and rapid expansion of the manpower required by Coastal Forces from 1942 led to the necessity for new methods of training, which could not always prepare men adequately for the tasks ahead. The twenty or so MTBs in commission in 1939 had become by 1945 a force approaching 2,000 MTBs, MLs and HDMLs, carrying about 25,000 men. Courses were shortened, and training depended more on the individual efforts of SOs, COs and coxswains in a working-up period for the crews before their boats began operating. For those fortunate enough (even if these were not the words they would have chosen) to work up at HMS *Bee*, first at Weymouth and later at Holyhead, this was very effective. But the Mediterranean 'short' boat flotillas rarely had that opportunity. Most of their craft arrived from the USA and the crews which took them over had first to familiarize themselves with each boat's characteristics, and then with their own duties. It was small wonder that the early years in the Mediterranean were fraught with difficulties.

There was one other decisive factor in the increase in success of the boats as the war progressed, which has deliberately not been touched upon in the text of the earlier chapters. It is now common knowledge that the development of 'Ultra' – the ability to decode enemy signals – had a profound effect upon the ability of Intelligence officers to pass to the operations officers at the bases uncannily accurate information on such matters as enemy convoy sailings.

Throughout the war, this was a closely guarded secret, kept so effectively that COs when given their sailing orders believed that the sources of information were mainly hidden observers ashore – spies in some form or other – or from aircraft reconnaissance.

It is because the significance of 'Ultra' was never realized by those despatched to seek

'The Dawn of Peace' – sunrise off Valletta, Malta, from the Coastal Force Base. (Courtesy, A.T. Robinson)

and destroy the enemy, that it has not been mentioned; it certainly accounts for the great proportional increase in the number of interceptions made, and therefore inevitably in the increasing success of patrols.

Many accounts of the operations of flotillas attempt to quantify success in terms of numbers of enemy ships claimed as sunk or damaged, or aircraft shot down.

The accuracy of such estimates must always be in doubt. In the case of MTBs, enemy engagement frequently involved many interruptions during which dispositions changed, leaving the possibility of duplicate claims. Even when a torpedo was seen to hit, or fire began to engulf an enemy ship, there was no certainty that it would sink, even if

severely damaged. The experience of our own MTBs confirms that there were many examples of crippled boats which limped or were towed back to harbour and later repaired to see service again.

Verification of sinkings is best achieved through the enemy's own records, unless a target was actually seen to sink. Sophisticated radar, as in the case of torpedo strikes by the 7th and 28th Flotillas in the later stages of the war, could also confirm a sinking by the sudden disappearance from the screen of an echo when others remained.

It is even more difficult to quantify the number of patrols the boats carried out, but there is some basis for presenting some figures of occasions on which the boats were in action with the enemy. A list of every recorded action mentioned in official reports was compiled in Admiralty in about 1952. Unfortunately close study reveals that it is rather incomplete and inconsistent, particularly because each Command used different methods to report, and there were, in any case, no specific criteria to define 'an action'. But the list is the best documented evidence available and a simple count based on classifications of types of enemy contact is possible, and may be of interest.

The list indicates that all types of Coastal Force craft were in contact with the enemy on 967 occasions. The MTBs, MGBs and SGBs were involved in 761 of those incidents; the remainder mostly concerned MLs. Three-quarters of those contacts (about 570) were in the form of what can be simply described as surface battles: exchanges of fire, usually at short range, with enemy ships. In addition, there were about 150 reports of engagements with aircraft, mining incidents, and close attacks by shore batteries. Support of landings and clandestine operations, although frequent, were not reported adequately and rarely appear in the list.

The Mediterranean MTBs (excluding the Dog Boats, as in this history) were involved in all these forms of engagement, and in many which were never reported in detail, often because of the detached service on which they were so frequently employed.

The list reveals that the 109 'short' boats of the Mediterranean flotillas are reported as taking part in 149 actions, 144 of them in direct conflict with the enemy. The figure of only five for landings, minelaying, mining, aircraft and attack by shore batteries is clearly wrong, and from the accounts in this history could well be increased tenfold.

Those accounts will also indicate that a very high proportion of the boats of the early flotillas were lost, many of them as a result of attack by aircraft in areas and in circum-

stances where the enemy had command of the air. Records show that in all, thirty-one were lost, of which twelve were in air attacks, two in surface action and four by mining. Damage in heavy seas accounted for four, another four were lost by grounding and four by collision – all hazards of MTB operations. The most unusual was the case of MTB 262 which had to be sunk by the crew when it broke down near an enemy island and faced capture if no action was taken.

In the Mediterranean, the fate of the surviving boats when hostilities ended is not very well recorded. Certainly the boats of later flotillas on lend-lease from the US Navy which were seaworthy, were returned to the US authorities at their bases at Palermo and Bizerta. The British boats when paid off were first employed usefully in a variety of ways and then disposed of within the Command.

The longer-serving officers and men were sent home according to their demobilization priority rating, largely by the 'Medlock' route which many recall as a very uncomfortable experience, borne with fortitude as they were 'going home'. It involved crowded troopships to Toulon, a night or two in tented camps with inadequate facilities, and a two-day rail journey across France, whose railway system was being restored after the ravages of war, aboard wooden-seated carriages to Dieppe. There, in another tented camp, they waited their turn for a ferry across the Channel to Newhaven before their individual journeys to their homes. In doing so they crossed the narrow strip of water where for many of them their experience in MTBs had begun in 1940/41, and which so often throughout history had been the saviour of Britain.

As in all MTB flotillas a tremendous spirit of brotherhood had been established, and the bond created is exemplified by the large number who maintain their links through the Coastal Forces Veterans Association. Almost universally, they retained an interest in the Royal Navy and particularly waited to see whether a force of some form of 'Fast Patrol Boats' would continue the traditions of the wartime flotillas. Many were aware of the mistakes made when the lessons learned from the First World War were quickly forgotten, leading to a very slow start to operational effectiveness in 1939. They wondered if the new and advanced boats of the 1950s would be developed and retained to carry forward the bitterly won experience of the Second World War.

By 1958, they knew that this was a forlorn hope. Other nations persisted with new generations of Fast Patrol Boats, some built in Britain by Vosper Thornycroft. But the decision of Admiralty – on economic grounds, and also because Britain's contri-bution to NATO concentrated on submarines, carriers and frigates – meant that Coastal Forces no longer had a future in the Royal Navy.

There is one constant irritation for the men of the MTBs of 1939–45. They search the naval histories of the war at sea and are astonished at the scant recognition of the work they did in disrupting enemy supplies all over the Narrow Seas, in which a thousand of them gave their lives.

They find it particularly strange, for instance, that in the major work entitled *Engage the Enemy More Closely* there is just one single mention of MTBs and MGBs, the naval units which undoubtedly *did* engage the enemy more closely than any other.

NOTES

Abbreviations frequently used both in footnotes and in these endnotes: PRO: Public Record Office; NHB: Naval Historical Branch; MO numbers are Admiralty references, found at NHB; ROP: Report of Proceedings; the ADM 199 series refers to operational reports at the PRO; WIR: War Intelligence Reports; NID: Naval Intelligence Department; CFPR: Coastal Forces Periodic Reviews; CFI: Coastal Forces Information Bulletins; CCF: Captain Coastal Forces.

CHAPTER 1

NOTE 1

General note on sources: The sources for definitive information of the period covered in this chapter are extremely slight. Navy Lists and Red and Pink Lists are not helpful, and even the Ships' Cards giving details of the boats of the 1st MTB Flotilla, most of which became C/T (Control and/or Towing) boats, were removed and cannot be found in the Naval Historical Branch.

It has therefore been necessary to rely on information gleaned from the small number of veterans of these boats who have been traced, or earlier articles by them in the authors' possession, particularly by C.M. Donner, H.L. Lloyd, and J.T. Mannooch.

NOTE 2

The nine 1st Flotilla COs who later commanded their own flotillas in action were:

Lt H.R.A. Kidston RN: (1st CO 04): 4th MGBs
Lt E.M. Thorpe RN: 2nd MA/SBs, 4th MGBs,
  19th MGBs (Ds)

Lt P.F.S. Gould RN: 3rd MGBs, 32nd MTBs (Ds)
Lt A.A.T. Seymour-Hayden RN: 1st MGBs
Lt L.J.H. Gamble RN: 5th MTBs, 31st MTBs (Ds)
Lt J.A. Eardley-Wilmot RN: 11th MTBs
Lt H.L. Lloyd RN: 4th MTBs
Lt D.H. Mason RN: 59th MTBs (Ds)
Lt J.T. Mannooch RN: 1st MTBs (from 1/40)
Lt D. Jermain RN: 10th and 15th MTBs.

CHAPTER 2

NOTE 3

General sources: The early history of the operations of the handful of Coastal Forces boats in 1939–41 is very poorly documented. The Navy Lists rarely help, and the records contain very few references to operational activity.

The development of the designs of craft by those firms mainly involved – British Power Boat, Thornycroft and Vosper – has largely been unravelled by Geoffrey Hudson's research into their records over fifty years. The operational aspects rely very heavily on information supplied by the surviving officers and men. Fortunately, there are enough accounts to provide corroborating evidence: in the case of the 10th MTB Flotilla supplied by Rear Adm C.C. Anderson CB, Charles Coles OBE VRD, Miles Coverdale, Capt I.A.B. Quarrie CBE VRD RNR, and David Souter VRD. The Imperial War Museum provided the Reports of Proceedings concerning the loss of five boats at Crete by the SO, Lt Cdr E.C. Peake RN. The only mention of the service of MA/SB3 in the Mediterranean in official records is the statement concerning her mining in the Suez Canal, but the personal memoir by the late Fred Coombes DSM sent to the authors gives graphic detail of her commission.

CHAPTER 3

NOTE 4

Operation Vigorous to take supplies to Malta from Alexandria, coinciding with Operation Harpoon from Gibraltar, mid-June 1942.

Sources: 1. ROP in PRO, Kew in ADM 199/680. 2. Roskill, *The War at Sea*, Vol. 2. 3. Rohwer and Hummelchen, *Chronology of the War at Sea*, Vol. 1. 4. Pope, *Flag 4*. This account includes information from R.A. Allan. At the time of the operation he was a Lieutenant RNVR commanding MTB 259. By the end of the war, he was Cdr Allan OBE DSO, Commander Legion d'Honneur, Croix de Guerre, Officer of Legion of Merit USA, and was five times mentioned in despatches. He later became MP for South Paddington. He died on 4 April 1979 as a Life Peer – Baron Allan of Kilmahew. 5. Information to H.F. Cooper from D.C. Souter VRD DL.

NOTE 5

The withdrawal from Tobruk – awards.

Source: *Seedie's List of Coastal Forces Awards* by Capt W. Chatterton Dickson RN Retd, pub. Ripley Registers 1992.

Denis Jermain's coolness and effective leadership were recognized by the award of a Bar to his DSC. Solomon (260) was awarded the DSC for his gallantry – especially in laying a smoke screen under the noses of the tanks and artillery ashore.

NOTE 6

Operation Agreement, the raid on Tobruk 12–15 September 1942.

Sources: The main official source is to be found in documents at PRO, originally in CB 04272. A summary can be found at Naval Historical Branch in their Search Document S8069. From these are derived the accounts in Pope, *Flag 4* and Smith, *Massacre at Tobruk*. The account in this history is amplified by personal contributions in letters to

H.F. Cooper from Capt Denis Jermain DSC RN (Retd), Charles Coles OBE VRD, and Norman Ilett DSC.

CHAPTER 4

NOTE 7

A general note on sources for Chapter 4.

Most of the more detailed descriptive information which supports the official record has been accumulated by H.F. Cooper in correspondence with those who served in the boats. In many cases they had written their own accounts soon after the war. The authors are grateful for help from Capt Denis Jermain DSC RN (Retd), Charles Coles OBE VRD, Norman Ilett DSC, Cdr R.A.M. Hennessy LVO DSC RN (Retd). Where Dudley Pope had help when preparing *Flag 4* in 1954, from participants who have since died, the value of such material is acknowledged.

CHAPTER 5

NOTE 8

The sinking of U-561, damage to U-375, and disabling of two E-boats on 12/13 July by boats of the 24th, 7th and 33rd Flotillas.

Sources: 1. Admiralty list MO 10163 and MO 9976. 2. ROP at PRO Kew in ADM 199/541. 3. Information by Cdr C.W.S. Dreyer given by Dudley Pope in 1953/4 in compilation of *Flag 4*.

Awards: Lt Dreyer was awarded the DSO, and Lt Strong the DSC for Operation Husky, and two DSMs and four MIDs to crew members involved – all clearly with this action in mind.

CHAPTER 6

NOTE 9

The Air Raid on Bari on 2 December 1943.

Sources: 1. Personal accounts by L.V. Strong, C.R. Holloway, E. Young, H. du Boulay, J.W.H. Collins, B.G. Syrett, collected by H.F. Cooper. 2. Awards from *Seedie's List of Coastal Forces Awards*.

Mustard Gas: The presence of a cargo of mustard gas aboard an American ship should be explained. It was to be held in reserve and would be available for use in a reprisal attack if first employed by the enemy.

CHAPTER 8

NOTE 10
Detail which amplifies the information in ADM 199/268 and in the Summaries of Recorded Actions has been provided by COs of the 7th Flotilla at this time – Lts N. Ilett DSC, R. Aitchison DSC, and R. Varvill DSC, and also by the Motor Mechanic of MTB 423, C/MM J.L. Lee DSM.

NOTE 11
Similarly, detail which amplifies the official record of operations by the 20th Flotilla has been provided by the following COs at the time: Lts P.H. Hyslop DSC, F. Frenzel DSC, and B. Syrett.

CHAPTER 9

NOTE 12
The sources from which the material for this chapter has been gathered by the authors are of two types. First, they arise from correspondence with the two Senior Officers and several of the Commanding Officers, who made available a full set of Reports of Proceedings, ensuring accuracy of detail. Secondly, the fact that H.F. Cooper, co-author and main researcher, himself served in the flotilla, adds greatly to the completeness of the history. Under the individual note for the source of information for each of the actions, there is therefore no need to repeat 'Report of Proceedings', and generally only the Admiralty List reference – an MO number – is quoted.

CHAPTER 10

NOTE 13
General note on sources.

Because of the circumstances which prevailed in Hong Kong in the last stages of the Japanese assault, the official record of the 2nd MTB Flotilla's operations was not submitted until 8 March 1942, when Lt Cdr G.H. Gandy and other COs reached Rangoon. The Imperial War Museum holds a copy of the remarkable handwritten copy of the draft of that report kept as a contemporaneous note throughout the last days in Hong Kong and during the journey through occupied China. The final typewritten report includes Reports of Proceedings of the actions of 19 December 1941 by Lt R.R.W. Ashby RHKNVR, Lt C.J. Collingwood RN and Lt A. Kennedy RNVR.

Even more complete and valuable is the material included in Alexander Kennedy's privately published memoir *Hong Kong Full Circle*, written in 1945 but printed in 1969.

APPENDIX 2

TABLES

TABLE 1: WAR LOSSES OF BOATS

(NB: 'CTL': 'Constructive Total Loss' – beyond economic repair)

1ST MTB FLOTILLA
16.11.39   MTB 06   Foundered off Sardinia.

INDEPENDENT
28.02.41   MA/SB 3   Mined in Suez Canal.

10TH/15TH/27TH MTB FLOTILLAS
16.10.40   MTB 106 Sunk by exploding acoustic mine while sweeping in the Thames Estuary.

23.05.41   MTB 67 ⎫
           MTB 213 ⎪
           MTB 214 ⎬ Lost during enemy air attack at Suda Bay, Crete.
           MTB 216 ⎪
           MTB 217 ⎭
14.12.41   MTB 68   Sunk after collision with MTB 215 off the coast of Libya.
29.03.42   MTB 215   Foundered near Tobruk en route to Alexandria after collision with MTB 68.
14.06.42   MTB 259   Lost during towing operation between Alexandria and Malta.
14.09.42   MTB 308 ⎫
           MTB 310 ⎬ Lost by air attack during raid on Tobruk (Operation Agreement).
           MTB 312 ⎭
14.09.42   MTB 314   Lost by grounding, and abandoned during raid on Tobruk.
24.02.43   MTB 262   Self-destructed after engine failure off Galita Island, Tunisia.
02.04.43   MTB 267   Broke back on passage to Malta, and sunk by gunfire.
02.05.43   MTB 311   Destroyed by mine off Bone, Algeria.
10.05.43   MTB 264   Destroyed by mine near Sousse, Tunisia.
17.07.43   MTB 316   Lost by direct hit from Italian cruiser *Africano Scipione* in the Strait of Messina.
17.04.44   MTB 266   CTL. Sank in Alexandria harbour, having suffered action damage on 09.03.44.
26.08.45   MTB 261   Destroyed after sinking in Alexandria harbour.

7TH/8TH MTB FLOTILLAS

02.04.43	MTB	63 ⎫	Total losses after colliding off Benghazi.
	MTB	64 ⎭	
08.05.43	MTB	61	Destroyed after grounding in sight of enemy in Kelibia harbour.
08.09.43	MTB	77	Bombed and sunk during landing at Vibo Valentia, Calabria.
24.11.43	MTB	73	Bombed and sunk at Maddalena, Sardinia.
26.04.44	MTB	79	Destroyed off Malta as target vessel after sinking when damaged alongside at Hayes Wharf.
14.03.45	MTB	95	Sunk as target off Malta.

20TH MTB FLOTILLA

21.07.43	MTB 288	Bombed and sunk, Augusta harbour, Sicily.
24.07.44	MTB 372	Sunk in action in the Adriatic.
24.11.44	MTB 287 ⎫	Destroyed by gunfire after grounding on Levrera Island, northern
	MTB 371 ⎭	Dalmatian islands.

24TH MTB FLOTILLA

| – .07.45 | MTB 243 | Reported as sunk as target. |
| 21.07.45 | MTB 242 | Sank on tow to Malta. |

Total 35; 11 in aircraft attack, 4 by mining, 3 in surface actions, 4 by grounding, 4 in collisions, 5 from damage in heavy weather, 3 destroyed in harbour and as targets, and 1 sunk by the crew.

2ND MTB FLOTILLA (IN HONG KONG)

16.12.41	MTB	08	Bombed on slip at Hong Kong.
19.12.41	MTB	12 ⎫	Lost, probably from shore battery fire, at Hong Kong.
	MTB	26 ⎭	
26.12.41	MTB	07 ⎫	
	MTB	09	
	MTB	10 ⎬	Scuttled in Mirs Bay on surrender of Hong Kong.
	MTB	11	
	MTB	27 ⎭	

TABLE 2: AWARDS OF DECORATIONS

(FROM *SEEDIE'S LIST OF COASTAL FORCES AWARDS*)

DISTINGUISHED SERVICE ORDER (DSO)

24th Flot.	Lt C.W.S. Dreyer DSC RN
20th Flot.	Lt H.A. Barbary RN
28th Flot.	Lt C.J. Jerram DSC

OFFICER OF THE ORDER OF THE BRITISH EMPIRE (OBE)
MTB 10   Lt R.W. Goodwin RNZNVR

MEMBER OF THE ORDER OF THE BRITISH EMPIRE (MBE)
MTB 243   Sub Lt J.E.H. Collins

2ND BAR TO THE DISTINGUISHED SERVICE CROSS (DSC**)
7th Flot.   Lt A.C.B. Blomfield DSC RN

BAR TO THE DISTINGUISHED SERVICE CROSS (DSC*)

MTB 260	Lt M.H.B. Solomon
260	Lt H.F. Wadds
309	Lt D. Jermain
400	Lt W.J. Archer
404	Lt E.H.G. Lassen
406	Sub Lt J.E.H. Collins
422	Lt A.H. Moore
7th Flot.	Lt A.C.B. Blomfield
20th Flot.	Lt Cdr J.D. Lancaster
28th Flot.	Lt C.J. Jerram
HMS *Mosquito*	Lt Cdr C.P. Evensen and Lt Cdr T.G. Fuller

DISTINGUISHED SERVICE CROSS (DSC)

MTB 07	Lt Cdr R.R. Ashby
77	Lt J.B. Sturgeon
	Lt E.H.G. Lassen
81	Lt L.V. Strong
84	Sub Lt F.A. Gilpin
89	Lt W.J. Archer
226	Lt P.H. Hyslop
260	Lt H.F. Wadds
266	Lt R.R. Smith
295	Sub Lt F.N. Frenzel
298	Lt F.M.A. Shore
307	Lt J.G.G. Muir
311	Lt Cdr J.D. Lancaster
315	Lt L.E. Newall
377	Lt R. Aitchison
378	Sub Lt G.P.H. James
397	Sub Lt R.J. Lubbock
405	Lt F.G.U. Scoble
406	Sub Lt J.E.H.Collins
407	Lt H.C.H. du Boulay
408	Lt R.P. Tonkin
409	Lt C.R. Holloway

410	Lt A.O. Woodhouse
419	Lt C.J. Finch
420	Lt N.L. Ilett
421	Lt R. Varvill
	Lt A.H. Moore
422	Sub Lt G.H.Bullwinkle
10th Flot.	Lt C.P. Evensen
24th Flot.	Lt D. Scott
HMS *Mosquito*	Lt G.W. Whittam

BRITISH EMPIRE MEDAL (BEM)

MTB	243	O/Sea P.T.F. Bickmore
	260	POMM J.N. Lawrence
	262	PO P. Ward
	10th Flot.	POMM E.B. Rafter

DISTINGUISHED SERVICE MEDAL (DSM)

MTB	57	A/B N.W. Turner
	73	L/Sea A.L. Harrison
	77	ChMM W.R. Stollery
		A/B G.T. Hammett
		Tel S. Fenwick
	81	L/Sea A.F. Currie
	84	L/Sea D.W.C. Evetts
	89	L/Tel F. Langford
		POMM R.S. Sutcliffe
	226	LMM W.J. Donovan
	260	Sto PO H. Cooke
		A/B B. Colgan
		POMM J.N. Lawrence
		Tel C. Clater
	264	POMM J.C. Jones
	266	POMM R.L. Capindale
		L/Sea J. Wilson
	298	L/Sea H. Bowers
	309	Sto E. Baynes
	311	PO R.R. Vittles
	313	PO M. Cregan
	315	POMM J.W. Littlejohn
		A/B J.H. Annetts
		PO G.H.H. Herbert
	376	Tel A. Stringer
	377	L/Sea B. Maguire
	378	L/Sea E. Pringle
	397	L/Sea A.E. Taylor

404	A/B R.S. Ellis
405	L/Sea C. Harte
406	L/Sea E.T. Brookes
407	A/B J.F. McCormick
408	L/Sea A.V. Lee
410	A/B F.J. Underwood
420	L/Tel G. Phipps
	POMM C.A.J. Joseph
	A/B C.A. Platt
421	Tel L. Mears
	A/B W.M. Thomson
423	ChMM J.L. Lee
	L/Sea W. Goulding
HMS *Mosquito*	A/B T.W. Nisbett.

'Mentioned in Dispatches' 55 officers, and 92 for other ranks were also gazetted.

TABLE 3: THE MEDITERRANEAN FLOTILLAS

1ST MTB FLOTILLA
In the Mediterranean 1937–9 (60-ft British Power Boats):
> 01, 02, 03, 04, 05, 06, 14, 15, 16, 17, 18, 19
> SOs: Lt G.B. Sayer RN
> Lt C.M. Donner RN

7TH MTB FLOTILLA
1) In Mediterranean from mid-1942 to December 1943 (71-ft Vospers, 1939 Class):
> 57, 58, 59, 60, 61, 62, 63, 64, 65
> SOs: Lt R.A.M. Hennessy RN to May 1943
> Lt A.C.B. Blomfield DSC RN
2) December 1943 to July 1945:
> 375, 376, 377, 378 (71-ft US Vospers)
> 419, 420, 421, 422, 423 (78-ft US Higgins)
> SOs: Lt A.C.B. Blomfield DSC RN to October 1944
> Lt A.H. Moore DSC RNVR

8TH MTB FLOTILLA
Merged with the 7th Flotilla on arrival in Mediterranean late in 1942 and early 1943 (71-ft Vospers, 1940 Class):
> 73, 75, 76, 77, 78, 79, 82, 84, 95
> SOs: Lt R.A.M. Hennessy RN
> Lt A.C.B. Blomfield DSC RN

10TH MTB FLOTILLA

1) Operational in UK from April to December 1940. All early Thornycroft boats, but different designs:

        67, 68 (55 ft); 104 (45 ft) 106, 107 (40 ft)

        SO: Lt C.C. Anderson RN

2) April 1941 to May 1941 (Crete):

        67, 68; 213, 214, 215, 216, 217 (55-ft Thornycrofts)

        SO: Lt Cdr E.C. Peake RN

3) May 1941 to December 1941:

        68, 215 only

        SO: Lt C.C. Anderson RN

4) January 1942 to September 1942. (ten 70-ft US Elcos):

        259, 260, 261, 262, 263, 264, 265, 266, 267, 268

        SOs: Lt Cdr C.D. Noakes RN to June 1942

               Lt R.A. Allan RNVR

15TH MTB FLOTILLA

Ten boats of the 15th joined operations with the 10th. May 1942 to September 1942 (Tobruk) (ten 77-ft US Elcos):

        307, 308, 309, 310, 311, 312, 313, 314, 315, 316

        SO: Lt D. Jermain DSC RN

10TH/15TH MTB FLOTILLA

1) The surviving boats of the 10th and 15th merged. September 1942 to September 1943:

        260, 261, 262, 263, 264, 265, 266, 267, 268, 307, 309, 311, 313, 315, 316

        SO: Lt D. Jermain DSC RN

2) September 1943 to September 1944:

        263, 265, 266, 307, 309, 313, 315

        SO: Lt Cdr C.P. Evensen DSC RNVR

27TH MTB FLOTILLA (10/27TH)

Joined the 10th in operations as one flotilla. September 1944 to May 1945:

        27th: 396, 397, 398, 399; 400, 401, 402, 403 (71-ft US Vospers) with 307, 309, 315, the surviving 77-ft US Elcos of the 10th

        SO: Lt R. Varvill DSC RNVR

20TH MTB FLOTILLA

1) May 1943 to January 1944 (71-ft US Vospers):

        287, 288, 289, 290, 295, 296, 297, 298

        SOs: Lt H.A. Barbary RN to October 1943

               Lt Cdr J.D. Lancaster DSC RNVR

2) January 1944 to May 1945:

        287, 289, 290, 295, 297, 298, joined by four more US Vospers 371, 372, 373, 374

        SOs: Lt Cdr J.D. Lancaster DSC RNVR to October 1944

               Lt P.H. Hyslop DSC RNVR

24TH MTB FLOTILLA
June 1942 to May 1943 in Britain. May 1943 to November 1944 in the Mediterranean (71-ft Vospers, 1940/41 Class):

       81, 84, 85, 86, 89, 97, 226, 242, 243
      SOs: Lt E.N. Poland RN to September 1942
              Lt B. Ward DSC RN to November 1942
              Lt C.W.S. Dreyer DSC RN to September 1943
              Lt D. Scott DSC RN to March 1944
              Lt B. Sturgeon DSC RNVR (killed on first operation, 2 April 1944)
              Lt R. Keyes RN to August 1944
              Lt C.R. Holloway RNVR to November 1944

28TH MTB FLOTILLA
November 1944 to May 1945 (continued in commission until November 1945) (71-ft US Vospers):

       404, 405, 406, 407, 408, 409, 410, 411
      SOs: Lt C.J. Jerram DSO DSC RNVR to May 1945
              Lt C.R. Holloway DSC RNVR

The Non-Mediterranean Flotillas

2ND MTB FLOTILLA
At Hong Kong 1938–41:

       07, 08, 09, 10, 11, 12 (60-ft British Power Boats)
       26, 27 (55-ft Thornycrofts)
      SOs: Lt Cdr D.G. Clark RN
              Lt Cdr G. Gandy RN

16TH AND 17TH MTB FLOTILLAS
In India and Ceylon 1943–4 (71-ft US Vospers):

       275, 276, 277, 278, 279, 280, 281, 282, 283, 285 (284 and 286 lost 9.9.43 in transport to India from USA)
       291, 292, 293, 294; 299, 300, 301, 302, 303, 304, 305, 306
       SO 16th: Lt Cdr K.A. Cradock-Hartopp RN
       SO 17th: Lt Cdr E.F. Hamilton-Meikle RN

19TH MTB FLOTILLA
In the West Indies 1942–3 (70-ft Canadian-built British Power Boats):

       332, 333, 334, 335, 336, 337, 338, 339, 340, 341, 342, 343
      SO: Lt H.A. Barbary RN

BIBLIOGRAPHY

PUBLISHED SOURCES

Agar, Capt Augustus, VC DSO RN. *Baltic Episode*, Conway Maritime Press, London, 1983

Anderson, Rear Adm Courtney C., CB. *Seagulls in my Belfry*, The Pentland Press, Durham, 1997

Barnett, Correlli. *Engage the Enemy More Closely*, Hodder and Stoughton, 1991

Bulkley, Capt Robert J. (Junr), USNR (Retd). *At Close Quarters*, PT Boats in the US Navy, Naval History Division, Washington, 1962

Beaver, Paul. *E-boats & Coastal Craft* (World War 2 Photo Albums), Patrick Stephens, 1980

Chatterton Dickson, Capt W., RN (Retd) ('Seedie'). *Seedie's List of Coastal Forces Awards for World War 2*, Ripley Registers 1992

Churchill, Winston S. *The Second World War* Volumes 1–6, Cassell, 1948–54

Cooper, Bryan. *The Buccaneers*, Macdonald, London, 1970

——. *The Battle of the Torpedo Boats*, Macdonald, London, 1970

——. *The E-boat Threat*, Macdonald and Jane's, 1976

Dorling, Capt Taprell, DSO FRHists RN ('Taffrail'). *Western Mediterranean 1942–1945*, Hodder and Stoughton, 1947

Lambert, John, and Ross, Al. *Allied Coastal Forces of World War 2*, Volume 2, 'Vosper MTBs and US Elcos', Conway Maritime Press, London, 1993

Lawrence, Hal. *Victory at Sea: Tales of His Majesty's Coastal Forces*, McLelland & Stewart Inc, Toronto, 1989

Lenton, H.T. and Colledge, J.J. *Warships of World War 2*, Ian Allan, 1964

Maclean, Fitzroy. *Eastern Approaches*, Jonathan Cape, 1949

McCoville, Michael. *A Small War in the Balkans*, Macmillan, London, 1986

Nolan, Brian, and Street, Brian Jeffrey. *Champagne Navy – Canada's Small Boat Raiders in the Second World War*, Random House, Toronto, 1991

North, A.J.D. *Royal Naval Coastal Forces 1939–1945*, Almark Publishing Co., London, 1972

Pickles, Harold, DSM. *Untold Stories of Small Boats at War*, The Pentland Press, Bishop Auckland, 1994

Pope, Dudley. *Flag 4, The Battle of Coastal Forces in the Mediterranean*, William Kimber, London, 1954

Rance, Adrian. *Fast Boats and Flying Boats* (a biography of Hubert Scott-Paine), Ensign Publications, Southampton, 1989

Reynolds, Leonard C., OBE DSC. *Gunboat 658*, William Kimber, London, 1955

——. *Dog Boats at War* (a history of the operations of the D class Fairmile MTBs and MGBs 1939–45), Sutton Publishing, 1998

Rohwer, J. and Hummelchen, G. *Chronology of the War at Sea 1939–1945*, Volume 1, 1939–1942, and Volume 2, 1943–1945, The Military Book Society by arrangement with Ian Allen Ltd, London, 1972

Roskill, Capt S.W., DSC RN. *History of the Second War, The War at Sea 1939–1945*, Volume 1: *The Defensive*, HMSO, London, 1954; Volume 2: *The Period of Balance*, HMSO, London, 1957; Volume 3: *The Offensive*, HMSO, London, 1960

Seligman, Adrian. *War in the Islands* (Undercover Operations in the Aegean 1942–4), Sutton Publishing, 1996

Smith, P.C. *Massacre at Tobruk*, Kimber, 1987

Whitley, M.J. *German Coastal Forces of World War 2*, Arms & Armour Press, a Cassell imprint, London, 1992

UNPUBLISHED SOURCES

PRIVATELY PRINTED AND DISTRIBUTED MEMOIRS

Blaxell, Lionel H., OBE DSC. *Through the Hawse Pipe 1939–1946*, Memoirs, 1990

Kennedy, Alexander. *Hong Kong Full Circle 1939–1945*, written 1946, printed 1969

Lynch, Mack. *Salty Dips*, Vol. 1 (Section 2, T.G. Fuller, 'MTB Skipper and Flotilla Commander'), compiled by the Ottawa Branch of the Naval Officers' Associations of Canada, 1983

PRIVATELY PREPARED HISTORIES IN BOOKLET FORM

Cooper, H.F. 'A history of the 28th MTB Flotilla', June 1993

——. 'A history of the 24th MTB Flotilla', October 1993

——. 'A history of the 7th and 8th MTB Flotillas', December 1993

——. 'The combined histories of the 10th, 15th and 27th MTB Flotillas', May 1994

——. 'A history of the 20th MTB Flotilla', January 1995

All deposited with the Imperial War Museum.

MEMOIRS, ARTICLES AND NOTES IN UNPUBLISHED FORM MADE AVAILABLE TO THE AUTHORS

Coombes, F.B., DSM. *Reminiscences of World War Two*, Part 2, date unknown

Mannooch, Lt Cdr J.T., RN (Retd). 'An account of the return to England of the 1st MTB Flotilla through the French Canals, November and December 1939', article written 1940

ACCOUNTS OF EVENTS, PROVIDED BY RETIRED OFFICERS OF THE FLOTILLAS, MANY WRITTEN SHORTLY AFTER THEY OCCURRED

Anderson, Rear Adm C.C., CB. Notes of the early days of the 10th MTB Flotilla, and the operations during the fall of Crete and its aftermath

Coles, Lt Cdr C., OBE VRD RNR (Retd). Notes on operations in the 1st, 10th, and 15th MTB Flotillas 1939–1943, and as a Prisoner of War

Gandy, Cdr G.H. RN (Retd). Notes from a log kept during the last days before the fall of Hong Kong on 25 December 1941 and during the journey of the surviving officers and men of the 2nd MTB Flotilla through Southern China to Rangoon, held at the Imperial War Museum

Jermain, Capt D., DSC* RN (Retd). Notes on operations in the 1st, 15th and 10th MTB Flotillas 1939–1943

Quarrie, Capt I.A.B., CBE VRD RNR (Retd). Notes on operations in 1st and 10th MTB Flotillas 1939–1942

NAVAL RECORDS
At the Naval Historical Branch
ADM 187, 'Pink Lists', weekly lists of movements of minor war vessels overseas

ADM 199/2327, Rear Admiral Coastal Forces Information Reports

Battle Summary Reports

Card Index of all MTBs and MGBs

List of Recorded Coastal Forces Actions
Navy Lists
Naval Historical Branch Search Documents
War Diaries
War Intelligence Reports

At the Public Records Office, Kew

ADM 199/257	Operations in the Adriatic and Aegean 1943–5
268	Coastal Forces in the Mediterranean 1943–4
269	Coastal Forces Actions, Adriatic 1944
537	MTB Operations in the Mediterranean
541	MTB Operations in the Mediterranean
597	Operation 'Rumble Bumble' (support for El Alamein)
677	Coastal Forces in the Mediterranean 1941–5
680	Operation Vigorous
858	Operation Husky
891	Reports on surrender of German Naval Forces in Northern Adriatic 1945
943, 944, 945, 947	Operation Husky
2195–2326	War Diary Summaries 9/39 – 12/45
CB 04272	Operation Agreement

Elsewhere

Newsletters of the Coastal Forces Veterans' Association
Questionnaires from Veterans – all sources

INDEX